Phonological and Phonetic Considerations of Lexical Processing

Benjamins Current Topics

ISSN 1874-0081

Special issues of established journals tend to circulate within the orbit of the subscribers of those journals. For the Benjamins Current Topics series a number of special issues of various journals have been selected containing salient topics of research with the aim of finding new audiences for topically interesting material, bringing such material to a wider readership in book format.

For an overview of all books published in this series, please see *http://benjamins.com/catalog/bct*

Volume 80

Phonological and Phonetic Considerations of Lexical Processing
Edited by Gonia Jarema and Gary Libben

These materials were previously published in *The Mental Lexicon* 8:3 (2013)

Phonological and Phonetic Considerations of Lexical Processing

Edited by

Gonia Jarema
Université de Montréal

Gary Libben
Brock University

John Benjamins Publishing Company
Amsterdam / Philadelphia

∞™ The paper used in this publication meets the minimum requirements of the American National Standard for Information Sciences – Permanence of Paper for Printed Library Materials, ANSI Z39.48-1984.

DOI 10.1075/bct.80

Cataloging-in-Publication Data available from Library of Congress:
LCCN 2015024524 (PRINT) / 2015032961 (E-BOOK)

ISBN 978 90 272 4268 6 (HB)
ISBN 978 90 272 6792 4 (E-BOOK)

John Benjamins Publishing Co. · https://benjamins.com

Table of contents

About the contributors

Gonia Jarema
Department of Linguistics
and Translation
Université de Montréal
Pavillon Lionel-Groulx
C. P. 6128, succ. Centre-ville
Montreal, Quebec, H3C 3J7
Canada

gonia.jarema@umontreal.ca

Gary Libben
Office of the Vice President Research
Brock University
500 Glenridge Ave.
St. Catharines, Ontario L2S 3A1
Canada

glibben@brocku.ca

Benjamin V. Tucker
Department of Linguistics
University of Alberta
4-32 Assiniboia Hall
Edmonton, Alberta T6G 2E7
Canada

bvtucker@ualberta.ca

Iris Hanique
Radboud University Nijmegen & Max
Planck Institute for Psycholinguistics
P.O. Box 310
6500 AH Nijmegen
The Netherlands

i.hanique@let.ru.nl

Ellen Aalders
Radboud University Nijmegen & Max
Planck Institute for Psycholinguistics
P.O. Box 310
6500 AH Nijmegen
The Netherlands

Ellen.Aalders@mpi.nl

Mirjam Ernestus
Radboud University Nijmegen & Max
Planck Institute for Psycholinguistics
P.O. Box 310
6500 AH Nijmegen
The Netherlands

m.ernestus@let.ru.nl

Kit W. Cho
Department of Psychology
University at Albany
State University of New York
1400 Washington Avenue
Albany, NY 12222, USA

kcho@albany.edu

Laurie B. Feldman
Department of Psychology
SS 399, University at Albany
State University of New York
1400 Washington Avenue,
Albany, NY 12222, USA

lfeldman@albany.edu

Joseph Paul Stemberger
Department of Linguistics
Totem Field Studios
University of British Columbia
2613 West Mall
Vancouver B.C. V6T 1Z4
Canada

Joseph.Stemberger@ubc.ca

Naoko Witzel
Department of Linguistics & TESOL
Box 19559
UT Arlington, Arlington, TX 76019, USA

naoko@uta.edu

Yujeong Choi
Department of East Asian Studies
University of Toronto
Robarts Library, 14087
130 St. George Street
Toronto, Ontario M5S 3H1
Canada

yujeong.choi@utoronto.ca

Marjoleine Sloos
Interacting Minds Centre
Jens Chr. Skous Vej 4,
Building 1483, 3rd floor
DK-8000 Aarhus C,
Denmark

marj.sloos@gmail.com

Isabelle Darcy
Second Language Studies
Indiana University
Memorial Hall 301
1021 E. Third St.
Bloomington, IN 47405, USA

idarcy@indiana.edu

Danielle Daidone
Second Language Studies
Indiana University
Memorial Hall 301
1021 E. Third St.
Bloomington, IN 47405, USA

ddaidone@indiana.edu

Chisato Kojima
Asian Studies
Knox College
2 East South Street
Galesburg, IL, 61401-4999, USA

ckojima@ knox.edu

Jeffrey Witzel
Department of Linguistics & TESOL
Box 19559
UT Arlington, Arlington, TX 76019, USA

jeffrey.witzel@uta.edu

Samantha Cornelius
Department of Linguistics & TESOL
Box 19559
UT Arlington
Arlington, TX 76019, USA

samantha.cornelius@mavs.uta.edu

Kenneth I. Forster
Department of Psychology
University of Arizona
Tucson, AZ 85721, USA

kforster@u.arizona.edu

Jonathan C. Forster
Department of Psychology
University of Arizona
Tucson, AZ 85721, USA

Michael Ramscar
Eberhard Karls Universität Tübingen
Wilhelmstrasse 19
72074 Tübingen
Germany

michael.ramscar@uni-tuebingen.de

Peter Hendrix
Eberhard Karls Universität Tübingen
Wilhelmstrasse 19
72074 Tübingen
Germany

petrus.hendrix@uni-tuebingen.de

Bradley C. Love
University College London
Experimental Psychology
26 Bedford Way, Room 228
London, UK WC1H 0AP

b.love@ucl.ac.uk

Harald Baayen
Eberhard Karls Universität Tübingen
Wilhelmstrasse 19
72074 Tübingen
Germany

harald.baayen@uni-tuebingen.de

The integration of phonological and phonetic processing

A matter of sound judgment

Gonia Jarema[i], Gary Libben[ii], and Benjamin V. Tucker[iii]
[i]Université de Montréal and Centre universitaire de gériatrie de Montréal / [ii]Brock University / [iii]University of Alberta

The goal of this book is to bring together research perspectives that both support and advance the investigation of phonological and phonetic factors in the functional architecture of the mental lexicon and in lexical processing.

It is paradoxical that a consideration of speaking and listening should warrant special treatment in the study of how words are represented and processed in the mind. It is clear that the ability to produce and comprehend written words is scaffolded upon our ability to say them and understand them aurally. Yet, there has been a strong tendency for researchers to employ the written forms of words to conceptualize how words may be represented in our minds. Indeed, even the term "mental lexicon" evokes images of a dictionary that is much more likely to be perceived as a repository of written words rather than of spoken words.

In many ways, the use of the written form of words as the unmarked metaphor in the scientific investigation of lexical representation and processing is innocuous. In order to refer to words in the pages of books and journals, they must be represented somehow – and it seems relatively obvious that the most convenient representations in such media are the visual written representations for which we already have conventionalized forms. Thus, we use representations such as 'BOOK' to refer to the representation – indeed the neurological instantiation – of the cognitive activities that correspond to the knowledge of 'book' and the ability to use that knowledge in acts of communication. This is primarily a matter of convenience. But that convenience carries with it some danger, for, to state this reflexively: *All metaphors are double-edged swords.*

This leads us to the question of why, in particular, and despite its convenience, the use of the written form of words as the unmarked metaphor may be a *double-edged sword.* In our view, there are two inter-related reasons for this: The first is that the written metaphor is by nature static and thus tends to de-emphasize

DOI 10.1075/bct.80.002int

the fundamentally dynamic nature of the mental lexicon and lexical processing. The second is that the relative dominance of the written form in the investigation of lexical processing has tended to de-emphasize the role of production in lexical ability among language users and therefore its importance in the modelling of that ability. As we discuss below, greater focus on the role of speech in lexical processing research will enhance considerations of the inherently dynamic nature of lexical ability and the importance of production in mental lexicon theory. Greater emphasis on the role of speech will also increase ecological validity and facilitate the development of new opportunities for knowledge advancement and integration.

The dynamic nature of the mental lexicon

At first blush, it may seem that the notion of dynamism is at odds with the inherently representational nature of the mental lexicon. In our view, however, this is not the case at all. Jarema and Libben (2007) present a definition of the mental lexicon, which has its dynamic nature as a core feature. Jarema and Libben (2007) define the mental lexicon as:

> the cognitive system that constitutes the capacity for conscious and unconscious lexical activity. (p. 2)

In this definition, the term *system* highlights the functional integrity that is characteristic of lexical activity. The key feature of the mental lexicon is the manner in which lexical representations are inherently linked in complex multidimensional networks. The definition situates the mental lexicon as not simply the repository of representations that enables lexical activity. Rather, it constitutes the claim that the mental lexicon *is* that lexical activity. Perhaps most importantly, the use of the term 'capacity' within the definition highlights the importance of the productivity and dynamism in lexical knowledge and lexical ability. For example, the lexical knowledge of a speaker of English includes not only the ability to acquire and retain a memory trace for a word such as *landscape* (common in English since 1800) but also to create and interpret words such as *seascape* (common since 1900), *cityscape* (common since 1950), *soundscape* (common since 1960), *textscape* and *screenscape* (both attested since 1990). The newness of many of these words and the ease with which they can be interpreted illustrate another key point – the lexical knowledge of an individual will change throughout the lifespan as new languages are acquired, as new words are learned, as words that have been previously learned fall into disuse, and as new connections among words and their sub-elements are formed and changed.

This phenomenon of change across the lifespan is addressed directly in this book by Michael Ramscar, Peter Hendrix, Bradley Love and Harald Baayen in their chapter entitled *Learning is not decline: The mental lexicon as a window into cognition across the lifespan*. The authors challenge the widely accepted view that healthy aging is linked to cognitive decline and claim that current models of learning in aging are based on erroneous assumptions about associative learning and are thus inaccurate, and cannot capture processing performance in the elderly in an adequate manner. Scores obtained from psychometric vocabulary tests are shown to distort and misrepresent performance, resulting in an underestimation of cognitive abilities in older adults. Ramscar et al. demonstrate that when learning models that adequately control for effects of lexical learning on performance are employed, there is little evidence of cognitive decline among older adults. Rather, they claim that "lexical knowledge becomes more and more attuned to the information structure of the lexicon". Under their view, the continued experience of acquiring lexical knowledge comes at a cost: it augments processing load over the lifespan. But the ability to learn vocabulary items is not fixed, it improves over time as increase in accuracy scores clearly demonstrates. Thus slow-down of lexical processing in the aging population should not be equated with cognitive decline. Ramscar et al. argue that, rather than adopting the prevalent stereotype of decline in aging, we should be placing emphasis on increased expertise through experience, a dynamic which can be captured through the use of discriminative learning models that provide a meaningful framework for the understanding of lexical processing across the lifespan.

Phonological and phonetic processing as a window to dynamic lexical knowledge and processing

Our discussion above of the fundamentally dynamic nature of the mental lexicon and the manner in which the lexical abilities of individuals change across the lifespan leads us to the question of the fundamental role that phonological and phonetic properties of words play in those representations and in their dynamic nature.

Perhaps the first place to begin the exploration of the role of phonological and phonetic properties is through a consideration of the individuality and variability associated with spoken words. The written word is, by design and by circumstance, considerably more invariant synchronically and more conservative diachronically than the spoken word. Consider, as an example, the word *light* in English. Its spelling has been relatively invariant for over 500 years, as evidenced in the title of the 1582 essay of the Puritan Christopher Fetherston "*A Dialogue*

Agaynst Light, Lewde, and Lasciuious Dauncing". In this essay, C. Fetherston cautioned against allowing singing and dancing on Sundays. We can expect that his and his contemporaries' pronunciation of 'light' in his reading of the essay would have differed rather dramatically from the current pronunciation, retaining the Germanic /xt/ as the final consonant cluster that has disappeared in modern English. But, of course, this does not mean that either the pronunciation 500 years ago or now would be invariant across dialects and speakers. We see, for example that, even in current North American pronunciation, there is considerable variation. Canadians will most likely produce *light* as /lʌɪt/, demonstrating the phonological phenomenon known as Canadian Raising. Americans will likely pronounce it as /laɪt/, with the diphthong being present or absent, depending on local dialect.

What effects does this inherent variability within the speech signal have on the representation of words in the mind and on an individual's ability to recognize words spoken by members of his or her own speech community, or by other individuals that they might perceive as having 'an accent'? The ability to answer this and related questions is central to the attainment of a comprehensive and ecologically valid science of lexical representation and processing. Moreover, in an increasingly multilingual world, more and more people vary in the manner in which they pronounce a word in a given language. As a consequence, listeners may need to be able to recognize words spoken with an accent that is quite different from their own.

Matters of lexical processing related to the issues noted above are treated in this volume by Kit W. Cho and Laurie Beth Feldman in their chapter *Production and accent affect memory*. They examined how native speakers of English recall and recognize words spoken in either a highly familiar accent (American English), or a less familiar accent (Dutch). The main purpose of the study was to determine whether production benefits recognition. They found that performance on a memory task benefits from production more than from listening, and that irrespective of whether one pronounces words in one's own accent or whether one imitates the accent of the speaker, producing words presented with an unfamiliar accent facilitates recall and recognition. They demonstrate that acoustic-phonetic details are retained in listening, but "overshadowed or attenuated by production", and thus provide empirical evidence in support of the view that acoustic-phonetic and articulatory information interact in memory tasks.

The chapter by Cho and Feldman raises the question of the fundamental nature of lexical representations generally and, more specifically, with respect to their encoding of the phonological and phonetic properties of words. Given that, in terms of acoustic detail, spoken words may be considered to be unique events, what kinds of representations in the mental lexicon are likely to be developed in order to accommodate this inherent variation? In their chapter *How robust are exemplar effects in word comprehension?*, Iris Hanique, Ellen Aalders, and Mirjam Ernestus address the central question of whether a word's pronunciation is stored in terms of abstract information about its acoustic properties, or rather in terms of exemplars, that is as a set of representations of exact pronunciations of each instance of the word as it is heard. They probed the validity of the exemplar model in four long-term priming experiments varying the distance in trials between prime and target, pronunciation (unreduced-reduced), speaker match between prime and target (same-different) and type and number of variation (degree of reduction and/or speaker voice). Exemplar effects were only found in the first of the four experiments, a short experiment with no speaker variation and a high proportion of repeated words. Hanique et al. argue that because, in spontaneous speech, degree of variation varies greatly, abstract lexical representations may play a more prominent role than exemplars. They conclude that spoken language comprehension can be accounted for in a hybrid model that combines abstract representations *and* exemplars, or in a model that posits only abstract lexical representation and that "assumes domain-general episodic memory". This leads them to suggest that in natural conversation, which is as a rule characterized by great reduction variation, exemplars do not play a prominent role.

Considering Second Language and bilingual processing as core phenomena

An important theme that emerges across this book is that second language acquisition across the lifespan plays a key role in the variable phonetic and phonological properties of speech that will be encountered by hearers of a language. As noted by Libben and Goral (2015), seminal contributions by authors such as Grosjean (1989) have stressed that language processing by speakers of more than one language must be taken as a theoretical primitive and cannot be well understood by simply combing models of monolingual processing (see also Grosjean, 2008). It has been repeatedly shown that bilinguals' performance in each of their languages differs from monolingual norms (e.g., Gollan & Goldrick, 2012). And, this is particularly so in the phonological and phonetic domains.

This phenomenon is taken up by Isabelle Darcy, Danielle Daidone, and Chisato Kojima in their chapter entitled *Asymmetric lexical access and fuzzy lexical representations in second language learners*. The authors begin with the observation that L2 learners have been demonstrated to exhibit less efficient word recognition abilities than native listeners, due to difficulties with the perceptual discrimination of sounds and/or with accurate (native-like) lexical encoding of words in L2. They expand previous studies on asymmetries in phonemic contrast discrimination by attempting to tease apart the "phonetic coding deficiency hypothesis" from the "lexical coding deficiency hypothesis" by studying phonetic categorization and lexical decision among native speakers of American English learning German and Japanese. Results revealed that both learners of Japanese and learners of German discriminate phonemic contrasts much like the control group of native speakers, at both the high and the intermediate levels of proficiency. In lexical decision, the previously reported asymmetrical pattern was observed in both groups, confirming that encoding of new and difficult phonemic contrasts is not fully target-like and is influenced by L1. This asymmetry, combined with accurate phonetic categorization, is interpreted as revealing that such contrasts are inadequately represented at the lexical level, thus supporting the lexical coding deficiency hypothesis. Darcy and colleagues suggest that fuzzy lexical representations may in fact increase lexical competition in spoken word recognition in early stages of L2 proficiency and that lexically imprecise representations triggered by deficient lexical encoding, rather than inadequate acoustic perception, are at the root of assymetric patterns in lexical access.

How do speech and writing influence each other?

As we move toward a world characterized by global literacy, spoken-only language processing is a term that is increasingly reserved for the first years of childhood, rather than for literacy differences among adults. Accordingly, the possible interaction between phonological and phonetic factors on the one hand and orthographic factors on the other hand is very important to the effective modeling of lexical processing in both domains. Almost all native speakers of English encounter their basic core vocabulary aurally before the onset of literacy. Thus, there is an important way in with spoken word processing is prior to visual word processing both ontologically, and perhaps logically. Yet, this should not lead us to suppose that, as a result, we will find psycholinguistic effects of speech on reading and writing, but not vice versa. Returning to our example of the word *light* above, one would expect that as a high frequency word characterized by early age of acquisition, it would almost certainly be among those words that are learned aurally before visually. Yet, how would adult native speakers of North American English, who, as we noted above, might have very differing pronunciations for the word, characterize those differences? It is very likely that they would characterize them as differences in how people from different regions pronounce the word spelled "l-i-g-h-t". In other words, they would use the written form as the underlying, core, unbiased reference point for the characterization of their pronunciation, or the pronunciation of others. This raises important implications when considering the orthographic effects on speech both within languages and between languages, because writing systems, as technical human inventions, are not, of course, unbiased at all, but rather represent particular engineering solutions constrained by a large number of factors, including the phonological and phonetic properties of the particular languages that they were designed to encode (bidirectional influence of this sort can also be a driver of spelling change, e.g., the use of *lite* for *light* in American spelling).

Perhaps one of the most successful writing systems developed is that used for Korean, and that which is the subject of the chapter in this volume by Naoko Witzel, Jeffrey Witzel, and Yujeong Choi, entitled *The locus of the masked onset priming effect: Evidence from Korean.*

Korean writing features both an alphabetic (Hangul) and a logographic (Hanja) script. The authors take as their starting point the view that producing words aloud involves computing the phonology of visually perceived letter strings and the experimental finding that in the presence of a masked prime, naming is facilitated when prime and target share an initial phoneme or phonemes, creating a masked onset priming effect, or MOPE. Under the assumption that the MOPE engages non-lexical grapheme-to-phoneme processes, they employed nonword Hangul prime-target pairs in order to force a non-lexical route in naming. Results obtained revealed that a MOPE emerges when primes and targets share an initial CV syllable or (but to a lesser degree) when they only share an initial phoneme, indicating that although Korean Hangul is a syllabary script, syllables are decomposed into individual units that operate during grapheme-to-phoneme conversion. Witzel et al. argue that their findings support the view that the MOPE reflects non-lexical grapheme-to-phoneme conversion processes and conflicts with an explanation in terms of a late facilitation in speech planning, because such an account would only predict priming at the level of a prosodic unit above the phoneme (i.e., the syllable) but not at the phoneme level.

The dynamics of dialect changes over time: Exemplar theory as capturing the interplay of phonology and orthography over time

As the discussion above indicates, understanding the roles of exemplars in the modeling of the phonological and phonetic properties of words and in the modeling of lexical representation is a key next step in mental lexicon research. This is, of course, particularly challenging if change is a ubiquitous characteristic of the system. Indeed, it may well be possible that this change is not constant in its trajectory. A very interesting case of such change in trajectory is brought to the foreground by Marjoleine Sloos in her chapter *The reversal of the Bären–Beeren merger in Austrian Standard German.* The starting point for this study is the general tendency for variation in pronunciation, whether dialectally or socially determined, to give rise to 'merging'. This is a phenomenon where two sounds become perceptually undistinguishable, thus blocking any potential reversal to the two distinct sounds. But, Sloos shows that a merger can be reversed under contextual pressures. In a corpus study of younger and older speakers, the author investigates the current reversal of the Bären-Beeren merger that had evolved historically in both the Austrian and German varieties of Standard German. She found that younger adults increasingly adopt the prestige variety of Standard German (a 'multicentric' language), that is German Standard German, where the vowel distinction is prevalent. Sloos proposes that merger reversals can best be accounted for within exemplar theory. Besides information on how words are pronounced, competing exemplars also store sociolinguistic and orthographic information. However, "Orthographical information becomes available as a cue for pronunciation if, and only if, linguistic as well as social information fall short in the selection process." Orthography is not an implicit process "because it is learned separately and memorized consciously, unlike auditory information" and is stored at a level that is connected to the auditory level. In the reversal of a merger, it comes into play in the presence of sociolinguistic motivation.

Morphology, phonology, and phonetics

Across the world's languages, most words do not consist of a single meaning-bearing form (e.g. *book*) but rather are composite forms. Sometimes the subunits are easily identifiable lexical subunits (e.g., *bookcase*). Sometimes, they contain subunits that are formally identifiable but do not exist as independent words (as in our example above of *landscape*, in which *-scape* is derived from Dutch, *-schap*, making English *landscape* cognate with German *Landschaft*). In other cases (e.g., *booking, books, bookish, prebook*), subunits are best describes as affix forms.

From the outset of research on the mental lexicon, a great deal of research has dealt with the formal morphological properties of words and the question of how the morphological subunits of words may influence their representations in the mind and how they are accessed during the processes of language comprehension and production. The chapter by Joseph Stemberger in this volume entitled *Phonological reduction in the first part of noun compounds* ties into a key discussion in this domain – this is the discussion concerning whether regular and irregular lexical forms, in particular plurals, are stored and processed differently in the mind.

Two main hypotheses have emerged from the literature. The first posits that regular and irregular plurals are processed differentially, with regulars being rule-generated, while irregulars are stored in the mental lexicon. In his chapter, Stemberger adopts an alternative position by arguing that this difference may in fact result from phonological differences between these forms. He bases himself on a previous study (Stemberger, 2007) that showed that young children tend to produce overtensing errors in monomorphemic past-tense forms with basic rimes (e.g., didn't broke; didn't played). He argues that this observation, rather than being reducible to strictly phonological effects, points to an interaction between phonology and morphology. In production, uninflected and inflected forms are in competition, and because as a rule English irregular past-tense forms are "phonologically simpler, less marked, and of higher-frequency", they are more accessible than regular forms. Stemberger further argues that similar effects could be at play in the first constituent of compounds and presents a study of a child who produced more phonological reduction on a compound's first constituent noun than on that same noun produced alone, independently of morphology (in both cases the noun was a singular form). This is interpreted as evidence for the late development of phonological complexity in compounds and for an account of the difference between regular and irregular plurals in terms of an interaction between morphological and phonological effects. This study is thus in harmony with the previous chapters of this volume in that it brings out ecological considerations and emphasizes the coming into play of interactive, rather than isolated, linguistic factors in compound processing.

Toward a modality-integrated science of lexical processing

The chapter by Joseph Stemberger discussed above points to the importance of considering phonological factors in what may otherwise be seen as a purely morphological phenomenon. Although one might expect that the potential interaction of phonological and morphological factors in lexical processing would constitute the norm in mental lexicon research, this has not been the case. As we have noted above, from the outset, reading has constituted the dominant domain for the investigation of the mental lexicon and lexical processing. In the early days of mental lexicon research, the principal driver of this trend was technological necessity. The field had its origins in chronometric analysis, in which response time to visually presented stimuli served as the dominant dependent variable. And, within this context, the lexical decision task (introduced into the literature by Meyer and Schwanefeldt (1971)) played a dominant role as the accepted experimental paradigm in the field. Although the lexical decision task could, in principle, be used for both visually presented and auditorily presented stimuli, it was simply easier for researchers to use visually presented stimuli. They were (and still are) easier to store in a stimulus list and easier to present to participants in experiments.

An additional important factor is that visual stimuli seem inherently more canonical. They use standardized abstract representations (characters and letters) rather than phonological and phonetic features that may be specific to a given speaker. Thus, for many researchers, having spoken stimuli presented by an individual speaker would be comparable to having visual stimuli presented in a single person's cursive handwriting. This is a methodological challenge that cannot be ignored, but neither does it constitute an insuperable obstacle (see Hanique, et al., this volume). In addition, it may be the case that by avoiding individualized pronunciation effects, we may have unwittingly, but systematically, failed to capture a fundamental characteristic of the lexical processing system – namely its ability to deal naturally with inherent speaker variation.

There is another key reason for the dominance of visual processing paradigms in mental lexicon research. This is basically that auditory stimuli unfold over time and visual stimuli can be presented all at once and, if necessary, for very brief durations. Thus, the visual presentation of stimuli is considerably more amenable to the management of ceiling effects in recognition through tachistoscopic presentation. They are more amenable to masked priming manipulations that, similarly, trade on the fact that visual stimuli can be presented in their entirety for very brief durations. This is a core difference (Mattys, 1997). Spoken language is inherently time dependent, while written language is static. When a written word is presented the complete word is presented simultaneously to a participant, while a spoken word may unfold over a period of 500 to 600 ms with individual parts of the word occurring over several instances of time. This basic difference in the characteristics of the modalities may require different processing mechanisms to be recruited. However, it is not clear that these two modalities are so different that we need to think of them as separate processing domains rather than aspects of a single language processing system.

As we noted above, it *is* clear that of the two modalities, it is spoken language that is the more natural, both in terms of our development as a species and our development as individual members of the species. This fact does not, in any way diminish the importance of visual processing (without which we would likely not have the cultural continuity that enabled psycholinguistics, or any other branch of scientific inquiry to develop). Rather, it may be the case that a useful metaphor for understanding the interplay between auditory and visual lexical processing is photography. A photograph of a bird in flight is not the same as a bird in flight. It is missing the inherent time-series dynamics. But, at the same time, it allows other kinds of scrutiny to be possible. In many ways, the written word is an attempt by a visual artist to use a static medium in order to capture a bird in flight. As much as it would be an error to not use the information that can be gained through the study of reading and writing, it would also be an error – and perhaps an even greater one – to miss the opportunities that can be gained by studying the fundamentally dynamic nature of language in its most natural form, namely speech.

Although, at present, there is little doubt that research on lexical processing is less developed in the domain of speaking and listening than in writing and reading, we see some evidence that this auditory-visual asymmetry might be lessened in coming years. Crucial to this effort will be the supporting research efforts in the speech domain that are under development. For example, there are about half a dozen big data experiments such as the English Lexicon Project (e.g., Balota et al., 2007) and others (e.g., Ferrand et al., 2010; Keuleers, Lacey, Rastle, and Bysbaert, 2012), often having over 30,000 stimuli of interest. There is, as yet, no such equivalent for spoken language. The closest is BALDEY which is a survey of about 2,000 lexical items (Ernestus & Cutler, 2015). The third author of the present chapter is preparing one such big data set for spoken language and the creation of the stimuli alone has required several years and hundreds of hours of work by a small group of researchers preparing the stimuli.

Despite the time-intensiveness of lexical research in the speech domain, key technical innovations have made speech processing research considerably easier that it has been in the past. The advent of digital technologies have made working with speech stimuli much simpler, allowing anyone with a personal computer to work with speech recordings. Of course, researchers need training in speech and speech acoustics, but we expect that here as well, we can look to a near-future in which the work of individual researchers is scaffolded by the availability of large spoken corpora, software for stimulus creation, and databases of lexical speech production and recognition performance.

We also expect that considerable opportunity to combine speech and lexical processing research will come from web-based experiment delivery. The methodological chapter in this volume by Jeffrey Witzel, Samantha Cornelius, Naoko Witzel, Kenneth I. Forster, and Jonathan C. Forster entitled "Testing the viability of webDMDX for masked priming experiments" demonstrates the steps that have already been taken in this domain. The authors examine whether highly time-sensitive experiments can be reliably run using webDMDX, as conducting such experiments online can present a number of problems. These are related to the speed and stability of the participants' internet connections, the synchronization of webDMDX with the screen, the refresh interval of the testing computer, and the calculation of the number of refresh intervals of host computers for experiments involving tachistoscopic displays. To evaluate the viability of the web-deployable implementation of DMDX, Witzel et al. compared the webDMDX to the labDMDX in three experiments. Following minor adjustments, the webDMDX and the labDMDX yielded similar results on both the lexical decision and the letter detection tasks. However, as the authors note, it remains the case that running DMDX in a laboratory offers the advantages of stable hardware, a quiet environment with constrained attentional demands. These are factors that are clearly also important for web-based experiments involving speech processing as well as for those in which speech production data are obtained.

Conclusion: The shape of the future

It seems to us self-evident that, in order to truly understand *language*, we need to investigate spoken language. However, whether visual lexical processing and auditory lexical processing can be brought together under a single theory of lexical comprehension and whether speech and writing can be brought together under a single theory of lexical production will be a matter of crucial debate in coming years. The quality of this debate and our ability to arrive at evidence-based conclusions will crucially depend on how successful we are in integrating speech research and visual processing research into the same theoretical conversation. On the way – and whatever the final outcome – we are sure to learn a great deal about how details of writing systems and phonological systems interact and affect individual language users. A more integrated approach would also likely place individual and situational variation (which are much attenuated in reading print) in a much more central position in the design and analysis of experiments. The investigation of questions concerning spontaneous vs. laboratory speech, dialect processing, and accentedness would add significantly to the richness of the lexical processing literature and enhance the ecological validity of experimental designs as well as the knowledge obtained from them.

References

Balota, D. A., Yap, M. J., Cortese, M. J., Hutchison, K. I., Kessler, B., Loftis, B., Treiman, R. (2007). The English Lexicon Project. *Behavior Research Methods*, *39*(3), 445–459.

Ernestus, M. & Cutler, A. (2015). BALDEY: A database of auditory lexical decisions. *Quarterly Journal of Experimental Psychology* 68, 8, 1469–1488.

Ferrand, L., New, B., Brysbaert, M., Keuleers, E., Bonin, P., Méot, A., Pallier, C. (2010). The French Lexicon Project: Lexical decision data for 38,840 French words and 38,840 pseudowords. *Behavior Research Methods*, *42*(2), 488–496. DOI: 10.3758/BRM.42.2.488

Fetherston, C. (1582). *A Dialogue Agaynst Light, Lewde, and Lasciuious Dauncing* [facsimile published by Geizer Press, Leicester, UK, 1973]

Gollan, T. H., & Goldrick, M. (2012). Does bilingualism twist your tongue? *Cognition*, 125, 491–497.

Grosjean, F. (1989). Neurolinguists beware! The bilingual is not two monolinguals in one person. *Brain and Language*, 36, 3–15.

Grosjean, F. (2008). *Studying Bilinguals*. Oxford: Oxford University Press.

Jarema, G. & Libben, G. (2007). Matters of Definitions. In G. Jarema & G. Libben (Eds.) *Core Perspectives on the Mental Lexicon*. Oxford: Elsevier, pp. 1–12.

Keuleers, E., Lacey, P., Rastle, K., & Brysbaert, M. (2012). The British Lexicon Project: Lexical decision data for 28,730 monosyllabic and disyllabic English words. *Behavior Research Methods*, *44*(1), 287–304. DOI: 10.3758/s13428-011-0118-4

Libben, G. & Goral, M. (2015). How bilingualism shapes the mental lexicon. In J. W. Schwieter (Ed.) *Cambridge Handbook of Bilingual Processing*, Cambridge, England: Cambridge University Press.

Mattys, S. L. (1997). The use of time during lexical processing and segmentation: A review. *Psychonomic Bulletin & Review*, *4*(3), 310–329. DOI: 10.3758/BF03210789

Meyer, D. E., & Schvaneveldt, R. W. (1971). Facilitation in recognizing pairs of words: Evidence of a dependence between retrieval operations. *Journal of Experimental Psychology*, 90, 227–234.

Stemberger, J. P. (2007). Children's overtensing errors: Phonological and lexical effects on syntax. *Journal of Memory and Language*, 57, 49–64. DOI: 10.1016/j.jml.2007.02.003

How robust are exemplar effects in word comprehension?

Iris Hanique,[i, ii] Ellen Aalders,[i] and Mirjam Ernestus[i, ii]
[i] Centre for Language Studies, Radboud University Nijmegen, the Netherlands / [ii] Max Planck Institute for Psycholinguistics, Nijmegen, the Netherlands

This paper studies the robustness of exemplar effects in word comprehension by means of four long-term priming experiments with lexical decision tasks in Dutch. A prime and target represented the same word type and were presented with the same or different degree of reduction. In Experiment 1, participants heard only a small number of trials, a large proportion of repeated words, and stimuli produced by only one speaker. They recognized targets more quickly if these represented the same degree of reduction as their primes, which forms additional evidence for the exemplar effects reported in the literature. Similar effects were found for two speakers who differ in their pronunciations. In Experiment 2, with a smaller proportion of repeated words and more trials between prime and target, participants recognized targets preceded by primes with the same or a different degree of reduction equally quickly. Also, in Experiments 3 and 4, in which listeners were not exposed to one but two types of pronunciation variation (reduction degree and speaker voice), no exemplar effects arose. We conclude that the role of exemplars in speech comprehension during natural conversations, which typically involve several speakers and few repeated content words, may be smaller than previously assumed.

Keywords: speech comprehension, exemplar effects, pronunciation variation, acoustic reduction

Several models of speech comprehension assume that the mental lexicon stores the pronunciation of a word with two types of representations, namely abstract representations and exemplars (e.g., Goldinger, 2007; McLennan, Luce, & Charles-Luce, 2003). Abstract representations are strings of sound symbols like phonemes or phonological features, which only contain information about acoustic properties that distinguish between these symbols. In contrast, clouds of exemplars

DOI 10.1075/bct.80.01han

represent many occurrences of words that the language user has uttered or heard. Each exemplar is a detailed representation corresponding to the speech signal of one occurrence and thus contains subtle acoustic information, for example about the word's exact pronunciation or the speaker's voice. Many articles in the literature point to a role of exemplars in word comprehension. This study investigates the robustness of these exemplar effects.

Exemplar effects have been established in several priming experiments (e.g., Bradlow, Nygaard, & Pisoni, 1999; Craik & Kirsner, 1974; Goh, 2005; Goldinger, 1996; Janse, 2008; Mattys & Liss, 2008; McLennan et al., 2003; McLennan & Luce, 2005; Palmeri, Goldinger, & Pisoni, 1993). These experiments contained repeated words and the comprehension of the second occurrence of a word (the target) was expected to be facilitated by the first occurrence (the prime). Primes and targets were completely identical, that is the same token, or they differed in speech rate, time-compression, the realization of a certain segment (e.g., intervocalic /t,d/ produced as [t,d] or as a flap in American English), or the speaker's voice. Most experiments showed that participants reacted more quickly or produced fewer errors on the target if it was identical to the prime. Presumably, participants stored primes with all their acoustic detail and, if targets were acoustically identical to these primes, they could quickly recognize them via these exemplars formed by the primes.

Not all experiments showed these exemplar effects. McLennan, Luce, and Charles-Luce (2003) studied allophonic variability and found exemplar effects only when participants processed stimuli relatively fast. Conversely, for indexical variability (e.g., variability in speaker voice and speech rate) McLennan and Luce (2005) only observed exemplar effects if processing was slow. To account for this, McLennan and Luce suggest that more abstract features are generally dominant early in processing and show effects when participants are fast, while surface features (e.g., indexical details) dominate later stages and show effects when participants are slow. However, surface representations can still show effects at an early stage if they represent variants that are relatively frequent (e.g., representations containing flaps instead of underlying /t/ and /d/).

Palmeri et al. (1993) also observed that exemplar effects do not always occur. In an old-new judgment task they investigated whether exemplar effects remain if primes and targets are separated by a large number of words, and therefore they varied the lag between primes and targets (1, 2, 4, 8, 16, 32, or 64 words). In addition, the authors examined whether exemplar effects are influenced by the number of speakers heard (1, 2, 6, 12, or 20 speakers). Primes and targets were produced by either the same or a different speaker. Their results suggest that exemplar effects are only present at lags smaller than 64 words. Exemplar effects did not differ for the different numbers of speakers.

Goldinger (1996) investigated similar issues. He studied the extent to which exemplar effects decrease if the time interval between primes and targets increases (from five minutes, to one day, to a week). In the same experiment, Goldinger investigated whether exemplar effects arise if stimuli are produced by two, six, or ten speakers. Speaker voice for a given prime and corresponding target was either the same or different and participants performed one of two tasks (identifying the words in white noise or judging whether the word had been presented before). The identification task showed exemplar effects for all time intervals, yet for the old-new judgments a week's interval was enough to block these effects. This provides additional evidence that exemplar effects become more difficult to access over time. The effect of the number of speakers in the experiment is less clear.

Our study also investigates the issue of when exemplar effects arise in speech comprehension. More specifically, this study investigates whether exemplar effects are robust under more natural conditions than those typically tested in the literature, providing us with information about the role of exemplars in the comprehension process. Following McLennan and Luce (2005), we conducted four long-term priming experiments using lexical decision only. This way, participants had to process words completely – unlike in, for example, phoneme monitoring or shadowing – and did not have to rely on explicit memory (as in old-new judgment).

Our targets were Dutch verbs that start with the unstressed prefixes *be-* or *ver-*. Words of this type are common in Dutch and their prefixes often contain reduced schwas in casual speech (Hanique, Ernestus, & Schuppler, 2013; Pluymaekers, Ernestus, & Baayen, 2005). In all four experiments, primes and targets could differ in their degree of reduction: Segments in the reduced tokens were shorter than in the unreduced tokens, and some segments were completely missing. Our unreduced tokens therefore represent tokens that are typically found in slow speech, while our reduced tokens represent tokens that can be found at a high speech rate in casual speech. We hypothesized that if participants react more quickly to targets showing the same degree of reduction as their primes, participants must have accessed the exemplars of these primes.

First, we examined whether exemplar effects arise for different speakers, by using two very different speakers. Speakers tend to differ in whether and how they reduce words at high speech rates in casual conversations (e.g., Hanique, Ernestus, & Boves, 2015). In Experiments 1 and 2, we investigated whether exemplar effects were larger if the difference in degree of reduction between the reduced and unreduced tokens was larger. Both experiments consisted of two subexperiments that were identical except for speaker voice.

Second, we investigated whether exemplar effects also occur if the repetition of words is less clear for participants in our experiment than in experiments reported in the literature. In the experiments in the literature, the number of trials varied from 48 (McLennan & Luce, 2005) to 436 (Craik & Kirsner, 1974) and between 33% and 50% of the trials formed word repetitions. Furthermore, the majority of these experiments used an explicit memory task (old-new judgments). Since it was clear to the participants that many words were repeated, they may have used a strategy in which they directly accessed exemplars. In Experiments 1 and 3 of our study, participants listened to 288 trials in which 34% of the trials formed word repetitions (similar to McLennan and Luce, 2005). In Experiments 2 and 4, we increased the number of trials to 800 and 864 respectively, and decreased the percentage of trials constituting word repetitions to less than 20% (almost 16% in Experiment 2 and 18% in Experiment 4).

Third, in previous experiments, listeners only heard one type of variation in the speech signal. For instance, in Bradlow et al. (1999), speech rate, amplitude, and speaker were varied, but each participant only heard one of these variations. In Experiments 3 and 4, we investigated whether exemplar effects also arise if the stimuli in the experiment differ in two indexical properties: degree of reduction and speaker voice.

Finally, our experiments differ from previous experiments in that the prime and the target were never completely identical. We chose to always have different productions of the same word in order to obtain results that are ecologically more valid. In real life, listeners are very unlikely to hear a given word produced twice in exactly the same way.

Experiment 1

Method

Participants

We tested 48 native speakers of Dutch aged 18 to 28 (mean 21 years). Nine were left-handed and ten were male. In this experiment, as in all other experiments presented in this paper, none of the participants reported any hearing impairment, all were paid for their participation, and they had not participated in any of the other experiments in this study.

Materials

The materials consisted of an equal number of real Dutch words and pseudo-words; all were tri-syllabic infinitives. Half of them started with the prefix *be-* and the other half with *ver-* (e.g., *beschrijven* 'to describe' and *vertolken* 'to

Table 1. The number of stimuli presented in Experiment 1. The stimuli are broken down for prefix (*be-* or *ver-*), whether they function as primes, targets, or foils (which are subdivided into repeated and non-repeated foils), whether they are real words or pseudo-words, whether they occur in Part 1 or Part 2 of the experiment, and whether within this part they occurred in Block 1 (B1) or Block 2 (B2).

		Primes	Targets	Repeated foils		Foils		Total	
		Real		Pseudo		Real	Pseudo	Real	Pseudo
		B1	B2	B1	B2	B1/B2	B1/B2	B1/B2	B1/B2
Part 1	*be-*	12	12	12	12	12	12	36	36
	ver-	12	12	12	12	12	12	36	36
Part 2	*be-*	12	12	12	12	12	12	36	36
	ver-	12	12	12	12	12	12	36	36
Total		48	48	48	48	48	48	144	144

interpret'). The pseudo-infinitives did not contain phonotactically illegal phoneme sequences. All primes were real infinitives and primes and targets represented the same word types.

Table 1 presents an overview of the numbers of the different types of stimuli. The experiment contained 48 pairs of primes and targets. We wished to keep the number of trials intervening between primes and targets small so that, at least in this respect, our experiment resembled the experiments in the literature that showed exemplar effects. These 48 prime-target pairs were therefore divided over two parts. Each part consisted of two blocks: the first block had 24 primes and 48 foils and the second block contained the corresponding 24 targets and 48 foils. Each word type occurred in only one part of the experiment. In order to better hide the aim of the experiment, in the second block of each part, we repeated real words (the targets) as well as 24 pseudo-infinitives (foils).[1]

We used two pronunciation variants for the primes, targets, and foils: an unreduced one, carefully articulated at a slow speech rate, and a reduced one, with shorter and possibly absent segments. A prime and target represented either the same or a different pronunciation variant. All stimuli were recorded by two Dutch native speakers: one male (henceforth *Speaker A*) and one female (*Speaker B*). Stimuli were recorded over the course of multiple recording sessions. Since speakers typically do not produce casual speech in front of a microphone, we had to tell our speakers that the reduced stimuli had to sound as if uttered in casual speech. The instructions given to the speakers determined whether tokens were categorized as reduced or unreduced. For each word type that occurred as prime and target or as repeated foil, each speaker recorded several unreduced and reduced tokens (see Figure 1 for an example). From these tokens we selected the

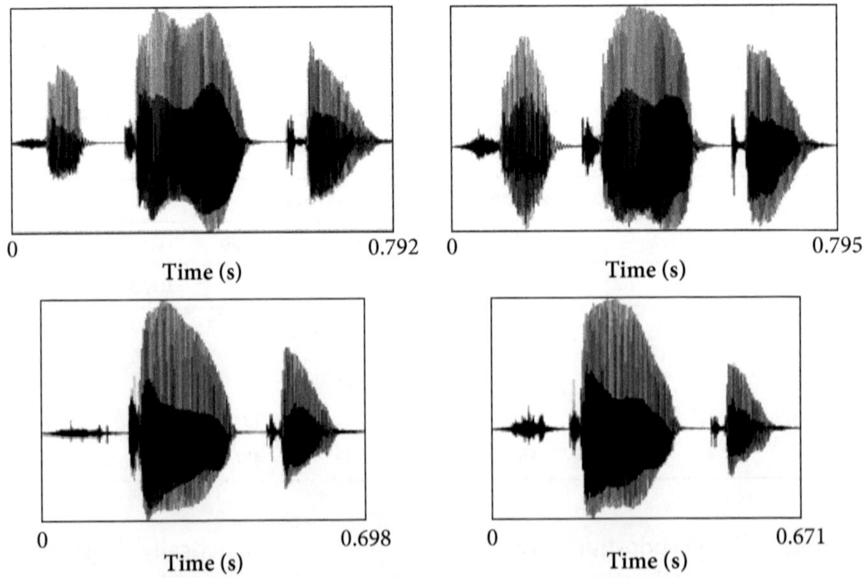

Figure 1. Examples of recorded stimuli: two unreduced and two reduced variants of *vertolken* /vərtɔlkə/ 'to interpret', produced by Speaker B.

two best tokens for each pronunciation variant for a given speaker, so that primes and targets (and repeated foils) were always different tokens. For the remaining foils, we recorded either reduced or unreduced variants and selected the best token for a given speaker.

We analyzed the recordings to examine whether the reduced and unreduced stimuli differed in degree of reduction, and whether the speakers varied in the degree of the pronunciation difference between reduced and unreduced stimuli. For the 384 recorded primes and target tokens, we created broad phonetic transcriptions using the forced alignment procedure described by Schuppler, Ernestus, Scharenborg, and Boves (2011). From these transcriptions we extracted the duration of the whole word and determined whether schwa was present. The averages are presented in Table 2. Subsequently, we analyzed these two measures as dependent variables. For the presence of schwa, we fitted logistic mixed effects regression models and for word duration we fitted mixed effect regression models, with *prefix* (*be-* vs. *ver-*), *speaker* (Speaker A vs. B), and *variant* (reduced vs. unreduced) as fixed effects and *word type* (e.g., *vertolken* or *beschrijven*) as random effect. Table 3 shows the resulting models. As shown in Figure 2, reduced stimuli were significantly shorter than unreduced stimuli. This difference was larger for stimuli produced by Speaker B. Similarly, schwa was more often absent in reduced stimuli and in stimuli produced by Speaker B. The automatically generated

Table 2. Average word duration and average percentages of word tokens produced with schwa split for speaker and pronunciation variant.

Measure	Speaker A		Speaker B	
	Reduced	Unreduced	Reduced	Unreduced
Word duration	588 ms	664 ms	485 ms	616 ms
Schwa presence	52.1%	100%	13.5%	89.6%

Table 3. Statistical models of the phonetic analysis of the recorded primes and targets.

Fixed effects	Word duration			Presence of schwa		
	$\hat{\beta}$	t	$p <$	$\hat{\beta}$	z	$p <$
Prefix (*ver*)	56.78	4.01	.0001	0.75	1.97	.05
Speaker (Speaker A)	101.51	22.14	.0001	2.33	6.21	.0001
Variant (unreduced)	131.21	28.96	.0001	4.69	10.11	.0001
Speaker × variant	−53.20	−8.23	.0001	–	–	n.s.

transcriptions suggest that schwa was frequently absent even in Speaker B's unreduced realizations (10.4%). In general, our analyses clearly demonstrate that the reduced tokens are more reduced than the unreduced tokens. In addition, Speaker B shows a larger difference between the reduced and unreduced tokens than Speaker A.

To test whether the differences between the unreduced and reduced tokens and between two speakers could also be perceived by naive listeners, we conducted a rating experiment. We asked 50 participants aged between 18 and 29 (mean 21) to rate 60 foils and all primes and targets on a 6-point scale ranging

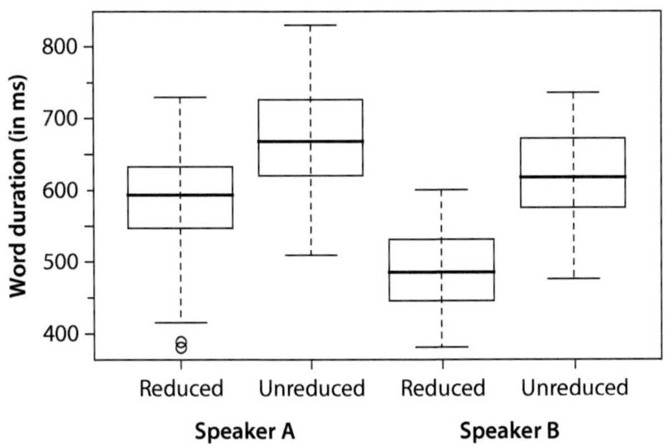

Figure 2. Boxplot of word duration split to speaker and pronunciation variant.

from very unintelligible (rating score 1) to very intelligible (rating score 6). We created eight different pseudo-randomized orders of the stimuli, so that together the eight lists contained every token of each word (i.e., two primes and two targets produced by each speaker). Each participant heard one list in which each word type occurred once and which contained both reduced and unreduced stimuli produced by Speaker A as well as Speaker B. Since the rating scores were not normally distributed, we converted the scores to a factor in which scores 1, 2, and 3 were treated as unintelligible and scores 4, 5, and 6 as intelligible. We then fitted a logistic linear mixed effects model (Faraway, 2006) based on all primes and targets with *word type* and *participant* as crossed random effects. This model yielded significant effects of *speaker* ($\hat{\beta} = 2.89$, $z = 10.51$, $p < .0001$) and *pronunciation variant* ($\hat{\beta} = 3.86$, $z = 9.46$, $p < .0001$) and their interaction ($\hat{\beta} = -2.39$, $z = -3.51$, $p < .001$), indicating that reduced items were less intelligible than unreduced items, especially if the items were produced by Speaker B (Speaker A: reduced 96.7% intelligible and unreduced 99.2%; Speaker B: reduced 72.5% and unreduced 98.7%). The two speakers clearly differed in their pronunciation and intelligibility of the reduced variants and it is therefore interesting to compare exemplar effects for these two speakers.

In the main experiment, the order in which the stimuli were presented to the participants was identical for those listening to Speakers A and those listening to Speaker B. We created four master lists for each speaker which tested priming for a given word only once. In each of the blocks of these lists, half of the primes or targets and approximately half of the foils were unreduced, and the other half were reduced. The four lists represented four different pseudo-randomizations of the trials. These randomizations had to obey four restrictions: (1) each block started with at least one foil; (2) each prime and target was followed by at least one foil; (3) at most eight words or eight pseudo-words occurred in succession; (4) prime and target were separated by a maximum of 100 trials (average: 67; range: 19 to 100). Trials with primes and targets were randomly assigned to one of the four possible combinations of the prime and target's pronunciation types: unreduced prime and unreduced target, unreduced prime and reduced target, reduced prime and unreduced target, and reduced prime and reduced target. For each master list, we created three other lists with the same words in the same order: together the four lists formed a set that represents all four possible combinations of the prime and target's pronunciation variants for each word. The combination of these four sets of four lists for each speaker resulted in 32 stimulus lists. Each list was randomly assigned to one or two participants with half of the participants receiving lists with Speaker A and the other half receiving lists with Speaker B.

Procedure
The experiment was conducted in a sound-attenuated booth, and participants were tested individually. Participants listened to the stimuli over headphones and performed a lexical decision task. They responded by pressing buttons on a button box; yes-responses were always given with the dominant hand and no-responses with the other hand. In each trial, one stimulus was presented and the next trial was initiated one second after a response was given or 3.5 seconds after the end of the stimulus. There was a pause between the two parts of the experiment, and one session lasted approximately 15 minutes.

Analyses
We analyzed the accuracy of the answers to the targets by means of logistic mixed effects models and the log-transformed response times (RTs) to the targets by means of mixed effects regression models, with *word type* and *participant* as crossed random effects. Random slopes were tested for all fixed effects. The analysis of the response times was based only on those trials that received a correct response and for which the corresponding prime had also elicited a correct response. Response times for which the residual standard errors deviated more than 2.5 times from the values predicted by the statistical model were regarded as outliers and discarded. Subsequently, the model was refitted.

We tested the influences of three predictors of interest, namely *variant match*, which indicated whether the prime and target represent the same (i.e., match) or a different pronunciation variant (i.e., mismatch), *speaker* (Speaker A vs. B) and *the distance in trials between the prime and target*. In addition, we added several control predictors to the statistical models which, in earlier studies, have been shown to affect speech processing (e.g., Van de Ven, Tucker, & Ernestus, 2011): *trial number*, *experiment part* (part 1 vs. 2), the *pronunciation variant* of the target (reduced vs. unreduced), *prefix* (*be*- vs. *ver*-), the log-transformed *target duration*, the log-transformed response times to the prime (*RT prime*) and to the preceding trial (*RT preceding*), and the log-transformed *word frequency* (based on counts from the Spoken Dutch Corpus; Oostdijk, 2002). Interactions were tested for the predictors of interest only. All non-significant effects and random slopes were excluded from the model.

All correlating variables were orthogonalized before they were added to our statistical model: If a continuous predictor A was correlated with predictor B, we replaced predictor A by the residuals of a linear regression model predicting predictor A as a function of predictor B. If the correlation involved two continuous predictors, the influence of the least interesting one (in the example above, predictor B) was partialled out. Thus, in Experiment 1 we had four residualized predictors in our model: *frequency* (correlated with *prefix*), *target duration* (correlated with *speaker* and *prefix), RT preceding* (correlated with *speaker*), and *RT prime* (correlated with *RT preceding*, *speaker*, and *prefix*).

Results and discussion

Participants made errors in 5% of the target trials. Analysis of these trials did not show an effect of any of the variables of interest. The same holds for the errors in Experiment 2, 3, and 4.

As none of the participants made errors in more than 20% of the trials, none were excluded from our analyses of the response times. We restricted our analyses to those target words for which more than 80% of the responses were correct, which led to the exclusion of the word *bekransen* 'to garland'. Table 4 shows the statistical model based on the remaining 1980 trials (85.9% of all trials). Response times measured from word onset were 943 ms on average and ranged from 522 to 2375 ms. The effects of our control predictors showed that responses were faster to words carrying the prefix *be-* (mean: 913 ms) than *ver-* (971 ms); to words produced by Speaker B (mean: 879 ms) compared to Speaker A (1003 ms); and to words with a higher frequency of occurrence. In addition, responses were faster if the word itself or its prime was shorter. Finally, responses were faster the faster the response to the prime or the preceding trial.

Table 4. Statistical models for the response times of Experiments 1 and 2. Estimated standard deviation is indicated by sd.

Fixed effects	**Experiment 1**			**Experiment 2**		
	$\hat{\beta}$	t	$p <$	$\hat{\beta}$	t	$p <$
Prefix (*ver-*)	0.06	5.9	.0001	0.08	7.23	.0001
Speaker (Speaker A)	0.13	4.9	.0001	0.08	4.91	.0001
Word frequency	−0.01	−2.3	.001	−0.02	−3.63	.0001
Target duration	0.39	14.2	.0001	0.40	19.26	.0001
RT prime	0.16	8.5	.0001	0.07	6.61	.0001
RT preceding trial	0.21	10.2	.0001	0.12	12.37	.0001
Variant match (mismatch)	0.02	3.5	.0001	–	–	n.s.
Random effects			**sd**			**sd**
Word type	intercept		0.03	intercept		0.03
Word type	RT preceding trial		0.08			
Participant	intercept		0.09	intercept		0.10
Participant				target duration		0.09
Residual			0.15			0.14

Importantly, we found a significant main effect of *variant match*, which indicated that responses were faster if the prime and the target represented the same pronunciation variant (mean: 933 ms) compared to different variants (952 ms). *Variant match* did not significantly interact with the random effects *word type* or *participant*, suggesting that the effect does not depend on a subset of word types or participants. Furthermore, the interaction between *variant match* and *speaker* was not significant, which suggests that the effect of *variant match* does not differ for the two speakers. We examined whether the effect was also significant for the two speakers separately and it was (Speaker A: $\hat{\beta} = 0.018$, $t = 2.29$, $p < .05$; Speaker B: $\hat{\beta} = 0.021$, $t = 2.61$, $p < .05$). Although our phonetic analyses and the rating study clearly showed differences between the stimuli produced by the two speakers, the effect of *variant match* is thus similar for both speakers. A possible explanation is that each participant heard only one speaker. As listeners typically adapt very rapidly to a new speaker (e.g., Dahan, Drucker, and Scarborough, 2008), participants had probably already adapted to the speaker during the first block. Consequently, the differences between the speakers did not play a substantial role.

To further investigate the robustness of exemplars, in Experiment 2 we increased the number of non-repeated foils. This experiment consisted of 800 trials. As only 16% of the trials formed word repetitions, this setup closely approximates natural conversations, in which speakers avoid repetition by often replacing content words by pronouns. As we were not able to create large numbers of stimuli using the prefixes *be-* and *ver-* only, Experiments 2 also contained foils with the prefixes *in-*, *aan-*, and *ont-*. In addition, we increased the average number of trials between primes and targets. Since we thought these manipulations would make it harder to find exemplar effects, we tested more participants.

Experiment 2

Method

Participants

All 130 participants were native speakers of Dutch (21 male), aged between 18 and 31 (mean 21); 14 were left-handed.

Materials

We used the same stimuli as in Experiment 1 plus additional foils. The Dutch lexicon contains approximately 500 tri-syllabic infinitives with the prefix *be-* or *ver-* and a unique stem (Celex; Baayen, Piepenbrock, & Gulikers, 1995), including very low frequency infinitives (e.g., *verzoeten* 'to sweeten', *bewolken* 'to cloud

Table 5. The number of stimuli presented in Experiment 2. The stimuli are broken down for prefix (*be*, *ver-*, *in-*, *aan-*, or *ont-*), whether they function as primes, targets, or foils (which are subdivided in repeated and non-repeated foils), whether they are real words or pseudo-words, and whether they occurred in Block 1 (B1) or Block 2 (B2).

Prefix	Primes	Targets	Repeated foils				Foils		Total	
	Real		Real		Pseudo		Real	Pseudo	Real	Pseudo
	B1	B2	B1	B2	B1	B2	B1/B2	B1/B2	B1/B2	B1/B2
be-	24	24			24	24	32	32	80	80
ver-	24	24			24	24	32	32	80	80
in-			5	5	5	5	76	64	86	74
aan-			5	5	5	5	76	64	86	74
ont-			5	5	5	5	58	82	68	92
Total	48	48	15	15	63	63	274	274	400	400

over', and *verzagen* 'to saw up'). The additional foils therefore also represented three other prefixes: *aan-*, *in-*, and *ont-*. In order to ensure that each of the five prefixes was presented 160 times in the entire experiment, we added 32 infinitives starting with *be-* and *ver-* and 480 infinitives carrying either the prefix *aan-*, *in-*, or *ont-* (see Table 5). The number of real and pseudo-infinitives starting with *in-*, *aan-*, or *ont-* was unequal, as only a limited number of real *ont*-infinitives are available. To avoid repetition of the prefixes *be-* and *ver-* only, 30 foils with the prefix *in-*, *aan-*, and *ont-* were also presented twice.

Furthermore, we increased the number of trials between primes and targets and presented all stimuli in one part with two blocks. The first block consisted of 48 primes and 352 foils, and the second of 48 targets and 352 foils. The number of trials between the primes and targets was entirely random (average: 405; range: 79 to 765 trials).

Both speakers recorded all new foils only once, in either a reduced or unreduced pronunciation variant. As each participant only heard stimuli from one speaker, both occurrences of the 30 repeated foils with the prefixes *in-*, *aan-*, and *ont-* were the same recording (token).

Procedure

We used the same procedure as in Experiment 1, except that all stimuli were presented in one part with a pause between the two blocks. A session lasted approximately 37 minutes.

Results and discussion

We analyzed the response times of Experiment 2 with the same method and predictors[2] as used in Experiment 1 except for the predictor *experiment part*. Three participants and the word *bekransen* 'to garland' were excluded from analyses as their error rates were above 20%. Table 4 shows the statistical model based on the remaining 5111 trials (81.9% of all trials). The average response time was 981 ms (range: 525 to 2108 ms). All control predictors that were significant in Experiment 1 were also significant in this experiment.

Although the statistical power of Experiment 2 was greater than that of Experiment 1 (due to the larger number of participants), we found no main effect of *variant match* or an interaction between *variant match* and *speaker*. Hence, in an experimental setting with a smaller proportion of repeated words and more trials between prime and target, targets preceded by primes representing the same or a different pronunciation variant are recognized equally quickly. This experiment therefore suggests that the exemplar effects found in Experiment 1 only arise in short experiments with little variation.

In Experiment 3, we further investigated the robustness of exemplar effects. We returned to the stimuli and setup of Experiment 1 and investigated whether exemplar effects are found if the prime and target may differ in two, instead of one, indexical property. The experiment tested four experimental conditions: (1) speaker match and variant match between primes and targets, (2) speaker match and variant mismatch, (3) speaker mismatch and variant match, (4) speaker mismatch and variant mismatch.

Experiment 3

Method

Participants

All 49 participants were native speakers of Dutch (six male), aged between 18 and 26 (mean 20); four were left-handed.

Materials and procedure

We used the same stimuli and recordings as in Experiment 1. In contrast to the previous experiments, half of the trials in a stimulus list were produced by Speaker A and the other half by Speaker B. Furthermore, whereas primes were either reduced or unreduced, targets were always reduced. We created three different pseudo-randomizations of the trials with the same restrictions as Experiment 1. We created eight lists for each randomization by varying the variant and speaker of the prime and the speaker of the target, which resulted in 24 different stimulus lists. A prime and target were again separated by 67 trials on average. The procedure and duration of a session were identical to those of Experiment 1.

Analyses

Except for the *pronunciation variant* of the target, which was always reduced, we used the same predictors[3] as in Experiment 1; note that *speaker* refers to the speaker of the target. In addition, we used the new predictor of interest *speaker match* (match vs. mismatch between the speaker of the prime and target).

Results and discussion

As the error rates of all participants were lower than 20%, no participants were excluded from analyses. The word *bekransen* 'to garland' had an error rate above 20% and was again omitted from further analyses. The statistical model of Experiment 3 was based on the remaining 2004 trials (85.2% of all trials) and is shown in Table 6. Response times were, on average, 943 ms (range: 540 to 1943 ms). The control predictors that were significant in the preceding experiments were again significant and showed similar effects. In addition, we found a difference between

Table 6. Statistical models for the response times of Experiment 3 and 4. Estimated standard deviation is indicated by sd.

Fixed effects	**Experiment 3**			**Experiment 4**		
	$\hat{\beta}$	t	$p<$	$\hat{\beta}$	t	$p<$
Prefix (*ver-*)	0.05	3.9	.0001	0.05	4.07	.0001
Speaker (Speaker A)	0.08	7.9	.0001	0.08	11.09	.0001
Word frequency	−0.02	−2.3	.05	–	–	.0001
Target duration	0.40	6.3	.0001	0.29	5.27	.0001
RT prime	0.12	6.2	.0001	0.11	3.76	.0001
RT preceding trial	0.14	8.4	.0001	0.22	13.27	.0001
Variant match (mismatch)	−0.05	−4.6	.0001	–	–	n.s.
Random effects			**sd**			**sd**
Word type	intercept		0.05	intercept		0.04
Word type	speaker		0.05	RT prime		0.11
Participant	intercept		0.09	intercept		0.08
Participant	experiment part		0.06	RT prime		0.14
Residual			0.14			0.17

the two experiment parts, indicating that responses obtained in the second part (mean: 921 ms) were faster than in the first part (966 ms).

Importantly, neither *variant match* nor *speaker match* showed a significant effect, nor did they interact with each other or with *speaker*. An effect of *variant match* is absent although the statistical power of Experiment 1 was similar to the power of Experiment 3 (Experiment 1: 24 match responses from 24 participants for both speakers; Experiment 3: 12 match responses from 49 participants also for both speakers).

The difference found between Experiments 1 and 3 was supported by an analysis of the combined dataset of the responses to Speaker A in Experiment 1 and the responses in Experiment 3, which shows an interaction between *experiment* and *variant match* ($\hat{\beta} = -0.031$, $t = -2.7$, $p < .05$): Whereas *variant match* explains variance in Speaker A's part of Experiment 1, it does not in Experiment 3. An analysis of the combined dataset of the responses to Speaker B in Experiment 1 and the responses in Experiment 3 gave the same result ($\hat{\beta} = -0.023$, $t = -2.1$, $p < .05$). These results suggest that exemplar effects were greater in Experiment 1, if they were present in Experiment 3 at all.

Neither Experiment 2 nor Experiment 3 showed exemplar effects. Nevertheless, we decided to conduct Experiment 4, which is a combination of Experiments 2 and 3: Participants heard the targets in the same four conditions as in Experiment 3, while the experiment was identical to Experiment 2 in the number and diversity of the foils and in the distances between primes and targets. If the null results in Experiments 2 and 3 were due to Type II errors, we would expect to find exemplar effects in Experiment 4. Moreover, we can combine the results from Experiment 4 with those from Experiments 2 and 3 to see whether these increased datasets present evidence for exemplar effects.

Experiment 4

Method

Participants

The participants were 68 native speakers of Dutch (17 male), aged between 18 and 27 years (mean 21); seven were left-handed.

Materials and procedure

The stimuli were the same set as those presented in Experiment 2. In line with Experiment 3, half of the stimuli presented to each participant were produced by Speaker A and the other half by Speaker B. Furthermore, as in Experiment 3, all targets were reduced. To make sure that not all reoccurring stimuli were reduced, we added 32 foils (16 real and 16 pseudo-words) with the prefixes *be-* and *ver-* that also reoccurred and were unreduced in Block 2 (these were reduced or unreduced in Block 1). Each participant was presented with a stimulus list of 864 trials. The procedure was identical to that of Experiment 2. One session lasted approximately 40 minutes.

Results and discussion

To analyze the response times, we used the predictors[4] from Experiment 3, except for *experiment part*. All participants and target words were included in the analyses, except for the target words *bekransen* 'to garland' and *beschaven* 'to civilize', as they had error rates higher than 20%. The statistical model of Experiment 4, based on the remaining 2459 trials (75.3% of all trials), is presented in Table 6. The average response time was 956 ms (range: 549 to 2444 ms). The same significant control effects were found as in Experiment 3, with the exception of *word frequency*.

Similar to Experiments 2 and 3, we found no effects of the predictors of interest. Hence, in the experimental setting with the most variation and in which only a small proportion of stimuli were primed, no evidence for the use of exemplars was found.

In an analysis of the combined data of Experiments 2, 3, and 4, we found no main effect of *variant match* nor an interaction of *variant match* with *experiment*. This indicates that exemplars did not play a substantial role in any of these experiments.

Additional analysis of all experimental data

So far, we investigated the presence of exemplar effects by analyzing the datasets with two categorical predictors (*variant match* and *speaker match*). The variation between a reduced and an unreduced realization differs between speakers (see Figure 2), word types, and word tokens. We therefore also analyzed all datasets with a continuous predictor indicating the similarity in reduction between the prime and target, namely the absolute difference between the log-transformed duration of the prime and the log-transformed duration of the target. Only the analysis of Experiment 1 showed a significant main effect of this continuous predictor ($\hat{\beta} = 0.17$, $t = 2.2$, $p < .05$), indicating that responses were faster if the duration difference between prime and target was smaller. In addition, none of the experiments showed an interaction between this predictor and *speaker*. These results indicate that even a more sensitive predictor shows no exemplar effects in Experiments 2, 3, and 4, and thus confirm the results obtained with the categorical predictors *variant match* and *speaker match*.

General discussion

In this paper, we investigated exemplar effects in a series of priming experiments with lexical decision tasks, in which primes and targets represented the same or a different pronunciation variant. We examined the robustness of exemplar effects under more natural conditions than in experiments reported in the literature so far (e.g., Craik & Kirsner, 1974; Goldinger, 1996; Palmeri et al., 1993) and did so in four ways. First, we studied the generalizability of exemplar effects over two very different speakers. Second, we investigated whether exemplar effects arise if the repetition of words is less clear for participants than in experiments showing exemplar effects reported in the literature. Third, we investigated if exemplar effects arise when listeners are exposed to not one but two types of pronunciation variation in the experiment (i.e., degree of reduction and speaker voice). Finally, in contrast to earlier studies, primes and targets were never completely identical.

In Experiment 1, 34% of the 288 trials formed word repetitions and each participant only listened to one of the two speakers. This experiment showed a clear exemplar effect: responses were faster to targets that represented the same pronunciation variant as their primes. In contrast to earlier studies (e.g., Mattys & Liss, 2008; McLennan et al., 2003; McLennan & Luce, 2005; Palmeri et al., 1993), in our experiments, primes and targets were always different recordings, even when they represented the same pronunciation variant produced by the same speaker. The results of Experiment 1 thus show that even if the target is not completely identical to the prime, its processing can be facilitated by the exemplar formed by its prime.

The exemplar effects arose regardless of the number of trials intervening between the prime and target. This shows that the priming effects remained constant during the first five minutes following the presentation of a prime. In this respect, our results differ from those obtained by Palmeri et al. (1993), who found that exemplar effects were only present if the interval between prime and target was smaller than 64 trials. A likely explanation for this difference in results is that Palmeri et al. used an old-new judgment task while we used lexical decision.

The exemplar effect was significant for both speakers, who clearly differ in their pronunciations and intelligibility. Hence, exemplar effects can be found for very different speakers. Our results appear to contrast with those obtained by Mattys and Liss (2008), who found that the size of exemplar effects depends on the level of intelligibility of the speakers: Participants who listened to dysarthric speakers showed longer response times and larger exemplar effects. Following McLennan and Luce (2005), the authors argue that exemplar effects are larger if performance latencies are longer. In our study, the less intelligible speaker did not elicit longer response times. Therefore, these authors would correctly predict similar exemplar effects for both speakers.

Experiment 1 provides data that are informative about speech processing in natural conditions. The percentage of words repeated within an interval of 100 words in lectures and classes from the Spoken Dutch Corpus (i.e., component n of the corpus; 53045 words) is as high as 46.6% (18.8% if only content words are taken into account). Our results thus hold for a substantial number of word tokens that listeners hear during classes and when listening to, for instance, news bulletins.

In Experiment 2, we made the repetition of words less obvious by simultaneously increasing the number of trials between a prime and target from 67 to 405 on average and reducing the proportion of trials forming word repetitions to 16%. This more closely approximates natural conversations, in which the frequent replacement of content words by pronouns decreases the repetition of content words. Although the statistical power of Experiment 2 was greater than Experiment 1 (due to the larger number of participants), Experiment 2 showed no exemplar effects. This indicates that exemplars effects are negligible when the repetition of words is less clear for participants.

The difference in delay between primes and targets in Experiments 1 and 2 may explain why we found priming effects in Experiment 1 but not in Experiment 2. The decay of the primes' exemplars (or of their activation) may have been too large at the moment the target was presented in Experiment 2. Only a small percentage of prime-target pairs (1.1%) were separated by maximally 100 trials and only 9.8% was separated by maximally 180 trials. Moreover, the block of primes was separated from the block of targets by a pause. Earlier findings that exemplar effects can be present even after one week (Goldinger, 1996) seem to contradict this explanation. However, exemplars may contain information about the context in which the occurrence was heard (e.g., the laboratory). If so, words presented in the laboratory after one week are more similar to exemplars with the same context information than exemplars encountered in a different context in that intervening week. When participants re-entered the laboratory after a week in Goldinger's experiment, they may have re-activated the exemplars specific to that laboratory. Consequently, at the moment a target word was presented, the number of different activated exemplars was probably larger in Experiment 2 than in Goldinger's experiment after one week, resulting in smaller priming effects. Further research is necessary to test this explanation.

Like Experiment 1, Experiment 2 did not show an effect of the distance between the prime and the target. This was probably due to the high number of prime-target pairs that were separated by a large number of trials. These pairs may not have shown priming effects at all, precluding a main effect of or interaction with the distance between prime and targets.

Experiment 3 studied the role of exemplars if the speech signal contained more than one type of variation (i.e., degree of reduction and speaker voice). Although the proportion of reoccurring words was the same as in Experiment 1, we found no effect of the similarity in pronunciation variant nor of the similarity in speaker voice. The statistical powers of Experiment 1 and 3 were the same, as were the average response latencies. A possible explanation comes from the earlier finding that if memory load is higher, listeners tend to use less acoustic detail in speech comprehension (e.g., Mattys & Wiget, 2011). The combination of two types of variation in Experiment 3 made Experiment 3 more demanding than Experiment 1, since the greater variation made linking the acoustic signal to semantic representations more effortful for the participants. As a consequence, participants may have paid less attention to acoustic similarity.

Another possible explanation for the absence of exemplar effects has to do with the difference in reduction patterns between our speakers. As illustrated in Figure 2, a reduced pronunciation produced by Speaker A may be very similar in word duration to an unreduced pronunciation produced by Speaker B. Primes and targets which constitute a variant mismatch may therefore be very similar, whereas those that constitute a match may be very dissimilar. This may explain why we did not find an effect of variant match. In order to test this hypothesis, we conducted additional analyses (presented above, after Experiment 4) investigating whether the difference in word duration between the prime and target predicts reaction times. This appeared not to be the case for Experiments 2, 3, and 4, which may be taken as evidence that the absence of an effect of variant match in Experiment 3 is not due to differences in reduction patterns between the two speakers. However, the speakers may not only differ in their speech rate in the two pronunciation variants, but also in their exact realization of the different segments of these variants. For instance, Speaker B may always weaken liquids after vowels, whereas Speaker A may produce them very clearly, at least in the unreduced tokens. Therefore, the absence of an effect of pronunciation variant in Experiment 3 may be due to substantial differences between the tokens representing one single variant produced by the two speakers. This explanation implies that listeners do not classify a given word token as unreduced or reduced depending on the speaker, which is in line with models assuming acoustically detailed representations for pronunciation variants.

This second possible explanation can also account for why Experiment 3 did not show a main effect of speaker match. If substantial exemplar effects only arise if a speaker match is combined with a variant match, they can only be expected in one of the four conditions in the experiment. Possibly, our experiment had too little power to show the difference between this condition and the three other ones. Future research has to show which of these explanations is most likely.

Regardless of the underlying cause, the absence of exemplar effects in Experiment 3 raises the question of what role exemplars play in speech comprehension in daily life. Most speech that people perceive is produced in spontaneous conversations involving several speakers in which degree of reduction varies greatly. The absence of exemplar effects in Experiment 3 suggests that, under these conditions, abstract lexical representations play a more important role than exemplars.

Finally, to complete the series of experiments, in Experiment 4 we examined the two types of variation simultaneously, in an experiment in which only a small proportion of stimuli reoccurred. In line with the results of Experiments 2 and 3, this experiment also showed no exemplar effects. These results confirm our findings that exemplar effects are absent in experimental setups like those of Experiments 2 and 3.

The results of this study have implications for modelling spoken word comprehension. The absence of exemplar effects in Experiments 2 to 4 disqualifies pure exemplar models but leaves hybrid models a viable option. Hybrid models do require further specification to explain under which conditions exemplars can affect comprehension. Our findings can also be accounted for in a model assuming only abstract lexical representations, provided that it assumes domain-general episodic memory. The exemplar effect found in Experiment 1 should then be reinterpreted as an episodic effect that arose because it was so obvious to participants that many words were repeated: Participants were encouraged to base decisions on episodic rather than abstract representations.

In conclusion, we conducted four priming experiments, and found exemplar effects in only the simplest experiment with no speaker variation and the largest proportion of repeated words. In spontaneous conversations, listeners may hear more than one speaker and content words are often replaced by pronouns. Hence, this paper suggests that, in a situation where more variation is available to the listener, like natural conversation, exemplars play a smaller role than previously assumed.

Acknowledgments

The authors would like to thank Lou Boves and Louis ten Bosch for their useful comments. This work was partly funded by a European Young Investigator Award and by an ERC consolidator grant (284108) to the third author.

Notes

1. By accident we also repeated the real word foil *besmetten*.

2. We residualized the following predictors: *frequency* (correlated with *prefix*), *target duration* (correlated with *speaker* and *prefix*), and *RT preceding* (correlated with *speaker*).

3. We residualized the following predictors: *frequency* (correlated with *prefix* and *experiment part*), *target duration* (correlated with *speaker*, *prefix*, and *experiment part*), *RT preceding* (correlated with *prefix* and *experiment part*), and *RT prime* (correlated with *RT preceding* and *experiment part*).

4. We residualized the following predictors: *target duration* (correlated with *speaker* and *prefix*) and *RT prime* (correlated with *RT preceding* and *prefix*).

References

Baayen, R., Piepenbrock, R., & Gulikers, L. (1995). *The CELEX lexical database (CD-ROM).* University of Pennsylvania, Philadelphia, PA: Linguistic Data Consortium.

Bradlow, A., Nygaard, L., & Pisoni, D. (1999). Effects of talker, rate, and amplitude variation on recognition memory for spoken words. *Perception & Psychophysics*, 61, 206–219. DOI: 10.3758/BF03206883

Craik, F., & Kirsner, K. (1974). The effect of speaker's voice on word recognition. *Quarterly Journal of Experimental Psychology*, 26, 274–284. DOI: 10.1080/14640747408400413

Dahan, D., Drucker, S., & Scarborough, R. (2008). Talker adaptation in speech perception: Adjusting the signal or the representations? *Cognition*, 108(3), 710–718. DOI: 10.1016/j.cognition.2008.06.003

Faraway, J. (2006). *Extending linear models with R: generalized linear mixed effects and nonpara metric regression models*. Boca Raton, FL: Chapman and Hall/CRC.

Goh, W. (2005). Talker variability and recognition memory: Instance-specific and voice-specific effects. *Journal of Experimental Psychology: Learning, Memory, and Cognition*, 31, 40–53. DOI: 10.1037/0278-7393.31.1.40

Goldinger, S. (1996). Words and voices: Episodic traces in spoken word identification and recognition memory. *Journal of Experimental Psychology: Learning, Memory, and Cognition*, 22, 1166–1183. DOI: 10.1037/0278-7393.22.5.1166

Goldinger, S. (2007). A complementary-systems approach to abstract and episodic speech perception. *Proceedings of the 16th International Congress of Phonetic Sciences* (pp. 49–54). Saarbrücken, Germany.

Hanique, I., Ernestus, M., & Boves, L. (2015). Choice and pronunciation of words: Individual differences within a homogeneous group of speakers. *Corpus Linguistics and Linguistic Theory* 11, 161–185. DOI: 10.1515/cllt-2014-0025

Hanique, I., Ernestus, M., & Schuppler, B. (2013). Informal speech processes can be categorical in nature, even if they affect many different words. *Journal of the Acoustical Society of America*, 133(3), 1644–1655. DOI: 10.1121/1.4790352

Janse, E. (2008). Spoken-word processing in aphasia: Effects of item overlap and item repetition. *Brain and Language*, 105, 185–198. DOI: 10.1016/j.bandl.2007.10.002

Mattys, S., & Liss, J. (2008). On building models of spoken-word recognition: When there is as much to learn from natural "oddities" as artificial normality. *Perception and Psychophysics*, 70(7), 1235–1242. DOI: 10.3758/PP.70.7.1235

Mattys, S., & Wiget, L. (2011). Effects of cognitive load on speech recognition. *Journal of Memory and Language*, 65, 145–160. DOI: 10.1016/j.jml.2011.04.004

McLennan, C., & Luce, P. (2005). Examining the time course of indexical specificity effects in spoken word recognition. *Journal of Experimental Psychology: Learning, Memory, and Cognition*, 31(2), 306–321. DOI: 10.1037/0278-7393.31.2.306

McLennan, C., Luce, P., & Charles-Luce, J. (2003). Representation of lexical form. *Journal of Experimental Psychology: Learning, Memory, and Cognition*, 29(4), 539–553. DOI: 10.1037/0278-7393.29.4.539

Oostdijk, N. (2002). The design of the Spoken Dutch Corpus. In P. Peters, P. Collins, & A. Smith (Eds.), *New frontiers of corpus research* (pp. 105–112). Amsterdam: Rodopi.

Palmeri, T., Goldinger, S., & Pisoni, D. (1993). Episodic encoding of voice attributes and recognition memory for spoken words. *Journal of Experimental Psychology: Learning, Memory, and Cognition*, 19, 309–328. DOI: 10.1037/0278-7393.19.2.309

Pluymaekers, M., Ernestus, M., & Baayen, R. H. (2005). Lexical frequency and acoustic reduction in spoken Dutch. *Journal of the Acoustical Society of America*, 118(4), 2561–2569. DOI: 10.1121/1.2011150

Schuppler, B., Ernestus, M., Scharenborg, O., & Boves, L. (2011). Acoustic reduction in conversational Dutch: A quantitative analysis based on automatically generated segmental transcriptions. *Journal of Phonetics*, 39, 96–109. DOI: 10.1016/j.wocn.2010.11.006

Van de Ven, M., Tucker, B., & Ernestus, M. (2011). Semantic context effects in the comprehension of reduced pronunciation variants. *Memory and Cognition*, 39, 1301–1316. DOI: 10.3758/s13421-011-0103-2

Appendix

Stimuli in all experiments

Targets

begieten begluren begraven begrijpen begroeten bekladden beklimmen bekransen bekrassen beschaven beschermen beschrijven besmeren bestelen bestoken bestraffen bestralen besturen betasten betrappen bevriezen bevruchten bezingen bezorgen verbannen verbranden vergeven vergrijzen verkiezen verklappen verkleumen verkreuken vermoeien verprutsen verslapen verslikken verspelen versperren verspreiden verstijven verstoten vertellen verteren vertolken vertragen vertrappen vertrekken verzachten

Repeated pseudo-word foils

bedangen bedinken begannen begoeren begranzen begruien beklegen bekonnen bekrapen bekrempen benotten bepleuten beplonten beporken beschakken beschoeten besmotten bestermen bestraaien betaffen betroeren bevichten bevrammen bezeiten verbloffen verbrissen verdechten verdilgen verdoepen verdrooien verfalmen verfrinsen vergippen vergoeten vergreuzen verguilen verklenen verknillen verkoezen verscharpen versnallen verstoemen verteuven vertiemen vertilmen verwilken verzekken verzwukken

Additional foils in Experiments 1 and 3

Real words

bedanken bedaren begeren beginnen begroten beheksen beheren bejagen bekeren bekronen beleggen belonen bemerken bereiden besmetten besmetten bestraten betreffen betwisten bevolken bevrijden beweren bewerken bezetten verbergen verbouwen verdampen verdenken verduren verdwalen vergoeden vergokken vergroeien verkleuren verknallen verlangen vermaken vermengen verplaatsen verplichten verrekken verstikken verstoppen vertakken vertalen vertoeven verzenden verzinnen

Pseudo-words

bedelken bedirven bedoeren begennen begrooien bekliegen bekreipen belamen bemonnen benoeten benuiden bepelen bepraven beristen beschekken beslatten bespraaien bestroeien betreuden bevengen bewirken bezekken bezieten bezoelen verbliffen verblijmen verbrussen verdetsen verdirven vergroemen vergussen verkirsen verknaren verloenken verlunken verniemen verpatten verpippen verrosten versmeuden versmieden verspallen vertoelen verwalken verwijpen verzoepen verzwekken verzweugen

Additional foils in Experiments 2 and 4

Real words

aanbellen aanblazen aanblijven aanboren aanbraden aanbreken aanbrengen aandienen aandikken aandragen aandraven aandrijven aandringen aandrukken aanduiden aandurven aanduwen aangrijpen aanhaken aanhalen aanhangen aanharken aanhebben aanhechten aanheffen aanhoren aanhouden aankaarten aankijken aanklagen aanklampen aankleden aankloppen aanknopen aankomen aankopen aankunnen aanladen aanleggen aanleren aanliggen aanmaken aanmanen aanmelden aanmeren aanmerken aanmeten aannaaien aannemen aanpakken aanpappen aanpassen aanplakken aanplanten aanpoten aanpraten aanprijzen aanraden aanraken aanreiken aanrichten aanrijden aanroepen aanroeren aanrukken aanschaffen aanscherpen aansluiten aansnellen aansnijden aanspannen aanspoelen aansporen aanspreken aanstampen aantreffen bedanken bedaren begeren beginnen begrenzen begroten beheksen beheren bejagen bekeren bekronen beleggen belichten belijden belonen bemerken beschimpen besluipen besluiten besmetten bespatten bestraten betrachten betreffen betrekken betwisten bevallen bevolken bevrijden beweren bezatten bezetten inbedden inbeelden inbeuken inblazen inblikken inbreken inbrengen inchecken indammen indekken indelen indenken indeuken indienen indikken indraaien indringen indrinken indrogen indruisen indrukken induiken indutten induwen inenten ingieten ingooien ingrijpen inhouden inhuren inkerven inkijken inklemmen inkleuren inkomen inkopen inkorten inkrimpen inladen inlassen inleiden inleven inlezen inlichten inlijsten inlijven inlopen inlossen inluiden inpakken inpassen inperken inplannen inprenten inprikken inrichten inroepen inruilen inschenken inscheuren inschikken inseinen insluipen insluiten insneeuwen insnoeren inspannen inspringen inspuiten instappen insteken instemmen instoppen instromen intoetsen invallen ontbieden ontbijten ontbinden ontbloten ontbossen ontbreken ontdekken ontdooien ontduiken onteren onterven ontfermen ontgelden ontglippen ontgroeien ontgroenen onthalen ontharen ontheffen onthullen onthutsen ontkennen ontkiemen ontkleuren ontkomen ontkrachten ontkurken ontladen ontlasten ontlopen ontluiken ontnemen ontpitten ontplooien ontpoppen ontroeren ontroven ontruimen ontschepen ontschieten ontsluiten ontsmetten ontsnappen ontspannen ontsporen ontspringen ontstemmen ontstijgen ontstoppen ontvallen ontvellen ontvetten ontvlammen ontvluchten ontvolken ontwaken ontzeggen ontzuilen verbergen verbluffen verdampen verdenken verdoffen verdoven verduren verdwalen vergelden vergoeden vergokken vergroeien vergulden verkleuren verklikken verknallen verkopen verkroppen vermaken verpakken verplaatsen verplichten verrekken versjouwen verstikken verstoppen vertalen vertikken vertoeven vertonen verzenden verzinnen

Pseudo-words

aandonnen aandriegen aandrieven aandrikken aangoeven aanhachten aanhiffen aanhoffen aankliegen aanklijzen aankloeden aankluigen aanknoepen aankuimen aanmekken aanmetten aanmoenen aanmolden aanmonnen aanmorken aanpatten aanpemmen aanpepsen aanpeuten aanplenten aanplikken aanploeken aanpretten aanproeten aanproetsen aanproezen aanprossen aanpruiten aanpuiten aanrakken aanrappen aanrijtsen aanriksen aanroeden aanruiden aanschieven aanschorpen aansnieden aansnoelen aansoeren aanspallen aansprokken aanstatten aanstempen aanstijken aanstoempen aanstopen aanstrappen aantekken aantisten aantoeken aantuiken aanvollen aanvregen aanwannen aanwienen aanwoeken aanwoezen aanwooien bededden bedirven bedoeren bedrakken bedwilmen begennen begronzen begrooien bekliegen bekreipen bemonnen benoeten bepelen bepraven beproeten beristen beschekken beslatten besnuien bespodden bespraaien bestarmen bestirmen bestroeien bestroeken betreuden bewirken bezanken bezekken bezeuken bezieten bezoelen inbeuten inbingen inboerken inbriksen inbummen indieken indinnen indoenen indommen indonken indremmen indrokken indrouwen indruigen indutsen ingitten ingoetsen ingoeven ingrannen inkarven inkeeuwen inkimmen inkloepen inkluipen inkummen inlijgen inlissen inloepen inloesten inloezen inmekken inmonten inplinnen inpranten inprekken inproetsen inraksen inralen inrannen inrensen inrutten inschekken inschoezen insienen inslappen insnieren inspienen insprangen instenden instijken instramen instreppen instreumen instrupsen intaben intaren intetsen intotsen intrieken invollen invruizen invuigen inweggen inwoetsen ontbatten ontblammen ontblitten ontboeden ontboesen ontbrikken ontbrinden ontbrotsen ontbunnen ontfilken ontfirmen ontflepsen ontgalden ontgirten ontglappen ontgleppen ontgratsen ontgreben ontgreeuwen ontgrennen ontgreunen ontgrooien ontgruinen onthatsen onthuitsen ontkarken ontkemmen ontkidden ontkloeren ontkoerken ontkrechten ontkrichten ontkrippen ontladden ontledden ontleppen ontlietsen ontlodden ontluitsen ontpatten ontpeuten ontplaaien ontpuiten ontschuipen ontslatten ontslitten ontsmatten ontsmoeren ontsmouten ontsmudden ontsmuiten ontsnieken ontsnippen ontsprengen ontsteugen ontstiepen ontstimmen ontstotsen ontstuigen ontveeuwen ontvelken ontveuzen ontvieten ontvilken ontvlachten ontvlichten ontvlimmen ontvloemen ontvollen ontvuiten ontwannen ontwienen ontwietsen ontwirren ontwoenen ontwoetsen ontworren ontwotsen ontwuinen ontzallen ontzelen ontzuiken verbiegen verbleuven verbliffen verbrussen verdappen verdetsen verdirven verdotsen verdwiezen vergellen vergeppen vergetten vergroemen vergussen verkessen verkirsen verkruggen verloenken verlunken verniemen verpatten verpippen verschorpen versloenzen versluppen versmeuden versmieden verspallen vertoelen verwalken verzwekken verzweugen

Repeated real words

aanbakken aanbieden aanstellen aansterken aanstichten inbakken inbinden instellen instinken instorten ontaarden ontberen ontvouwen ontwarren ontwennen

Repeated pseudo-words

aanbreuden aanbrinden aandinnen aanstotten aanstruipen inbetsen inbieben inweuden inzanken inzuien ontbaaien ontbetten ontbissen ontziggen ontzoegen

Additional foils in Experiment 4

Repeated real words

Stimuli are the same as in Experiment 2 with the following additions:
bedwingen bereiden beschijnen beslissen betuigen bevinden bewerken bezuren verbouwen verdwijnen verlangen vermengen verplegen verschuilen vertakken verzuimen

Repeated pseudo-words

Stimuli are the same as in Experiment 2 with the following additions:
bedelken bekeugen belamen benuiden beseppen besmieren bevengen bezwuren verblijmen verknaren verlienen verrosten verslaten verwijpen verzanen verzoepen

Production and accent affect memory

Kit W. Cho[i] and Laurie Beth Feldman[i, ii]
[i] University at Albany, State University of New York, Albany, NY, USA /
[ii] Haskins Laboratories, New Haven, Connecticut

In three experiments, we examined the effects of accents and production on free recall and yes/no recognition memory. In the study phase, native English participants heard English words pronounced by a speaker with an accent that is highly familiar to the participant (American English) or with a less familiar accent (Dutch). Participants had to either say aloud (produce) the word that they heard in their natural pronunciation (Exp. 1a) or imitate the original speaker (Exp. 1b) or simply listen to the word. In all experiments, in both recall and recognition, produced words and words spoken in an unfamiliar accent were more likely to be recalled and more likely to be recognized, than words that were listened to or words spoken in a more familiar accent. In recognition but not in recall, listening to words spoken in an unfamiliar accent improved memory more than listening to words spoken in a familiar accent. Results suggest that listening allows the acoustic-phonetic details of a speaker to be retained in memory, but that production attenuates access to details about the original speaker's pronunciation. Finally, the benefit of production for memory does not differ whether one produces in one's natural accent or imitates that of the speaker.

Keywords: accent, phonetic/memory interactions, production effect, recognition memory

In our multicultural world, we communicate with individuals who speak with different accents on a daily basis. It is therefore not surprising that accent has long been the focus of studies showing the influence of first (L1) language phonology on the perception and production of the phonology of a second (L2) language (for reviews see Flege 1987; Flege, Bohm, & Jang, 1997; Kuhl, 2000, 2004; Meador, Flege, & MacKay, 2000). Typical themes include how proficiency, type of noise mask and similarity of phonemes across particular pairs of languages impact intelligibility of L2 speech (Lecumberri, Cooke, & Cutler, 2010). Variability in the

DOI 10.1075/bct.80.02cho

pronunciation of words, especially those articulated in a foreign accent also provides a window on how the retention of low-level phonetic variation affects not only intelligibility, but also higher-order levels of cognition including memory in L1 speakers.

At the sentence level, previous research has shown that the transcription of an unfamiliar relative to a familiar accent is slower and less accurate (Adank, Evans, Scott, & Stuart-Smith, 2009; Floccia, Butler, Goslin, & Ellis, 2009; Munro & Derwing, 1995a) and that syntactic errors are difficult to detect (Schmid & Yeni-Komshian, 1999). While these studies demonstrate that accented speech can be less intelligible, electrophysiological measures show that L1 speakers show different P600 patterns to syntactic errors in foreign accented and native accented utterances (Hanulikova, van Alphen, van Goch, & Weber, 2012). At an even higher level of cognition, L1 speakers judge statements (e.g., ants don't sleep) spoken with an accent as less believable than those same sentences spoken in the listener's native accent (Lev-Ari & Keysar, 2010). This finding demonstrates diminished credibility for messages delivered in an unfamiliar accent (see Eisenstein, 1983, for a overview of native speakers' reaction to non-native speech).

Although these outcomes show that foreign accented speech can have negative consequences, there is debate as to whether it is accent per se that is responsible. Munro and Derwing (1995a, 1995b, see also Derwing & Munro, 1997) have identified three variables that can affect comprehension of foreign-accented speech: (a) accentedness, (b) comprehensibility, and (c) intelligibility. Both accentedness and comprehensibility are subjective measures, derived from Likert-type ratings by listeners who judge how "strong" the speaker's accent is and how easy it is to understand, respectively. These measures differ from intelligibility, which is a more objective measure of understanding, typically assessed by evaluating transcription accuracy. Munro and Derwing (1995a) showed that low comprehensibility increased reaction time in their sentence verification task more than did accent per se. However, overall, they (Munro & Derwing 1995a, 1995b; Derwing & Munro, 1997) reported strong correlations (based on the standards set by Cohen, 1992), between the three variables. Specifically, comprehensibility is positively correlated with intelligibility and negatively correlated with accentedness, and intelligibility is negatively correlated with accentedness.[1] Overall, the results show that foreign-accented speech negatively impacts both subjective (comprehensibility) judgments and objective (intelligibility) performance.

Words spoken in an unfamiliar accent, may be hard for listeners to process because the articulation deviates from the listener's experience in ways that seem unsystematic (e.g., Adank et al., 2009). For example, comprehensibility may be reduced when listening to a foreign accent because certain phonemic contrasts required for the speaker's second language are absent in the speaker's first language, and what replaces them differs across speakers in ways that are not immediately obvious (Best & Strange, 1992; Best, Bradlow, Guion-Anderson, & Polka, 2011). Some researchers have focused on methods intended to help listeners adapt to an unfamiliar accent more quickly (Adank, Hagoort, & Bekkering, 2010; Nguygen, Dufour, & Brunellière, 2012). For example, Adank et al. (2010) presented sentences composed of English words, but spoken by a native speaker of Dutch, to different groups of participants under varied training conditions, e.g., transcribing the sentences, saying aloud the sentences in one's own accent, saying aloud the sentences by imitating the accent of the speaker. (In that study, they created an unfamiliar accent by artificially substituting altered vowel pronunciations within the words). Participants were tested on their ability to transcribe words in novel sentences under adverse listening condition (background noise). Training by imitation led to the best intelligibility relative to the other training procedures.[2] Notwithstanding the results by Adank et al. (2010), the evidence supporting imitation as a method to enhance comprehension of a novel accent is not conclusive. Nguyen, Dufour, and Brunellière (2012) failed to replicate the benefits of imitating relative to simply listening to an unfamiliar dialect of a native accent in a lexical decision task. In that study the training and test stimuli were different words, and the experimenter did not design the novel pronunciations. As a result, the pronunciation of the to-be-learned accent was likely more natural than in Adank et al.'s (2010) study. Of course, contrasting demands of the lexical decision and transcription tasks or the role of prosodic information across a sequence of words, may be particularly relevant when words are accented.

While some researchers have examined intelligibility of accents in short time frames, others have introduced accent to study how variability influences the time course of learning. In a recent study, Muench and Creel (2013) required participants to learn novel labels that were associated with unfamiliar shapes when the labels were articulated by one speaker (one accent) or by two different speakers (two accents). Muench and Creel (2013) reported that the group that learned the voice-word associations with two accents needed more trials to reach criterion and were less accurate to produce those word labels at a later time. Interestingly in that study, speaker-specific effects were minor and restricted to a particular vowel domain. The authors attributed the impediment at learning of two accents relative to one to greater form-word inconsistency for a word in different voices and to phonological competition between the different form-word mappings that participants encountered. While this particular study demonstrates that the variability introduced by multiple accents can hinder learning, with semantically better-defined terms, others have demonstrated that accent variability can facilitate learning.

A series of experiments by Barcroft and Sommers (2005, see also Sommers & Barcroft, 2007, 2011), reported that introducing *more* variations of voice-word mappings within the same accent can promote better second-language learning of vocabulary words. Specifically, in Barcroft and Sommers (2005; Experiment 2), native American English speakers learned novel Spanish vocabulary words under one of three conditions: (a) no variability: six repetitions of each word by only one speaker, (b) moderate variability: two repetitions of each word, each by three speakers, and (c) high variability: six repetitions of each word, each by a different speaker. (Note that in all conditions, participants experienced six voice-word pairings.) The learning phase entailed presenting participants with a picture of a familiar object (e.g., clock) and the Spanish word for the picture's referent (e.g., *reloj*) that was presented auditory and spoken by a native speaker(s) of Spanish. Participants took two types of cued-recall tests: (1) one that was similar to the condition under which they learned the words (i.e., a picture served as a cue and they had to articulate the Spanish translation of the picture's referent), and (2) the Spanish translation of a target was presented auditory and served as a cue for participants to produce the English translation. For both types of tests, greater variability at learning increased the proportion of words recalled and decreased the latency to produce the correct response. The authors asserted that exposure to voice-word pairings from multiple speakers produces more robust representations of lexical items than does exposure to voice-word pairings from a single speaker. The outcomes of this study and that of Muench and Creel (2013) demonstrate that information about different speakers (voices or accents) can be stored and accessed and thus are consistent with Goldinger's (1998) claim that indexical information associated with acoustic-phonetic detail of the speaker's voice and style of speaking is stored in memory rather than being abstracted away (Goldinger, 1996; Goldinger, Pisoni, & Logan, 1991; Nygaard & Pisoni, 1998).

There are at least two differences that could lead to the discrepant results between Barcroft and Sommers (2005), who showed a benefit of variability and those reported by Muench and Creel (2013), who reported a decrement with greater variability. Most obvious is that Barcroft and Sommers (2005) had participants learn concepts (e.g., watch) that are well established in the participants' lexicon whereas Muench and Creel (2013) had participants learn novel labels for novel objects. It could be that voice-word variability is beneficial only when word form variability can be mapped onto an already established concept. In addition, whereas Barcroft and Sommers (2005) used a natural accent (Spanish), Muench and Creel (2013) taught an artificial accent to native American English speakers. (As suggested above, the use of an artificial as opposed to a more naturally occurring accent may have contributed to the discrepant findings between Adank et al., 2010 and Nguyen et al., 2012).

In the memory domain, Cho and Feldman (under revision) conducted two experiments to compare accented and non-accented words by having the same participants listen to words silently or listen to words and say them aloud (hereafter "produce"). Half of the words were presented in an American English accent, which is the accent that is most familiar to the participants who were native English speakers, and half of the words were presented in a Chinese accent, which, by comparison, is unfamiliar to the participants. There was one speaker of each accent and words were rotated through conditions across participants. Although participants were not forewarned of the upcoming memory tests, after study, they completed a free recall and a yes/no recognition tests. In both experiments, they observed a *production effect* (see MacLeod et al., 2010) in recall and recognition – words that were said aloud were remembered better than those that were listened to. In the recognition test, there was also a main effect of accent and an interaction of action by production: words that were presented in a Chinese accent were remembered significantly better than those same words when presented in an American English accent, but differences between the two accents were absent when participants produced those words during study. To rule out the possibility that the benefit of listening to a word in a foreign accent was an overcompensation for low intelligibility, in Experiment 2 they included words that varied on intelligibility (viz., transcription accuracy to auditorily presented single words in a pilot study). At the end of each study trial, they presented the visual form of each word so as to resolve challenges to intelligibility and ensure that participants eventually activated the lexical and semantic properties of the intended word. Cho and Feldman (under revision) reasoned that if the superior memory of accented words were attributable to augmented processing at encoding to compensate for low intelligibility of the auditory presentation at study, then the benefit of an accented presentation would be more robust for words with low transcription accuracy; however, they observed no effect and no interaction with the intelligibility of the word. In keeping with the benefit of encoding variability, the authors interpreted the outcome as evidence that listening to accented words produced more elaborated traces of those words that were likely due to the contribution of more variable indexical information; Accent effects were not a consequence of reduced intelligibility per se. In summary, the consequence of listening to a word pronounced in a foreign accent is a more distinctive or memorable episode because the variability in acoustic and phonetic detail that characterizes accented speech enriches the form-meaning relation more than the speech of another native whose accent more closely resembles prior episodes with that word. Most novel was that saying an accented word aloud after hearing it benefitted memory but the increase was not additive with any benefit of accent. The act of repeating a word requires mapping an acoustic-phonetic pattern onto the requisite code for articulation. Therefore, they concluded that the act of production results in the potential loss or overshadowing of acoustic and phonetic detail about the input from the original speaker. In essence, accent and indexical information contribute to better recognition performance when participants only listen but, when participants must produce the word, their own articulatory information seems to take precedence over indexical information about the original speaker.

The present study

In the present study, we sought to generalize the results and begin to explore the mechanisms underlying the benefit of production documented in Cho and Feldman (under revision). We first wanted to replicate our findings with a speaker of a different, unfamiliar accent. In Cho and Feldman (under revision), the unfamiliar accent was Chinese; in the present study, it was Dutch. Experiment 1a was a direct replication of the experiments in Cho and Feldman (under revision) with the following modifications (1) the accent of the unfamiliar speaker, (2) identities of the speakers, (3) the selection of words to remember (we chose a new set of words), and (4) the words were presented twice in two separately randomized blocks before test, in an attempt to strengthen the encoding of the words. In Experiment 1b, we asked whether imitating the accent of the speaker conferred an additional benefit beyond that of simply repeating the word in one's own accent; therefore, in Experiment 1b, participants were told that when they repeated the word, they should imitate the accent of the speaker. To our knowledge, no one has systematically investigated whether imitating the accent in which individual words are presented makes them more memorable than naturally repeating them. Any difference in outcomes between production with and without imitation could provide insights into how the phonetics and acoustics of the input map onto the articulatory code that underlies the benefit of production.

Two issues motivated Experiment 2. Methodologically, we wanted to see whether the effects in the recognition data persist when participants do not first complete a free recall test. Eliminating the recall task precludes any possible carryover effect from successful recall of words onto latter recognition. If present, such an effect could inflate performance on the recognition test for successfully recalled words. More important was that we explored a potential mechanism contributing to improved performance in recognition memory of accented words. Specifically we tested the hypothesis that the benefit of accent arises from increased activation of a studied word's phonological neighbors during encoding. For example, when presented with the word *map* in an unfamiliar accent, the unfamiliar pronunciation or phonological deviation from what one usually hears may activate phonological neighbors that share the same initial phoneme (e.g., *math*), or neighbors that rhyme with the target (e.g., *gap*). This hypothesis is congruent with the Neighborhood Activation Model that posits that a word activates those words with similar acoustic-phonetic patterns (Luce & Pisoni, 1998). In a recognition test participants do not generate words. However they may be more likely to indicate that they have studied a word that is phonologically similar to the studied target as compared to one with no phonological overlap. Experimentally, phonological activation of partially similar words may increase the likelihood that participants indicate that both *map* and *math* were studied. We ask whether, when words pronounced in an accent increase hits, that benefit comes at a cost of increasing false alarms on words that are phonologically similar to the targets. To test this hypothesis, we included two types of lures in the recognition test: those that are phonologically dissimilar to the targets, that is, unrelated, and those that are phonologically similar to the target like *math* and *gap* for the target *map*. If the benefit of accent at recognition derives from imprecise phonological specification and activation not only of the target but also of phonologically similar words, then the tendency for participants to indicate that phonologically similar lures were studied more often than phonologically dissimilar lures should be greater for accented than for unaccented targets. That is, false alarms should be higher to phonologically similar than to dissimilar lures and differences should be greater for the accented version of a target.

In the present experiments, during the study phase, half the words was listened to whereas the other half was listened to and repeated aloud by the participant. Half of the words was spoken by a native speaker of American English, whose accent was familiar to the participants in this study who also are native speakers, and half the words was spoken by a native speaker of Dutch, an accent that is unfamiliar to the participants by comparison. This manipulation allowed us to replicate the effects of accent on memory as reported in Cho and Feldman (under revision). Finally, we included accented words that were either easy or hard to transcribe in isolation in an attempt to demonstrate that perceptual (or cognitive) processing in response to low intelligibility is responsible for the effect of accent.

Experiments 1a and 1b

With the exception of the instructions for the production condition (viz., repeat or imitate), the procedure was identical in Experiments 1a and 1b.

Method

Design

The design was a 2 (Action: Listen or Produce) × 2 (Accent: American English or Dutch) × 2 (Ease of Identification: Easy vs. Hard) within-participants design. Memory was assessed using a free-recall and a yes/no recognition task. In Experiment 1a, participants produced the words in their natural-pronunciation; in Experiment 1b, participants produced the word by imitating the accent of the speaker.

Materials and counterbalancing

Eighty mono- and di-syllabic words were selected as study words; an additional 40 unrelated words were selected as lures on the recognition test (see the Appendix for the words). The study (target) words and lures were matched on word length, frequency, orthographic and phonological neighborhood size (see Table 1 for the characteristics of the items). There were two versions of each word: one pronounced by a male native American English speaker (American accent) and one pronounced by a male native Dutch speaker (Dutch accent). Words differed on intelligibility operationalized as ease of identification. This was determined by the transcription accuracy of the word when presented in a Dutch accent.[3] The mean identification rates for easy and hard words are 83% (range: 80–100%; standard deviation: 7%) and 26% (range: 0–40%; standard deviation: 18%), respectively. This difference is statistically significant $t(78) = 18.921, p < .001$.

Table 1. Mean values of the stimuli characteristics used in Experiments 1a, 1b, and 2.

Characteristic	Experiment	Item Type		
		Study (Targets)	Lures: Unrelated	Lures: Phon
Word Length	1a, 1b	4.64	4.55	–
	2		4.69	4.80
Frequency (log HAL)	1a, 1b	9.84	9.48	–
	2		9.84	9.54
Orthographic Neighborhood	1a, 1b	6.41	5.70	–
	2		7.06	6.63
Phonological Neighborhood	1a, 1b	16.41	13.78	–
	2		15.98	18.05

Note. Phon: Phonologically Similar; separate one-way ANOVAs were computed, for each characteristic in each experiment, all $Fs < 2.1$, $ps > .15$.
The same targets were used in all three experiments.
Phonologically Similar lures were not included in Experiments 1a and 1b.

For counterbalancing purposes, the words were divided into four sets of 10 and each set was rotated through each of the four conditions formed by crossing Accent and Action, with an equal number of participants seeing each of the four counterbalancing list. Across participants, each word in each of its accented pronunciations appeared in the listen and the production condition.

Participants
Thirty-two undergraduates from the Psychology Department participant pool at the University at Albany, State University of New York participated in each experiment in exchange for research credit; all reported English as their native language.

Procedure
Each participant was tested individually using E-Prime 2.0. In the first phase of the experiment, the study phase, participants were told that they would hear a list of words presented one at a time and that they would be asked either to listen to or to listen to and then produce the word. The action for each trial was cued using either a blue or yellow circle (counterbalanced across participants which color denoted listen or listen and repeat) that remained on the screen for 1500 ms. Participant were asked not to move their lips when they were listening to a word so as to avoid the possibility that mouthing enhanced memorability of an item. Immediately after the offset of the colored cue, a word was presented through speakers for 2000 ms, followed by a blank screen that lasted for 1500 ms, during which participants repeated the word or sat silently. Once the action was completed, the printed form of the word appeared on the screen for 1500 ms and then the screen went blank for 500 ms; thus, the total time for each trial was 7000 ms. Participants cycled through the study words twice in two separate blocks, with the words presented in a different randomized order for each participant, in an attempt to strengthen the encoding of the words. As noted above, participants were not informed of the upcoming memory tasks.

After completing the study phase of the experiment, participants completed a two-minute filler task in which they solved addition problems. They then completed the test phase that consisted of a three-minute free recall task in which they wrote down all the words they remembered from the study phase. After the recall task, there were an additional two minutes of math problems. Finally, participants performed a self-paced yes/no recognition test in which words were presented visually one at a time. Participants were instructed to respond "old" ("0" key on the keyboard) if they remembered having heard the word in the first part of the study and "new" ("1" key on the keyboard) if they did not. The entire session took approximately 25 minutes to complete.

Results and discussion

In all experiments, the effect sizes for ANOVAs on percent correct are reported using partial eta-square (η_p^2), and the effect sizes for independent t-test are reported using Cohen's d (d) and paired t-tests are reported using Cohen's d_{CD} (d_{CD}) based on the recommendation of Dunlap, Cortina, Vaslow, and Burke (1996). Separate analyses are reported with participants (F_1 or t_1) and items (F_2 or t_2) as random effects (see Clark, 1973).

We analyzed the recognition data using d', computed using z-Hits minus z-False Alarms. In computing the z-Hits and z-False Alarms, we followed the recommendation by Snodgrass and Corwin (1988) of adding a value of 0.5 to the hit and false alarm counts and adding 1 to the number of target and distractor items in each condition. (This procedure avoids undefined z-scores when participants had a hit rate of 1 or a false alarm rate of 0.) A higher d' represents greater memory discriminability.

Experiment 1a

The data from the recall task are presented in the top half of Table 2. Overall, items that were produced were remembered better than items that were listened to, .22 vs. .10, respectively, replicating the production effect. Items that were hard to identify were recalled at a higher rate than items that are easy to identify (.19 vs. .12, respectively). Finally, items spoken in a Dutch were better recalled relative to in an American accent (.19 vs. .12, respectively). These observations were confirmed in a 2 (Accent: American vs. Dutch) × 2 (Action: Listen vs. Produce) × 2

Table 2. Proportion of words recalled and intrusions in Experiments 1a and 1b.

Experiment	Intelligibility	Accent	Action		Production Effect	Intrusions
			Produce	Listen		
1a	Easy	Dutch	.18	.12	.06	.03
		American	.15	.04	.11	
	Hard	Dutch	.33	.14	.19	
		American	.21	.09	.12	
1b	Easy	Dutch	.23	.10	.13	.06
		American	.19	.07	.12	
	Hard	Dutch	.31	.13	.18	
		American	.20	.09	.11	

Note. In Experiment 1a, participants repeated the word in their own accent.
In Experiment 1b, subject imitated the accent of the speaker.

(Ease of Identification: Easy vs. Hard) repeated-measures ANOVAs that revealed main effects of all three variables (Accent: $F_1(1,31) = 27.312, p < .001, \eta_p^2 = .468, F_2(1,78) = 22.634, p < .001, \eta_p^2 = .225$; Action: $F_1(1,31) = 50.009, p < .001, \eta_p^2 = .617, F_2(1, 78) = 24.243, p < .001, \eta_p^2 = .237$, and Ease of Identification: $F_1(1,31) = 27.312, p < .001, \eta_p^2 = .468, F_2(1,78) = 3.042, p = .085, \eta_p^2 = .038$). In addition, there was a 3-way interaction ($F_1(1,31) = 6.903, p = .013, \eta_p^2 = .182, F_2(1,78) = 3.777, p = .056, \eta_p^2 = .064$) showing that the difference between saying aloud and listening (the production effect) was numerically greater for American-accented than Dutch-accented words when the words were easy to identify (.11 vs. .06, respectively, $t_1(31) = 1.708, p = .098, d_{CD} = .26$; $t_2(39) = 2.692, p = .010, d_{CD} = .36$), but that the reverse was true when the words were hard to identify (.12 vs. .19, respectively, $t_1(31) = 1.851, p = .074, d_{CD} = .32$; $t_2(39) = .053, p = .958, d_{CD} = .05$). Because this interaction was not replicated in Experiment 1b nor was it observed in the experiments reported by Cho and Feldman (under revision), we treat this finding as a Type I error. Finally, there was an interaction of Action by Ease of Identification, ($F_1(1,31) = 6.415, p = .017, \eta_p^2 = .171, F_2(1,78) = 3.495, p = .065, \eta_p^2 = .043$). Follow-up analyses to the significant interaction showed that the difference between producing and listening was larger in the hard to identify words (.27 vs. .12, $t_1(31) = 4.228, p < .001, d_{CD} = .50$; $t_2(78) = 3.943, p < .001, d = .39$) than in the easy to identify words (.17 vs. .08, $t_1(31) = 2.075, p = .046, d_{CD} = .34$; $t_2(78) = 2.326, p = .023, d = .20$). A likely explanation is that this is a hypercorrection effect (e.g., Butterfield & Metcalfe, 2001). To elaborate, for words that are hard to identify, participants sometimes generated phonological errors when producing the word. We speculate that providing visual feedback after an error may have made the learning episode particularly salient and memorable. The shortcoming of this account is that we could not document this interaction when the final test was recognition. All other 2-way interactions were not significant ($F_{1\&2}$s < 1.50, ps > .23, η_p^2s < .046).

For recognition, the data are presented in the top half of Table 3. The overall pattern of results replicate those of recall in that memory discriminability, as indicated by *d'* values, were higher for (1) words that were produced (2.25) as compared to those that were listened to (1.64), (2) words that were harder to identify (2.00) as compared to those that were easy to identify (1.89), and for (3) words that were presented in a Dutch (2.08) relative to an American (1.81) accent. A 2 (Accent: American vs. Dutch) × 2 (Action: Listen vs. Repeat) × 2 (Ease of Identification: Easy vs. Hard) repeated-measures ANOVAs confirmed these observations. With the exception of Ease of Identification whose F_2 analysis was only close to the conventional level of statistical significance, there were significant main effects of Accent ($F_1(1,31) = 26.129, p < .001, \eta_p^2 = .457, F_2(1,78) = 101.280, p < .001, \eta_p^2 = .565$), Action ($F_1$ $(1,31) = 109.353, p < .001, \eta_p^2 = .779, F_2(1,78) =$

27.184, $p < .001$, $\eta_p^2 = .258$), and Ease of Identification ($F_1(1,31) = 6.784$, $p = .014$, $\eta_p^2 = .180$; $F_2(1,78) = 2.908$, $p = .092$, $\eta_p^2 = .036$). Most interesting is that the interaction of Accent by Action was significant ($F_1(1,31) = 7.559$, $p = .010$, $\eta_p^2 = .196$, $F_2(1,78) = 10.778$, $p = .002$, $\eta_p^2 = .121$) revealing that Dutch-accented words were remembered better than American-accented words when the words were repeated (1.85 vs. 1.43, respectively, $t_1(31) = 4.438$, $p < .001$, $d_{CD} = .39$; $t_2(79) = 5.386$, $p < .001$, $d_{CD} = .33$) but less so when they were listened to (2.31 vs. 2.19, $t_1(31) = 2.233$, $p = .033$, $d_{CD} = .14$; $t_2(79) = 1.325$, $p = .189$, $d_{CD} = .17$). This finding replicates those reported by Cho and Feldman (under revision) suggesting that accented words may provide an additional source of indexical information for memory when listening but that accent information can be offset or rendered negligible by the articulatory information required for production. All other interactions were not significant ($F_{1\&2}$s < 2.85, *ps* > .10, η_p^2s < .077).

Experiment 1b

The data from the recall task are presented in the bottom half of Table 2. Similar to Experiment 1a, produced (with imitation) words were remembered better than those that were listened to (.23 vs. .10, respectively), those in a Dutch accent were remembered better than those in an American accent (.19 vs. .14, respectively), and those that were hard to identify better than those that were easy (.18 vs. .15, respectively). A 2 (Accent: American vs. Dutch) × 2 (Action: Listen vs. Produce) × 2 (Ease of Identification: Easy vs. Hard) repeated-measures ANOVAs revealed main effects of all three variables Accent ($F_1(1,31) = 26.330$, $p < .001$, $\eta_p^2 = .459$, $F_2(1,78) = 17.544$, $p < .001$, $\eta_p^2 = .184$), Action ($F_1(1,31) = 53.720$, $p < .001$, $\eta_p^2 = .634$, $F_2(1,78) = 14.524$, $p < .001$, $\eta_p^2 = .157$), and Ease of Identification ($F_1(1,31) = 4.755$, $p = .037$, $\eta_p^2 = .468$, $F_2(1,78) = 4.389$, $p = .039$, $\eta_p^2 = .053$). The Action by Difficulty interaction, which was significant in Experiment 1a did not replicate in this experiment ($F_1(1,31) = 2.166$, $p = .151$, $\eta_p^2 = .065$, $F_2(1, 78) =.095$, $p = .759$, $\eta_p^2 = .001$). However, the pattern of means in F_1, was in the same direction as that of Experiment 1a. The failure to obtain statistical significance for the interaction could be due to power. We address this issue by performing a combined analysis that will be discussed below. No interactions were significant ($F_{1\&2}$s < 2.2, *ps* > .15, η_p^2s < .07).

For recognition (data presented in the middle of Table 3), the results mirrored those of Experiment 1a in that memory discriminability was better for (1) words that were produced (or imitated) (2.07) rather than for those that were listened to (1.41), (2) words that were harder to identify (1.79) relative to those that were easy to identify (1.68), and for (3) words that were presented in a Dutch (1.84) relative to an American (1.63) accent. Two (Accent: American vs. Dutch) × 2 (Action: Listen vs. Produce) × 2 (Ease of Identification: Easy vs. Hard) repeated-measures

Table 3. Hits, false alarms, and d' in Experiments 1a, 1b, and 2.

Exp.	Intelligibility	Accent	Hits		FA: UR	d′: UR		FA: Phono		d′: Phono	
			Action			Action		Action		Action	
			Produce	Listen		Produce	Listen	Produce	Listen	Produce	Listen
1a	Easy	Dutch	.88	.75	.18	2.27	1.70	–	–	–	–
		American	.86	.65		2.19	1.38	–	–	–	–
	Hard	Dutch	.90	.82		2.35	2.00	–	–	–	–
		American	.87	.67		2.19	1.47	–	–	–	–
1b	Easy	Dutch	.84	.69	.20	2.03	1.50	–	–	–	–
		American	.82	.59		2.00	1.20	–	–	–	–
	Hard	Dutch	.85	.74		2.17	1.66	–	–	–	–
		American	.84	.61		2.06	1.26	–	–	–	–
2	Easy	Dutch	.82	.67	.13	2.45	1.91	.16	.15	2.19	1.71
		American	.79	.53		2.31	1.50	.17	.15	2.02	1.28
	Hard	Dutch	.84	.73		2.51	2.11	.17	.17	2.22	1.78
		American	.80	.60		2.34	1.70	.16	.17	2.11	1.35

Note. FA: False Alarms; Phono: Phonologically Similar; UR: Unrelated d' values are computed by taking the difference between the z-score associated with the proportion of hits and the z-score associated with the proportion of false alarms for each condition.

ANOVAs confirmed these observations (Accent: $F_1(1,31) = 13.678, p = .001, \eta_p^2 = .306, F_2(1,78) = 4.158, p = .045, \eta_p^2 = .051$; Action: $F_1(1,31) = 66.663, p < .001, \eta_p^2 = .683, F_2(1,78) = 40.056, p < .001, \eta_p^2 = .339$; and Ease of Identification: ($F_1(1,31) = 4.530, p = .041, \eta_p^2 = .127; F_2(1,78) = 3.845, p = .053, \eta_p^2 = .047$). Notably, we replicated the Action by Accent interaction that occurred in Experiment 1a, ($F_1(1,31) = 9.633, p = .004, \eta_p^2 = .237; F_2(1,78) = 5.224, p = .025, \eta_p^2 = .063$). Follow-up analysis to the interaction showed that there was no difference between producing a Dutch vs. American accented word (2.10 vs. 2.03, respectively, $t_1(31) = 1.142$, $p = .262$, $d_{CD} = .08$; $t_2(79) = .142$, $p = .887$, $d_{CD} = .07$) but that there was a greater benefit of listening to a Dutch vs. American accented word (1.58 vs. 1.23, respectively, $t_1(31) = 4.121, p < .001, d_{CD} = .27; t_2(79) = 2.886, p = .005, d_{CD} = .18$). Overall, the pattern of results in Experiment 1b replicated those of Experiment 1a. However, a potentially informative question that remains is whether imitation improved memory beyond that of merely producing the word. We address this issue by analyzing the combined data from Experiments 1a and 1b.

Combined analyses

We combined then analyzed the recall and recognition data from Experiments 1a and 1b. For F_1 analyses, Accent (American vs. Dutch), Ease of Identification (Easy vs. Hard) and Action (Listen vs. Produce) were treated as within-participants variables and Production Instruction (Natural Accent vs. Imitate) as a between-participants variable. For F_2 analyses, Ease of Identification was treated as a between-items effect, with the remaining variables treated as within-items effects. The critical focus was whether instructions to focus on and imitate the pronunciation of the original speaker in the produce condition altered the results relative to producing in one's natural accent.

In recall, there was no main effect of Production Instructions nor did it interact with any other variable ($Fs_{1\&2} < 2.66, p > .1, \eta_p^2 < .041$). Not surprisingly, the main effects of Accent ($F_1(1,62) = 53.276, p < .001, \eta_p^2 = .462, F_2(1,78) = 27.219, p < .001, \eta_p^2 = .259$), Action ($F_1(1,62) = 103.661, p < .001, \eta_p^2 = .626, F_2(1,78) = 23.505, p < .001, \eta_p^2 = .232$), and Ease of Identification ($F_1(1,62) = 21.794, p < .001, \eta_p^2 = .260, F_2(1,78) = 4.431, p = .039, \eta_p^2 = .054$) were all significant. The 3-way interaction of Action, Accent, and Ease of Identification also was significant ($F_1(1,62) = 4.170, p = .045, \eta_p^2 = .063; F_2(1,78) = 3.401, p = .069, \eta_p^2 = .042$). In summary, the advantage of producing over listening to words in recall was comparable for easy-to-identify words in an American and in a Dutch accent (.12 vs. .10, respectively, $t_1(64) = .785$, $p = .435$, $d_{CD} = .08$; $t_2(39) = 3.376$, $p = .002$, $d_{CD} = .37$) but the advantage of producing over listening seemed to be greater for hard to identify words in a Dutch than in an American accent (.18 vs. .12, respectively, $t_1(64) = 1.938, p = .057, d_{CD} = .25; t_2(39) = .500, p = .620, d_{CD} = .14$). Hard to identify words produced comparable production effects without and with imitation in Dutch (.19 vs. .18) as did hard (.12 vs. .11) and easy (.11 vs. 12) words in English. The only evidence of an effect of imitation was in recall for easy to identify Dutch words where instructions to produce naturally resulted in lower performance than instructions to imitate (.06 vs. .13). The Action by Ease of Identification interaction was close to significant for the F_1 analysis only ($F_1(1,62) = 3.910$, $p = .052$, $\eta_p^2 = .059$; $F_2(1,78) = .275$, $p = .602$, $\eta_p^2 = .004$) as was the Accent by Ease of Identification ($F_1(1,62) = 3.592$, $p = .063$, $\eta_p^2 = .055$; $F_2(1,78) = .051$, $p = .823$, $\eta_p^2 = .001$). These should be interpreted in the context of the three way interaction described above. No other interactions approached significance ($F_{1\&2}$s < 1.373, $p > .24$, $\eta_p^2 < .025$; $F_2(1,78) < 1.8$, $p = .189$, $\eta_p^2 = .011$).

Similar to the recall data, in the recognition data, there was no main effect of or interaction with Production Instruction in any F_1 analysis ($F_1 < 2.4$, $p > .12$, $\eta_p^2 < .037$). However, the main effect of Production Instruction in F_2 was significant ($F_2(1,78) = 41.881$, $p < .001$, $\eta_p^2 = .394$). All other F_2 interactions with Production Instruction were not close to significant ($F_2 < 2.6$, $p > .11$, $\eta_p^2 < .03$). In the present study, producing words by imitating the accent of the original speaker improves memory beyond that of producing the word in one's own accent only under very limited circumstances. These results failed to conceptually replicate those of Adank et al. (2010) who reported that imitating the accent of the speaker can lead to better perceptual adaption. However, there are two critical differences between the present study and that of Adank et al.'s (2010) – namely (1) we measured participants' memory of the words presented in an accent whereas they measured their ability to transcribe new words, and (2) our stimuli were individual words whereas theirs were sentences. As noted in the introduction, Nguyen et al. (2012) also failed to find a facilitation due to imitation and our materials (specifically, single words) were structurally more similar to theirs than to those of Adank et al. (2010) who used sentences that necessarily include prosodic information. It could also be that the failure to find an effect of imitation was because our participants were not as adept in imitating the accent of the speaker as they could be with more extensive training. The main effects of Accent ($F_1(1,62) = 38.390$, $p < .001$, $\eta_p^2 = .382$, $F_2(1, 78) = 20.641$, $p < .001$, $\eta_p^2 = .209$), Action ($F_1(1,62) = 162.410$, $p < .001$, $\eta_p^2 = .724$, $F_2(1, 78) = 109.108$, $p < .001$, $\eta_p^2 = 583$), and Ease of Identification ($F_1(1,62) = 11.090$, $p < .001$, $\eta_p^2 = .152$, $F_2(1,78) = 4.906$, $p = .030$, $\eta_p^2 = .059$) remained significant. The Accent by Action interaction also was significant ($F_1(1,62) = 16.766$, $p < .001$, $\eta_p^2 = .213$, $F_2(1,78) = 13.263$, $p < .001$, $\eta_p^2 = .145$) showing that Dutch-accented words were remembered at a higher rate than American-accented words when they were listened to (1.72 vs. 1.33, respectively, $t_1(64) = 6.087$, $p < .001$, $d_{CD} = .27$; $t_2(79) = 5.421$, $p = .259$, $d_{CD} = .46$) but much less so when they were produced (2.20 vs. 2.11, respectively, $t_1(64) = 2.367$, $p = .021$, $d_{CD} = .09$; $t_2(79) = .875$, $p = .384$, $d_{CD} = .19$).

Experiment 2

It is evident that hearing accented words and producing words at study can benefit memory. One question that Experiments 1a and 1b did not attempt to address was whether the benefit to memory of hearing accented words derives from richer form-to-meaning variation when words presented in an unfamiliar accent get mapped to meaning or whether activation of more words due to generally more ambiguous pronunciations results in the activation of phonetically similar words and a tendency to believe that those words were studied. An overall activation locus for the effect of accent variation is particularly relevant in the context of the demands of a recognition task in which participants do not need to generate but only to recognize the targets and test items. It could be that the consequence of listening to words in an unfamiliar accent is to increase activation more broadly to include words that are phonologically similar to the presented word. If this were the case, then when listening to accented speech, participants should be more likely to indicate that not only the target but also some of its phonological neighbors have been studied, for example, hearing the word *map* in an unfamiliar accent would be more likely to activate the word *math* than hearing it in a familiar accent.

The major change in Experiment 2 was that we added to the phonologically dissimilar lures in the recognition test a set of lures that were phonologically similar to the targets in order to test an imprecise phonological activation account. In addition, we did not administer a free recall test prior to the recognition test thereby preventing any possible "contamination" of the recognition data from participants having been exposed to successfully recalled words in a recall task. Because we did not find systematic differences between participants' producing in their own accent and imitating the accent of the speaker, we opted to have participants produce the word in their own accent. The rational being that this task is more natural to the participants and conforms to the conventional procedure in other studies that demonstrate the benefits of production on memory (e.g., MacLeod et al., 2010).

Method

Design

Our design was a 2 (Action: Listen or Produce) × 2 (Accent: American or Dutch) × 2 (Ease of Identification: easy vs. hard) × (Type of Lure: Unrelated vs. Phonologically Similar) within-participants design. Memory was assessed using a yes/no recognition task.

Materials and counterbalancing

The study words were identical to those used in Experiments 1a and 1b. For the unrelated lures, we presented the same 40 lures from Experiments 1a and 1b along with 40 additional unrelated lures. Novel was that we added 80 words that were phonologically similar to the study words (see Appendix for words). These words were obtained using the orthographic neighborhood feature in the English Lexicon Project database (Balota et al., 2007). A total of 240 items appeared in the recognition test (80 targets, 80 unrelated lures, and 80 phonologically similar lures). All sets of targets and lures were matched on word length, frequency, orthographic neighborhood, and phonological neighborhood (see Table 1). The counterbalancing procedure was identical to that of Experiments 1a and 1b.

Procedure

The procedure was exactly the same as that of Experiment 1 with the exclusion of the free-recall task prior to the recognition test.

Results and discussion

The recognition data are presented at the bottom of Table 3. Overall *d′* values were higher for words that (1) were produced (2.27) rather than listened to (1.67), (2) presented in a Dutch (2.11) relative to an American (1.83) accent, (3) hard to identify (2.02) as compared to easy to identify (1.92), and (4) unrelated (2.11) as compared to phonologically similar (1.84) lures. The lower *d′* for phonologically similar lures relative to unrelated lures shows that the presentation of a target (e.g. map) did activate its phonological neighbors (e.g., math). More critical was whether the Type of Lure interacted with any other variable, in particular accent. If the benefit of listening to accented words derived from activating phonological neighbors of the studied word, then one would expect that participants would be more likely to commit false alarms to phonologically similar lures as compared to unrelated, phonologically dissimilar lures when targets were accented. Importantly, Type of Lure did not interact with Accent of the word it was similar to (or any other variable). This outcome allows us to conclude that activation in the phonological neighbors of targets cannot account for the benefit of producing an item or listening to a word in an unfamiliar accent. A 2 (Accent: American vs. Dutch) × 2 (Action: Listen vs. Produce) × 2 (Type of Lure: Unrelated vs. Phonologically Similar) × 2 (Ease of Identification: Easy vs. Hard) repeated-measures ANOVAs revealed significant main effects of Accent ($F_1(1,39) = 24.255, p < .001, \eta_p^2 = .383$; $F_2(1,78) = 7.047, p = .010, \eta_p^2 = .083$), Action ($F_1(1,39) = 90.039, p < .001, \eta_p^2 = .698$; $F_2(1,78) = 42.622, p < .001, \eta_p^2 = .353$), and Type of Lure ($F_1(1,39) = 26.614,$

$p < .001$, $\eta_p^2 = .387$; $F_2(1,78) = 14.299$, $p < .001$, $\eta_p^2 = .155$); the main effect of Ease of Identification did not reach the conventional level of statistical significance ($F_1(1,39) = 3.798$, $p = .059$, $\eta_p^2 = .089$; $F_2(1, 78) = 3.689$, $p = .058$, $\eta_p^2 = .045$) but the means are in the same direction as in the previous experiments. The interaction of Accent by Action once again was significant, ($F_1(1,39) = 5.817$, $p = .021$, $\eta_p^2 = .130$; $F_2(1,78) = 5.112$, $p = .027$, $\eta_p^2 = .062$), revealing that while overall Dutch-accented words were remembered better than American-accented words, this difference was larger in the listen condition (2.01 vs. 1.60, respectively) ($t_1(39) = 4.688$, $p < .001$, $d_{CD} = .32$; $t_2(79) = 3.695$, $p < .001$, $d_{CD} = .26$) than in the produce condition (2.49 vs. 2.33, respectively, $t_1(39) = 2.131$, $p = .039$, $d_{CD} = .15$; $t_2(79) = .133$, $p = .895$, $d_{CD} = .05$). All other interactions were not significant ($F_{1\&2}$s < 2.60, ps $> .12$, η_p^2s $< .077$).

General discussion

We examined the role of accent on memory under the assumption that the acoustic-phonetic details of a speaker can be retained in memory and that an unfamiliar accent introduces greater variability to that memory trace, rendering it more informative or distinctive. In the present study, our main goals were to demonstrate that accented words improve memory using a Dutch rather than the Chinese unfamiliar accent that Cho and Feldman (under revision) had used and, more importantly, to determine whether we could replicate the interaction of accent with production under varied conditions. In Experiment 1b, we examined whether instructions to imitate the accent of the speaker at production could further improve memory as compared to producing in one's own accent. In Experiment 2, we examined whether the advantage of accented words was a consequence of low intelligibility and the resulting increase in the activation of words that were phonologically similar to (phonological neighbors of) the target word. We observed no effect of intelligibility of the target words and no interaction of accent with intelligibility and concluded that superior memory of accented words is associated with more elaborated encoding as a consequence of less typical pronunciations at initial auditory presentation.

Overall in recall, words that were produced were remembered better than those that were listened to. This replicates the production effect (e.g., MacLeod et al., 2010), and more novel, the accent variant of that outcome in Cho and Feldman (under revision). In the present experiments but not in Cho and Feldman (under revision), there were main effects of Accent (Dutch-accented words remembered better than American-accented words) as well as Ease of Identification (harder to identify words remembered better than easier to identified words).

The differences between outcomes should not be over interpreted, however. Although sets of stimuli in both studies were equated on their intelligibility scores, there was no attempt to equate materials on other potentially relevant factors such as accentedness or comprehensibility. Both foreign accents were unfamiliar to our participants relative to American English, but we did not ascertain that they were equally unfamiliar. In addition to particular phonological similarities and differences of the L1 with English, future studies could systematically examine how accent familiarity, accentedness and comprehensibility influence performance on memory tasks.

In recognition across the three experiments in the present study, as in recall, we observed the benefit of production over listening. Results replicate the Action by Accent interaction that was reported in the two experiments of Cho and Feldman (under revision). The interaction shows that repeating an unfamiliarly (vs. familiarly) accented word produced a small (and generally non-significant) increase in memory discriminability whereas listening to an unfamiliarly (vs. familiarly) accented word resulted in a large difference. The reliable interaction of Action by Accent in recognition makes it implausible that L2 accented words are remembered better than familiarly accented words because participants put forth more effort or attention at encoding whenever words are less intelligible and comprehensible. Indeed, if increased effort during encoding accounted for better memory, one would expect an additive effect of accent and production.

We could detect no evidence for greater effort at encoding. In line with claims that the diversity that emerges from encoding the acoustic-phonetic details of different speakers can benefit subsequent recognition and recall, we propose that the benefit of accent derives from enhanced variability in the voice-word mappings at encoding. The account is consistent with claims of Barcroft and Sommers (2005) where variability facilitated learning for concepts that already existed in the participants' lexicon. The impact of multiple mappings of form to meaning appears to differ for less established concepts. For example, Muench and Creel (2013) showed that multiple accents hindered learning concepts that were novel. Collectively, accent variants appear to compete with one another when meaning is underspecified but when meaning is well defined then variability in the voice-word mappings appears to enhance learning.

Perhaps most revealing was that the effect of accent interacted with the effect of action. Our interpretation is that the indexical and phonetic information introduced by listening to an unfamiliar foreign accent is less important when the participant produces the word than when she/he simply listens. This arises because the phonetic and acoustic detail of the originally encoded word must be mapped onto the participant's own articulatory code in order for the participant to produce it. At present, this account cannot differentiate between accounts where the act of production replaces or only overshadows the indexical information associated with the foreign accent. In essence we have demonstrated that indexical and articulatory information interact but whether the indexical information is lost or only attenuated in the context of one's own production cannot be determined from our findings. A source-monitoring task in which participants are presented with studied words and asked to identify the speaker of the word that they heard during encoding, is one possible method to determine whether production is sensitive to accent-based information in the input.

One hypothesis we tested as to why unfamiliar accented words were remembered better than familiar accented words was that hearing the former was more likely to activate words that are phonologically similar to the studied words. We tested this hypothesis by including phonological neighbors of the studied words in a recognition test. Importantly, results showed that participants were more likely to false alarm to phonological lures as predicted by the Neighborhood Activation Model (Luce & Pisoni, 1998; see also Sommers & Lewis, 1999). Crucial was that this increase was equal for the familiar and unfamiliar accent. The failure to find that an unfamiliar accent is more likely to activate phonological neighbors of the word makes it unlikely that more ambiguous pronunciations result in a tendency to say that more words are familiar.

Finally, in Experiment 1a we failed to detect a reliable incremental benefit of imitating the accent of the speaker relative to producing the word in one's own accent with the exception of accented words that are easy to identify. Although this finding is incongruent with previous findings by Adank et al. (2010), it is congruent with those reported by Nguyen et al. (2012). As noted above, Nguyen et al. and the present study exposed and tested participants on individual words, whereas Adank et al. (2010) used sentences and therefore introduced prosodic as well as phonological, lexical and syntactic dimensions of context that could further facilitate learning and testing. Another possibility is that participants in Adank et al.'s (2010) study were much more precise and successful in their ability to imitate the foreign accent. Before asserting that imitating phonetic details at production have no impact on recall and recognition, it would be important to compare production and imitation when materials are linguistically richer and the standards for correct imitation are more rigorous.

Conclusions

In the present study, we found that words spoken in an unfamiliar accent were remembered better in both recall and recognition than words pronounced in a familiar accent, supporting the claims that indexical information is stored and that unfamiliarly accented words strengthen memory traces more than familiarly accented words. Crucially, in recognition when instructed to produce, there were minor differences between words articulated in a familiar or unfamiliar accent; differences were restricted to the listening only study condition. One interpretation of the results is that the acoustic phonetic details of a speaker are retained in memory in a listening task but are effectively lost when the participant engages in production. In our opinion, a more viable interpretation is that the phonetic-acoustic information is overshadowed or attenuated by production. Either demonstrates an interaction of phonetic-acoustic with articulatory codes in the context of a memory task. However, the failure to detect differences in production of words in one's own accent and production by imitation of the speaker's accent imposes limits on that interaction.

Acknowledgements

We thank Sarah Birdsall and Elizabeth Stevens for their assistance with data collection and Megan Streeter for her assistance with data entry. We also thank Janet Van Hell and Mirjam Ernestus for help creating the accented materials. The research reported here was supported by funds from the National Institute of Child Health and Development Grant HD-01994 to Haskins Laboratories and by a visiting professor award from the Dutch Royal Academy.

Notes

1. Although the aggregate correlations of these variables are large, the researchers noted that there is large variability in the strength of the correlations among participants.

2. Although Adank et al. showed no increased adaptation for participants exposed to additional sentences relative to no additional exposure, some studies have demonstrated greater adaptation with increased exposure (e.g., Bradlow & Bent, 2008; Maye, Aslin, & Tanenhaus, 2008).

3. Ease of identification was based on accuracy rates in a separate study in which 8 participants, who were not part of any of the experiments reported here, transcribed the correct spelling of 240 Dutch-accented words that were presented auditorially one at a time. Easy and Hard words were matched on number of orthographic and phonological neighbors, *ps* > .6.

References

Adank, P., Hagoort, P., & Bekkering, H. (2010). Imitation improves language comprehension. *Psychological Science*, 21, 1903–1909. DOI: 10.1177/0956797610389192

Adank, P., Evans, B.G., Stuart-Smith, J., & Scott, S.K. (2009). Comprehension of familiar and unfamiliar native accents under adverse listening conditions. *Journal of Experimental Psychology: Human Perception and Performance*, 35, 520–529. DOI: 10.1037/a0013552

Balota, D.A., Yap, M.J., Cortese, M.J., Hutchison, K.A., Kessler, B., Loftis, B., Neely, J.H., Nelson, D.L., Simpson, G.B., & Treiman, R. (2007). The English Lexicon Project. *Behavior Research Methods*, 39, 445–459. DOI: 10.3758/BF03193014

Barcroft, J., & Sommers, M.S. (2005). Effects of acoustic variability on second language vocabulary learning. *Studies in Second Language Acquisition*, 27, 387–414. DOI: 10.1017/S0272263105050175

Best, C.T., Bradlow, A.R., Guion-Anderson, S., & Polka, L. (2011). Using the lens of phonetic experience to resolve phonological forms. *Journal of Phonetics*, 39, 453–455. DOI: 10.1016/j.wocn.2011.08.006

Best, C.T., & Strange, W. (1992). Effects of phonological and phonetic factors on cross-language perception of approximants. *Journal of Phonetics*, 20, 305–330.

Bradlow, A.R., & Bent, T. (2008). Perceptual adaptation to non-native speech. *Cognition*, 106, 707–729. DOI: 10.1016/j.cognition.2007.04.005

Butterfield, B., & Metcalfe, J. (2001). Errors committed with high confidence are hypercorrected. *Journal of Experimental Psychology: Learning, Memory, and Cognition*, 27, 1491–1494. DOI: 10.1037/0278-7393.27.6.1491

Cohen, J.A. (1992). Power primer. *Psychological Bulletin*, 112, 155–159. DOI: 10.1037/0033-2909.112.1.155

Cho, K.W., & Feldman, L.B. (under revision). Memory of Repeating Accented Words: Phonological and phonetic influences on the production effect. Under Review.

Clark, H.H. (1973). The language-as-fixed-effect fallacy: A critique of language statistics in psychological research. *Journal of Verbal Learning and Verbal Behavior*, 12, 335–359. DOI: 10.1016/S0022-5371(73)80014-3

Derwing, T.M. & Munro, M.J. (1997). Accent, intelligibility, and comprehensibility. *Studies in Second Language Acquisition*, 1, 1–16.

Dunlap, W.P., Cortina, J.M., Vaslow, J.B., & Burke, M.J. (1996). Metaanalysis of experiments with matched groups or repeated measures designs. *Psychological Methods*, 1, 170–177. DOI: 10.1037/1082-989X.1.2.170

Eisenstein, M. (1983). Native reactions to non-native speech: A review of empirical research. *Studies in Second Language Acquisition*, 5, 160–176. DOI: 10.1017/S0272263100004836

Flege, J.E. (1987). The production of new and similar phonemes in a foreign language: Evidence for the effect of equivalence classification. *Journal of Phonetics*, 15, 47–65.

Flege, J., Bohn, O.-S., & Jang, S. (1997). The effect of experience on nonnative subjects' production and perception of English vowels. *Journal of Phonetics*, 25, 437–470. DOI: 10.1006/jpho.1997.0052

Floccia, C., Butler, J., Goslin, J., & Ellis, L. (2009). Regional and foreign accent processing in english: Can listeners adapt? *Journal of Psycholinguistic Research*, 38, 379–412. DOI: 10.1007/s10936-008-9097-8

Goldinger, S.D. (1996). Words and voices: Episodic traces in spoken word identification and recognition memory. *Journal of Experimental Psychology: Learning, Memory, and Cognition*, 22, 1166–1183. DOI: 0278-7393/96

Goldinger, S.D. (1998). Echoes of echoes? An episodic theory of lexical access. *Psychological Review*, 105, 251–279. DOI: 10.1037/0033-295X.105.2.251

Goldinger, S.D., Pisoni, D.B., & Logan, J.S. (1991). On the nature of talker variability effects on recall of spoken word lists. *Journal of Experimental Psychology: Learning, Memory, and Cognition*, 17, 152–162. DOI: 10.1037/0278-7393.17.1.152

Hanulikova, A., Van Alphen, P.M., Van Goch, M.M., & Weber, A. (2012). When one person's mistake is another's standard usage: The effect of foreign accent on syntactic processing. *Journal of Cognitive Neuroscience*, 24, 878–887. DOI: 10.1162/jocn_a_00103

Kuhl, P.K. (2000). A new view of language acquisition. *Proceedings of the National Academy of Science*, 97, 11850–11857. DOI: 10.1073/pnas.97.22.11850

Kuhl, P.K. (2004). Early language acquisition: Cracking the speech code. *Nature Reviews Neuroscience*, 5, 831–843. DOI: 10.1038/nrn1533

Lecumberri, M.L.G., Cooke, M., & Cutler, A. (2010). Non-native speech perception in adverse conditions: A review. *Speech Communication*, 52, 864–886. DOI: 10.1016/j.specom.2010.08.014

Lev-Ari, S., & Keysar, B. (2010). Why don't we believe non-native speakers? The influence of accent on credibility. *Journal of Experimental Social Psychology*, 46, 1093–1096. DOI: 10.1016/j.jesp.2010.05.025

Luce, P.A., & Pisoni, D.B. (1998). Recognizing spoken words: The neighborhood activation model. *Ear and Hearing*, 19, 1–36. DOI: 10.1097/00003446-199802000-00001

MacLeod, C.M., Gopie, N., Hourihan, K.L., Neary, K.R., & Ozubko, J.D. (2010). The production effect: Delineation of a phenomenon. *Journal of Experimental Psychology: Learning,Memory, and Cognition*, 36, 671–685. DOI: 10.1037/a0018785

Maye, J., Aslin, R.N., Tanenhaus, M.K. (2008). The weckud wetch of the wast: Lexical adaptation to a novel accent. *Cognitive Science*, 32, 543–562. DOI: 10.1080/03640210802035357

Meador, D., Flege, J.E., & Mackay, I.R.A. (2000). Factors affecting the recognition of words in a second language. *Bilingualism: Language and Cognition*, 3, 55–67. DOI: 10.1017/S1366728900000134

Muench, K.L., & Creel, S.C. (2013). Gradient phonological inconsistency affects vocabulary learning. *Journal of Experimental Psychology: Learning, Memory, and Cognition*. Advance online publication. DOI: 10.1037/a0032862

Munro, M.J., & Dewing, T.M. (1995a). Processing time, accent, and comprehensibility in the perception of native and foreign-accented speech. *Language and Speech*, 38, 289–306. DOI: 10.1177/002383099503800305

Munro, M.J., & Derwing, T.M. (1995b). Foreign accent comprehensibility, and intelligibility in the speech of second language learners. *Language Learning*, 45, 73–97. DOI: 10.1111/j.1467-1770.1995.tb00963.x

Nygaard, L.C., & Pisoni, D.B. (1998). Talker-specific learning in speech perception. *Perception & Psychophysics*, 60, 355–376. DOI: 10.3758/BF03206860

Nguyen, N., Dufour, S., & Brunellière, A. (2012). Does imitation facilitate word recognition in a non-native regional accent? *Frontiers in Psychology*, 3, 1–7. DOI: 10.3389/fpsyg.2012.00480

Schmid, P.M., & Yeni-Komshian, G.H. (1999). The effects of speaker accent and target predictability on perception of mispronunciations. *Journal of Speech, Language, and Hearing Research*, 42, 56–64. DOI: 10.1044/jslhr.4201.56

Snodgrass, J.G., & Corwin, J. (1988). Pragmatics of measuring recognition memory: Applications to dementia and amnesia. *Journal of Experimental Psychology: General*, 117, 34–50. DOI: 10.1037/0096-3445.117.1.34

Sommers, M. S., & Barcroft, J. (2007). An integrated account of the effects of acoustic variability in first language and second language: Evidence from amplitude, fundamental frequency, and speaking rate variability. *Applied Psycholinguistics*, 28, 231–249. DOI: 10.1017/S0142716410000469

Sommers, M. S., & Barcroft, J. (2011). Indexical information, encoding difficulty, and second language vocabulary learning. *Applied Psycholinguistics*, 32, 417–434. DOI: 10.1017/S0142716410000469

Sommers, M. S., & Lewis, B. P. (1999). Who really lives next door: Creating false memories with phonological neighbors. *Journal of Memory and Language*, 40, 83–108. DOI: 10.1006/jmla.1998.2614

Appendix

Words used in Experiments 1a, 1b, and 2

Target	Phono Lures	Target	Phono Lures	Target	Phono Lures
apple	apt	fox	folks	salt	halt
arrow	ammo	fruit	flute	sauce	sought
aunt	and	gold	goals	scar	spar
author	offer	head	fed	shoe	she
baker	faker	hell	shell	shop	shot
ball	bought	insect	infect	shoulder	boulder
bath	wrath	jaw	paw	sign	nine
block	flock	juice	loose	silver	sillier
body	bottle	lamb	lame	sock	doc
boot	shoot	leg	log	son	such
box	books	lighting	fighting	song	wrong
bread	thread	mail	jail	stone	stove
bride	pride	map	math	street	stream
brother	breather	meat	feat	tail	tape
bull	bush	metal	pedal	tea	we
butcher	booker	mountain	fountain	tear	tire
calf	laugh	pair	their	thief	chief
captain	caftan	part	port	thumb	theme
cloud	crowd	peach	teach	time	team
cotton	gotten	piece	cease	tongue	tough
dance	chance	pig	gig	town	turn
end	any	pin	thin	wall	wool
fashion	passion	pound	wound	wave	wage
field	yield	price	press	winter	wonder
fist	mist	queen	clean	wood	good
flood	flush	rain	chain	world	wild
foot	fought	road	rogue		

UR Lures	UR Lures	UR Lures	UR Lures
any^	filed	mined*	stills^
arcade	firm*	minute	stop*
bat	fish*	off*	sung
begs	flow*	over*	swap*
bike*	fond*	patch*	sweater
blight^	fools^	path*	swollen
blue*	funk*	played	talk
boasts^	funny	puts	tend*
boats	glass^	raging	then
boots	grace	rate	ticker
brains^	heels^	reader	tidal
buds	host*	rough*	tits
called	hound*	seed	told
calls	huh	seems	took
catch	joke*	sells	tour*
cease^	kept*	shakes	trains*
chat	lady*	shores*	tree^
create	less	shout	trumpet
credit	long	sir	waves^
cure	looks	slacks*	wells*
east	matter	soft*	were
fact*	meek^	stark	wing
feels	miles	stick	years

Phono: Phonologically similar.
^: Used in Experiments 1a and 1b only.
*: Used in Experiments 1a and 1b and 2.

Phonological reduction in the first part of noun compounds

A case study of early child language

Joseph Paul Stemberger
University of British Columbia

Regular plural nouns rarely appear as the first member of a compound noun in English under any circumstances, while irregular plurals are more likely under certain conditions. One explanation holds that this is a consequence of the fundamentally different ways in which regular and irregular plurals are stored and processed, while an alternative explanation suggests that it may be rooted in phonological differences between regular and irregular forms. If the first part of a compound is phonologically restricted, the restrictions may interact with lexical access in a way that disfavors regular plurals (especially given that plurals of any sort are of low frequency in the first part of a compound, so processing is far from ceiling). This paper provides evidence from a case study of one child that the first part of a compound can be phonologically restricted compared to nouns when they appear as independent words. The data address compounds whose first elements are monomorphemic nouns, rather than plurals, but document the existence of phonological restrictions within compounds for at least one child. This existence proof strengthens the hypothesis that differences between regular and irregular forms may derive partly from differences in phonological structure.

Keywords: noun compounds, regular morphology, phonological development, phonological constraints

In English, the first part of a compound noun is generally an uninflected noun, e.g. *catfood* rather than **catsfood* (despite the fact that it is food intended for cats, so that the plural would be semantically appropriate). Kiparsky (1982) proposed that irregular plurals are more likely than regular plurals to occur as the first part of a compound. Gordon (1985) showed that young children are more likely to produce novel compounds with irregular plurals (*mice-eater*) than with regular

DOI 10.1075/bct.80.03ste

nouns (*rats-eater*), in an experimental task where the child produced the plural form of the noun and then immediately produced a compound. A large amount of attention has been directed at this issue in the following decades. It is clear that in typical speech (without first priming the plural form), speakers rarely use either regular or irregular plural forms in the first part of a compound (Buck-Gengler, Menn, & Healy, 2004; Ramscar & Dye, 2010); but this fact does not by itself explain the observed differences between regular and irregular plurals. One position (e.g. Berent & Pinker, 2007; Pinker & Prince, 1988; Pinker & Ullman, 2002; among many others) is that regular and irregular plurals are produced by different mechanisms: irregulars are stored in the lexicon and hence are available for compounding, while (most) regular forms are generated by rule and are not available for compounding. An alternative position is that regular plurals tend to create different phonological sequences than irregular plurals (e.g. the word-final consonant cluster /ts/ in *rats* vs. the singleton consonant /s/ in *mice*), and that this phonological difference underlies the different behavior of regular vs. irregular nouns in compounds (Haskell, MacDonald, & Seidenberg, 2003; Ramscar & Dye, 2010).

Berent and Pinker (2007) showed that the different behavior of regular vs. irregular plurals cannot be reduced to *purely* phonological factors. They created novel words ending in e.g. /u:nz/ that were taught to subjects as either monomorphemic nouns or as plural nouns. Subjects rated compounds as highly acceptable when this sequence appeared as part of a monomorphemic noun, but as unacceptable when it was part of a regular plural form. Berent and Pinker concluded that phonology is not the culprit here (and that this strengthens the position of symbolic models of language learning and processing and weakens the position of nonsymbolic models).

Berent and Pinker did not, however, address whether their results could arise from the *interaction* of phonology with morpholexical processing as it relates to lexical access and the singular-plural contrast. English speakers generally produce compounds with an uninflected first noun, even with nouns that have irregular plurals (e.g. Buck-Gengler, Menn, & Healy, 2004; Ramscar & Dye, 2010). It is thus uncontroversial (a) that singular/uninflected nouns must be available to speakers when producing compounds containing a noun that has an irregular plural, even when plurality might be semantically appropriate, and (b) that speakers use irregular plurals in the first part of a compound in only a small minority of tokens. The literature can be interpreted as showing that irregular plurals are better competitors than regular plurals in the first part of a compound, but that they are nonetheless weak competitors that rarely occur in compounds. In such a situation, where the plural form is produced in only a tiny proportion of tokens, processing is far from ceiling and many factors that affect accessibility, including phonological factors, might have an effect.

Stemberger (2007) showed, using data from 36 English-speaking children in the CHILDES database (MacWhinney, 2000), that just such phonological effects are active in overtensing errors in the speech of young children, where children produce an inflected past-tense form after forms of the auxiliary *do* (e.g. *didn't broke*) rather than the target uninflected base (*didn't break*). While earlier research had suggested that overtensing errors occur at a higher rate for irregular past-tense forms than for regulars, Stemberger showed that past-tense forms with "basic" rimes (rimes that are legal in monomorphemic words in English, and hence have more statistical support) are subject to a high rate of overtensing errors whether irregular (e.g. *didn't broke*) or regular (e.g. *didn't played*), but that past-tense forms with "non-basic" rimes (e.g. *didn't closed*, where word-final /zd/ occurs only in past-tense, perfect-aspect and passive forms in English), which are always regular, are subject to a very low error rate. There is every reason to believe that this phonological factor is active independently in monomorphemic words, since both children and adults are sensitive to phonotactic probability (e.g. Fromkin, 1971; Storkel, Armbrüster, & Hogan, 2006; Storkel & Rogers, 2000). The effects on overtensing errors were not purely phonological (since Stemberger noted that these same children were correctly producing target past-tense forms such as *closed*), but are an interaction between phonological factors and the access or construction of past-tense forms. (Marshall & van der Lely, 2006, report similar effects on basic past tense forms for children with Specific Language Impairment (SLI).) Stemberger argued that uninflected and inflected forms are in competition in language production. Especially in instances where the uninflected base form usually wins, the less-frequent victory by an inflected form is facilitated if it is phonologically more accessible. Irregular past-tense forms in English often have simpler, less marked, higher-frequency phonological structure, and so are more likely to be favored in such output than are regular forms. Stemberger argued that equivalent effects could be active in the first member in a compound, where base forms are statistically predominant; any factor that increases the accessibility of a plural might be expected to have the same sort of effect as in overtensing errors.

While Berent and Pinker maintain that symbolic models posit differences due to rules for regular plurals vs. storage of irregular plurals, and that nonsymbolic models attribute differences between regulars and irregulars to phonological processing, Bernhardt and Stemberger (1998) point out that symbolic models also have the option of attributing differences to phonological factors. Optimality Theory (OT) is a symbolic approach to phonology (adapted from nonsymbolic connectionist models; Smolensky, 1999) in which constraints on output (surface pronunciations) interact to create the correct output. Bernhardt and Stemberg-

Table 1. OT constraint table showing a possible interaction between the complexity of the coda and the realization of plurality.

INPUT →	maʊs, <Plural>		ɹæt, <Plural>		bɑks	
	maɪs	maʊs	ɹæts	ɹæt	bɑks	bɑk
Survived(C)						*!
NotComplex(Coda)			*!		*	
<PluralConstraints>		*!		*		

er (1998) argue that an interaction between phonology and morphology could underlie the finding that children with SLI have a higher rate of correct use of irregular past-tense forms than of regular past-tense forms. In the family studied by Gopnik and Crago (1991), for example, SLI speakers reduced final consonant clusters in monomorphemic words to a single consonant almost half the time, but produced a base form instead of a regular plural almost 75% of the time. Gopnik and Goad (1997) argued that the difference in the magnitude of reduction in inflected forms vs. in monomorphemic nouns means that the morphological facts cannot be reduced to a phonological effect; but they did not consider the possibility of an interaction between phonology and morphology. Perhaps the phonological difficulty of the final cluster that resulted in 50% error on morphologically simple words decreased the competitiveness of regular plurals, resulting in 75% error. Consider the OT constraint table (or *tableau*) in Table 1.

In the top row are three different input forms (the plural of *mouse*, the plural of *rat*, and the word *box*), and at row headings on the left are constraints; this follows the constraint table format of Bernhardt and Stemberger (1998), rotating the standard OT orientation (where constraint names are across the top in column headings), in order to avoid the practice of truncating constraint names (with consequent loss of readability) in tables with many constraints. The second row gives some competing pronunciations of the three input words, each at the head of a column; the winning candidate has a special border. If a given pronunciation violates a given constraint, there is an asterisk in that cell. A violated cell in a column high in the table (for a high-ranked constraint), where there is no violation in the other column, is a fatal violation that rules out that output; there is an exclamation point after the asterisk and a special cell border. A violation in any cell below that point (for a low-ranked constraint) does not make a difference, and irrelevant cells are shaded. The highest-ranked constraint in Table 1, **Survived(C)** (the equivalent of MAX in Prince & Smolensky, 2004, renamed by Bernhardt & Stemberger in order to be more transparent for the non-linguist) prevents deletion of e.g. the /s/ of *box* or *mouse* or the /t/ of *rat*. The middle-ranked constraint (**NotComplex(Coda)**, also known as *Complex$_{CODA}$) prevents final consonant clusters such as /ts/ and /ks/, if they can be avoided without violating higher-ranked constraints. The lowest-ranked constraints (the exact nature of which does not matter for our purposes) require the expression of plural morphology (whether regular or irregular), as long as that can be accomplished without violating higher-ranked constraints. These are all independently motivated constraints used in analyses of adult languages (e.g. Prince & Smolensky, 2004) and child phonological development (e.g. Bernhardt & Stemberger, 1998). In Table 1, since the constraint against word-final consonant clusters is ranked higher than (and so is more important than) the constraint that plurality must be expressed, the system outputs the base form *rat* (with no consonant cluster) rather than the plural form *rats* (with a final cluster). Because neither *mouse* nor *mice* ends in a cluster, the constraint against clusters is irrelevant, and the system outputs the irregular plural *mice* rather than the base form *mouse*. Faithfulness to consonants of the base (high-ranked **Survived(C)**) leads to *box* ending in a consonant cluster; unlike *rats*, there is no morphological way to avoid outputting a cluster. Thus, phonological factors can express themselves via an interaction with morphology, wherein the system opts not to mark plurality in regular forms for phonological reasons, without affecting similar sequences in monomorphemic words and without affecting irregular plurals.

Note that a different ordering of the constraints would yield different results. If **NotComplex(Coda)** is ranked highest, then the /ks/ of *box* is reduced to a single consonant (either the /k/ or the /s/ depending on other constraints, and young children in fact vary on this point; Bernhardt & Stemberger, 1998). If the morphological constraints are ranked highest, then the regular plural *rats* is output despite having a cluster (the correct ranking for adult English). There is a typology of different patterns, expected to occur in different children or at different periods of development. The ranking in Table 1 gives absolute effects (never reducing the cluster in *box* to a single consonant, always producing the base form *rat* rather than the plural form *rats*, always producing the plural form *mice*). However, ranking can be variable (Bernhardt & Stemberger, 1998; Boersma & Hayes, 2001), such that the constraints are ranked differently for different tokens, leading to two or more different outputs for the same input; ranking variability is flexible enough to yield whatever percentages are actually observed in the speech of a particular child at a given period.

Phonological effects on morphology are thus an option in symbolic as well as in nonsymbolic models. Berent and Pinker are simply wrong if they are maintaining that symbolic models disallow a phonological analysis (though they are right that symbolic models also have nonphonological mechanisms that could be involved). Arguments for a rule-based analysis will not be compelling until the "joint" (symbolic and nonsymbolic) phonological account is disproven in an empirical fashion.

We can still ask, however, how strong the empirical support is for such interactions of phonology and plurality in the first part of a compound. When dealing with independent nouns, we can be sure, given extensive research on phonological development (see e.g. Bernhardt & Stemberger, 1998), that there are phonological constraints against word-final singleton consonants and consonant clusters, etc., that are expressed in the development of most children learning English. If a child has difficulty with /z/ in the word *cheese* and /ks/ in the word *box*, it is plausible that they will also have difficulty with the similar /z/ and /ks/ in the words *trees* and *rocks*. However, there is as yet no empirical evidence that /z/ or /ks/ can present greater difficulties at the end of the first member of a compound than at the end of a word. Only if /ks/ can present greater difficulties in the compound *box-top* than in the simple noun *box* do we have a basis for saying that /ks/ presents greater difficulties in the hypothetical compound **rocks-top* than in the simple plural noun *rocks*. Only then can we attribute differences between regular and irregular plurals in the first part of a compound to differences in the phonological form of regulars vs. irregulars.

The present paper reports a case study of a child who showed phonological effects on nouns in compounds, involving the basic phonological forms of monomorphemic nouns and having nothing to do with plurality. Bleile (1987) collected spontaneous pronunciations of words from two children, with relatively fine sampling over a short period of time (22 sessions for each child over a two month period), with the goal of identifying instances of u-shaped learning and with no special focus on compounding, and listed all pronunciations for all child word productions in an appendix. On inspection of the data from one of the children (Jake), it is clear that there was more phonological reduction (deletion of consonants, simplification of diphthongs) for monomorphemic nouns when they appeared as the first member of a compound than when they appeared as independent words; phonological factors led to reduction specifically of the first part of a compound. The present research is a demonstration proof that phonological complexity can develop later in compounds than in independent nouns. This demonstration strengthens the possibility that differences between regular and irregular plural forms in compounds may arise via an interaction with phonological factors.

Method

Bleile (1987) recorded Jake, a monolingual English-learning child living in Iowa, in the child's home in 22 sessions (three times a week) from 2;0.11 to 2;2.3 (24–26 months old). Recordings were made during play, reading, and snacks, and involved interactions with the child's father and/or the investigator. Jake's Mean Length of Utterance was measured as 2.2 during the third session. Jake's hearing was normal. Motor, language and comprehension skills were somewhat advanced for his age. Recordings were made using a Sony Cassette tape recorder with ZT microphones. Bleile transcribed the recordings using the IPA at a fairly broad level (e.g., not transcribing aspiration, glottal stops, or vowel length, but including diphthongization). Transcription reliability was checked for the first 10 minutes of the fourth session; intra-judge reliability for syllable-final consonants was 86%, and inter-judge reliability was 93%. All transcribed utterances occurred either spontaneously or in response to a general question such as "What's this?". All words that might have been immediate imitation of an adult model were excluded.

There is one unfortunate omission in Bleile's transcriptions. English compound nouns are generally treated as having two stressed syllables; e.g., in *sandbox*, the word *sand* is viewed as having primary stress, while *box* has secondary stress. Bleile transcribed only primary stress. It is possible that some of these compounds were reduced to a single stressed syllable, with an unstressed second syllable. However, almost every second member of the compound has an unreduced vowel, so this is unlikely. It should be noted that none of the previous research on this topic (e.g. Gordon, 1985) has provided any information about stress in the compounds, so this limitation is a standard one.

I identified all two-member compound nouns in the corpus, focusing on those compounds where the first noun was made up of a single stressed syllable. (The single token of a three-noun compound, *birthday cake*, was eliminated.) A few words could be argued to have an adjective as the first element, but are included here because they have compound stress rather than phrasal stress (e.g. *french fries*). In a few words, the semantic content of the first element is obscure (*strawberry, popsickle, charcoal*); their inclusion here does not affect the results.

The nouns that appeared in the first position of the compounds were identified when they appeared as independent words, so that the same (monomorphemic) noun could be compared in compounds vs. as independent words. For each noun, it was determined whether the noun was (a) adult-like in both compounds and as an independent noun; (b) equally reduced in both positions (i.e. in the same percentage of tokens); or whether the noun was reduced more (i.e. in a larger percentage of tokens) (c) in compounds or (d) as an independent word. Differences were tested for significance using chi-squared tests for a by-token analysis (based on the number of tokens that were reduced vs. not); chi-squared tests have the disadvantage that the results can be driven by a few lexical items with large differences in one direction, even when most lexical items show no difference or small differences in the opposite direction. To test whether differences are consistent across lexical items, I used a sign test for a by-item analysis, based on the number of noun types that were reduced more in compounds vs. as independent words.

Phonological accounts do not predict that there will be reduction (deletion of consonants or simplification of diphthongs to monophthongs) in all words. Rather, reduction is more likely in more phonologically complex forms than in simpler forms. Taking into account the relatively small number of types (since all compounds were used spontaneously by the child rather than prompted, and so were unpredictable in number of types and tokens), I divided the nouns into three groups as a function of complexity: words with no final coda (ending in a long vowel or diphthong), words with a simple coda (containing an obstruent or nasal, whether the vowel was short, long, or diphthongal), and words with complexity in the coda. Complexity in the coda could derive from the existence of more than one consonant (generally referred to as a "complex coda", as in Table 1 above; no word in the sample had more than two consonants in the coda), or a single consonant with inherent complexity: /r/ or /l/, which have two places of articulation (both coronal and dorsal) and which generally are not yet mastered by children at this age. I then did a more detailed analysis of exactly which phonological elements were reduced.

Unfortunately, about half of the nouns that appeared in compounds were never produced as independent words. In such cases, the nouns were matched to phonologically similar independent nouns in the corpus: (1) to all rhyming words (e.g. for *pine(cone)*: *fine, mine, nine, sign*); (2) if there were no rhyming words, to all words of the same level of complexity (matching for complexity of the nucleus) that contained the same coda (e.g. for *french(fries)*: *lunch*); (3) if the same level of complexity of the nucleus could not be achieved, to all other words that contained the same coda, ignoring whether the nucleus was a short vowel, long vowel, or diphthong (e.g. for *friend(bear)*: *hand, sand, ground, round, around*, where *friend* has a short monophthong but the matched words have either a phonetically long monophthong or a diphthong); or (4) if no words had the same coda, to words (preferably with the same level of complexity in the nucleus) that contained similar codas (e.g. for *dump(truck)*: words that end in nasal+voiceless-stop, *front, tent, cement, drink, sink*). The noun in the compound was then compared to the matched independent nouns as a group (the rate of reduction in the noun in the compound vs. the overall rate of reduction across all matched words), and analyzed statistically in the same way noted above.

In some compounds, an issue arises concerning reduction in typical adult pronunciations. For example, in *sandbox* and *sandcastle*, the first element *sand* can be pronounced [sænd], but the cluster can also be reduced to the nasal ([sæn]), and the nasal can assimilate the place of articulation of the following stop ([sæmbɑks], [sæŋkʰæsl̩]). Absence of the /d/ in *sandbox* cannot be considered reduction relative to the adult pronunciation; only further reduction in the compound (to [sæ]) would be counted as reduction here. As it happens, Jake tended to reduce final /nd/ clusters to [n] (*sand* [sæn] in all tokens). In the word *busstop*, adults often produce the /ss/ sequence with a duration shorter than would be expected for final /s/ plus initial /s/ independently; one could view any deletion of the final /s/ as an extension of the adult pronunciation. In words like *suitcase*, adults often assimilate place of articulation to the first consonant ([suːk̚kʰeɪs]); some phoneticians maintain that this is not true assimilation, but rather extension of the velar closure to an earlier point in time, with reduction of the anterior coronal gesture of the /t/ (Browman & Goldstein, 1986), but this (similar) alternative is equivalent for our purposes here. Complete loss of the /t/ (with a short /k/) is beyond the range of adult variation, but could be viewed as shortening of a long velar stop in the child's speech (still a form of reduction), which would not be as likely when *suit* is an independent noun. I address below whether this possibility could impact on the results.

Results

Results are shown in Table 2. Raw data about all the words and their pronunciations are given in the Appendix.

18 nouns (42.9%) showed no reduction in either position. No nouns showed equal rates of reduction in compounds and independent nouns. The remaining 24 nouns (57.1%) showed more reduction when in the first part of a compound than when an independent word, while none (0%) were more reduced as an independent word than as the first member of a compound. There was more reduction in the first member of a compound than in independent nouns, both by token ($\chi^2(1) = 37.08$, $p < .001$) and by item (two-tailed sign test, 24 vs. 0, $p < .001$). There was no difference between nouns in compounds that were matched with the same independent noun vs. those matched with phonologically similar words.

Some nouns, all with complexity in the rhyme, were reduced even as independent nouns. For a clearer view of the effects, we can pull out those nouns that are reduced more than 50% of the time when they are independent nouns, and look at type and token frequencies for reduction in this group vs. in nouns with less than 50% reduction when an independent noun, as shown in Table 3. The

Table 2. Number of noun types of each level of rhyme complexity, with number of types, number of tokens for independent nouns vs. nouns as the first member of compounds. For the same nouns in both positions, vs. different phonologically matched nouns in compounds vs. as independent nouns.

Rhyme type	No coda					Simple coda					Coda with complexity					Total				
		independent		compound			independent		compound			independent		compound			independent		compound	
	types	tokens	reduced	tokens	reduced	types	tokens	reduced	tokens	reduced	types	tokens	reduced	tokens	reduced	types	tokens	reduced	tokens	reduced
Same nouns																				
neither reduced	3	17	.000	3	.000	6	26	.000	11	.000	1	9	.000	4	.000	10	52	.000	18	.000
compound more	0	–	–	0	–	8	30	.033	31	.742	3	19	.053	31	.323	11	49	.041	63	.524
independent more	0	–	–	0	–	0	–	–	–	–	0	–	–	–	–	0	–	–	–	–
both reduced	0	–	–	0	–	0	–	–	–	–	0	–	–	–	–	0	–	–	–	–
SUBTOTAL	3	17	.000	3	.000	14	56	.018	42	.548	4	28	.036	35	.286	21	101	.020	81	.407
Matched nouns																				
neither reduced	3	75	.000	5	.000	5	54	.000	11	.000	0	–	–	–	–	8	139	.000	13	.000
compound more	0	–	–	0	–	4	14	.071	6	1.000	9	102	.696	21	1.000	13	116	.621	27	1.000
independent more	0	–	–	0	–	0	–	–	–	–	0	–	–	–	–	0	–	–	–	–
both reduced	0	–	–	0	–	0	–	–	–	–	0	–	–	–	–	0	–	–	–	–
SUBTOTAL	3	75	.000	5	.000	9	68	.015	17	.353	9	102	.696	21	1.000	21	255	.282	40	.675
GRAND TOTAL	6	97	.000	8	.000	23	124	.016	59	.492	13	130	.554	56	.554	42	356	.208	121	.500

Table 3. Distinguishing the first members of a compound with complexity in the coda that are reduced more than 50% when an independent word vs. less than 50%.

	Independent reduced < 50%					Independent reduced > 50%				
		independent		compounds			independent		compounds	
	types	tokens	reduced	tokens	reduced	types	tokens	reduced	tokens	reduced
same nouns	3	19	.053	31	.323	0	–	–	–	–
matched nouns	5	22	.045	5	1.000	4	80	.875	16	1.000
TOTAL	8	41	.049	36	.417	4	80	.875	16	1.000
GRAND TOTAL	38	276	.014	105	.419					

4 words that are reduced more than half the time as an independent noun are reduced in every token when in the first part of a compound. The remaining 20 words are reduced at a low level (about 5% of tokens) as independent nouns, but are reduced more than half the time (about 55% of tokens) when they are the first part of a compound. The difference between nouns in the two positions is not a subtle one.

The complexity in the rhyme influences the rate of reduction. As evident in Table 1, no reduction occurred in nouns without a coda, whether in a compound or as an independent noun. For this set of nouns, more-than-minimal reduction in independent nouns occurred only for words with complexity in the coda, suggesting primary difficulty with codas containing consonant clusters and liquid consonants (/r, l/). However, Tables 2 and 3 together show that, for those nouns that are rarely reduced in independent position, reduction in compounds does not affect a larger number of *tokens* in codas with complexity (41%) than in simple codas (49%); the small difference in the unexpected direction is not significant ($\chi^2(1) < 1$). However, reduction does affect a larger percentage of *types* with complexity in the coda (8/9, 89%) than with simple codas (12/23, 52%), a difference which is significant without correction for a 2x2 table ($\chi^2(1) = 4.52$, $p < .05$), but is only marginally significant with Yates' correction ($\chi^2(1) = 2.98$, $p = .084$). The probability of a type being reduced rises with complexity (0% for types with no coda, 52% for types with a simple coda, 89% for types with complexity in the coda), but this does not translate in a simple fashion into differences in the percent of tokens that are reduced.

I examined the singleton consonants that are reduced in the first part of a compound. There are nine singleton consonants that appear at the end of the first part of the compound. All five anterior coronals delete in some tokens of every word (the stops /t, d/) or at least of some words (the nasal /n/ and the fricatives

/θ, s/). The labial stop /p/ occurs in only one word and deletes in some tokens but not others, while the other non-anterior-coronal consonants never delete (the dorsal stop /k/, the labial nasal /m/, and the nonanterior coronal fricative /ʃ/). All words ending in consonant clusters at least sometimes undergo Cluster Reduction, with loss of one consonant, and in some instances loss of both consonants. In all words ending in /l/, the /l/ deletes. In words ending in /r/, the /r/ deletes after a simple vowel, but not after a diphthong (where it is converted into a second syllable, a different way of eliminating complexity in the coda). Reduction is thus most common when there is complexity in the coda, and also when the coda is made up of anterior coronal consonants. The fricative /s/ is affected, but is not implicated as the sole difficulty.

Discussion and conclusion

Jake showed greater phonological limitations on the end of a noun when it was the first member of a compound than when it appeared as an independent noun. Consonant clusters were reduced to single consonants or deleted entirely. Final /r/ and /l/ were often deleted in the first part of a compound (but were more often vocalized to vowels in independent nouns). Codas containing single consonants were often deleted, especially anterior coronal consonants. This establishes that the final portion of the first noun in the compound can be more phonologically restricted than the final portion of independent nouns, independently of morphological considerations. The evidence is from a single child, but this is enough for an existence proof. Given the basic principles of both symbolic and nonsymbolic models, an existence proof of this sort has important ramifications, which I address below.

This fact that reduction can be greater in compounds should not be a complete surprise. In order to produce these English compound nouns in a way that approximates the adult pronunciation, the child must be able to produce larger and more diverse consonant sequences than in morphologically simple words, such as /mptr/ in *dumptruck*.

An expanded set of consonant sequences also occurs at word boundaries in sentences, and several studies have reported that children can have difficulty with these cross-word "consonant clusters" (Klein & Liu-Shea, 2009; Menn & Matthei, 1992; Stemberger, 1993). Stemberger, for example, reported on one child who produced the first two-word combinations such as *gone moon* (where the sequence /nm/ is of very low type frequency within words in English) by reducing the initial consonant of the second word to [h] ([danhuːn]), and later by separating the two consonants with a schwa. But, insofar as this is a problem in two-word utterances, it is resolved quite early, and children (like adults) soon produce longer and more diverse sequences of consonants across word boundaries than internal to words. Bernhardt and Stemberger (1998) note that children generally develop word-final codas in stressed syllables (such as /m/ in *come*) before they develop medial codas in clusters (such as the /m/ in *number*), because the latter involves overcoming extra difficulties with consonant sequences. In adult English, compound nouns occupy a middle ground between syntax and simple words; they are a syntactic-like sequence of two elements that can appear as independent words, but have stress (and reduction patterns) that differ from true syntactic combinations. Children do generalize their mastery of phonological patterns from independent words to compounds, but it would be reasonable for that generalization to take time to develop.

The reduction of the codas of the first member of a compound in this child's speech shows some resemblance to reductions that are familiar in the phonological development literature. Preferential deletion of anterior coronal consonants (irrespective of manner of articulation or voicing) has been reported before. Kehoe and Stoel-Gammon (1997) reported that, when a syllable deletes in a Sww word (a word made up of a stressed syllable followed by two unstressed syllables), unstressed syllables that begin with an anterior coronal (such as the second syllables of the words *animal* and *elephant*) are more likely to delete. That phonologically-driven reductions can be mistaken for purely morphological phenomena also has precedents. Gerken (1991) showed that English-learning children's lack of subject pronouns in early sentences may be due to the fact that such pronouns are generally unstressed in adult speech, since problems with initial unstressed syllables in morphologically simple words such as *balloon* are common at the same age.

It was noted above that there are some reductions in adult speech that may affect the first element in a cluster more often than independent nouns. The loss of /d/ in the words *sandbox* and *sandcastle* was not counted as a child-phonological reduction; and the child always produced *sand* without the /d/ even as an independent word, but deleted the nasal only in the compounds and never in the independent word. A few words can be argued to show assimilation or merger in adult speech that leads to a long or long-ish consonant: *busstop* with half-long [sˑ], *nighttime* and *suitcase* with long [kːʰ], *lawnmower* with long [mː] (though there are often subtle traces of the anterior coronal articulation). One could argue that reduction in these compounds is due to shortening of consonants in a way that is less likely to happen to independent nouns; and in fact all four of these nouns showed more reduction than the same independent nouns. I simply note here that the effects reported above are so strong that a few uncertain words of this sort make no difference. Jake's reductions affected codas that would never be reduced in adult speech, such as the /θ/ of *toothpaste*, the /mp/ of *dumptruck*, and the /d/ of *sidewalk*.

An existence proof of this sort has strong ramifications within all current theories, since all assume that a phenomenon that arises for one speaker could in principle arise for other speakers. Consider a symbolic approach such as Optimality Theory. A surface phonological pattern, no matter how complex, is the result of interactions between simple constraints; depending on the ranking of a set of constraints (i.e. on whether a given constraint is strong enough to prevent or require particular outputs), different surface patterns result. A particular constraint can play a role in many diverse surface patterns. The causes of different surface patterns lie in the componential organization of constraints; any surface pattern can be analyzed as a particular combination of constraints that express themselves more generally. If we can show that a particular constraint or ranking of constraints occurs in some adult language or in the speech of some child, we then predict that it will be generally available for others. This is true whether we hold that constraints are strictly innate to human language (e.g. Prince & Smolensky, 2004) or arise as the result of general principles not restricted to language (e.g. Bernhardt & Stemberger, 1998; Hayes, 1999). Universal availability is obvious in innate systems that specifically assume universal availability. In systems in which something emerges from general cognition, if all humans have basically the same general cognitive systems for learning, storing, and processing information, if something can arise for one individual, it must be able to arise more generally. A similar argument applies to nonsymbolic systems such as connectionist approaches to human language (e.g. Ramscar & Dye, 2010): if a pattern can arise for one learner, it must in principle be able to arise for all.

It is thus possible that the restriction against plurals in the first member of English compounds has a phonological component. Use of plural forms of any sort as the first member of a compound is of low frequency under typical conditions, because English speakers prefer singular/uninflected forms (e.g. Buck-Gengler et al., 2004). Under less typical conditions (including priming of the plural form), plural forms do occur there. Phonological restrictions may interact with morphology: speakers select the uninflected base/singular form rather than the regular plural form in order to avoid a disfavored phonological output (a more complex rhyme with a consonant cluster or a singleton anterior coronal consonant), in the first member of a compound but not when the noun appears independently in the sentence. This phonological factor disfavors regular plurals more than irregular plurals, due to the statistically different phonological properties of regulars vs. irregulars. On the other hand, Jake's data provides no direct evidence that it is /s/ and /z/ specifically that are the problem, as proposed by e.g. Haskell et al. (2003); but one might well ask whether the adult data require such a specific difficulty as opposed to the more general phonological difficulties involved here. However, since children can have difficulties with specific consonants in specific positions in the word, while being able to produce others in a more adult-like fashion, if it turns out that the restrictions in English compounds are due to /s/ and /z/ specifically, that is still compatible with symbolic systems such as Optimality Theory.

The results of this study show that phonological restrictions can differentially affect nouns that are the first member of a compound, as compared to independent nouns in the sentence. It is thus plausible that the restriction against regular plurals as the first member of a compound is at least partly phonologically driven, but mediated by morphological factors as well. The phonological component explains why regular plurals are disadvantaged relative to irregular plurals, but non-phonological factors must underlie the fact that even irregular plurals are disfavored in the first part of a compound. It is plausible that it is an interaction between independently needed phonological and non-phonological factors that leads to the (statistically) different behavior of regular and irregular plurals in compounds. This may hold true even if regular and irregular plurals are produced by different cognitive mechanisms, as assumed by e.g. Berent and Pinker (2007). The behavior of regular and irregular plurals in compounds perhaps provides no information that is relevant to that issue.

References

Berent, I., & Pinker, S. (2007). The dislike of regular plurals in compounds: Phonological or morphological. *The Mental Lexicon*, 2, 129–181. DOI: 10.1075/ml.2.2.03ber

Bernhardt, B. H., & Stemberger, J. P. (1998). *Handbook of phonological development: From the perspective of constraint-based nonlinear phonology*. San Diego: Academic Press.

Bleile, K. M. (1987). *Regressions in the phonological development of two children*. Unpublished doctoral dissertation, University of Iowa.

Boersma, P., & Hayes, B. (2001). Empirical tests of the gradual learning algorithm. *Linguistic Inquiry*, 32, 45–86. DOI: 10.1162/002438901554586

Browman, C. P., & Goldstein, L. M. (1986). Towards an articulatory phonology. *Phonology Yearbook*, 3, 219–252. DOI: 10.1017/S0952675700000658

Buck-Gengler, C. J., Menn, L., & Healy, A. (2004). What "mice-trap" tells us about the mental lexicon. *Brain and Language*, 90, 453–464. DOI: 10.1016/j.bandl.2003.12.001

Fromkin, V. A. (1971). The non-anomalous nature of anomalous utterances. *Language*, 47, 27–52. DOI: 10.2307/412187

Gerken, L. (1991). The metrical basis for children's subjectless sentences. *Journal of Memory and Language*, 30, 431–451. DOI: 10.1016/0749-596X(91)90015-C

Gopnik, M., & Crago, M. B. (1991). Familial aggregation of a developmental language disorder. *Cognition*, 39, 1–50. DOI: 10.1016/0010-0277(91)90058-C

Gopnik, M., & Goad, H. (1997). What underlies inflectional error patterns in Genetic Dysphasia? *Journal of Neurolinguistics*, 10, 109–137. DOI: 10.1016/S0911-6044(97)00003-1

Gordon, P. (1985). Level ordering in lexical development. *Cognition*, 21, 73–93. DOI: 10.1016/0010-0277(85)90046-0

Haskell, T.R., MacDonald, M.C., & Seidenberg, M.S. (2003). Language learning and innateness: Some implications of compounds research. *Cognitive Psychology*, 4, 119–163. DOI: 10.1016/S0010-0285(03)00007-0

Hayes, B. (1999). Phonetically-driven phonology: The role of optimality theory and inductive grounding. In M. Darnell, E. Moravscik, M. Noonan, F. Newmeyer, & K. Wheatly (Eds.), *Functionalism and formalism in linguistics*, vol. 1 (pp. 243–285). Amsterdam: John Benjamins. DOI: 10.1075/slcs.41.13hay

Kehoe, M., & Stoel-Gammon, C. (1997). Truncation patterns in English-speaking children's word productions. *Journal of Speech Language and Hearing Research*, 40, 526–541. DOI: 10.1044/jslhr.4003.526

Kiparsky, P. (1982). From cyclic phonology to lexical phonology. In H. van der Hulst & N. Smith (Eds.), *The structure of phonological representations*, part 1 (pp. 130–175). Dordrecht, Holland: Foris.

Klein, H.B., & Liu-Shea, M. (2009). Between-word simplification patterns in the continuous speech of children with speech sound disorders. *Language, speech, and hearing services in schools*, 40, 17–30. DOI: 10.1044/0161-1461(2008/08-0008)

MacWhinney, B. (2000). *The CHILDES Project: Tools for analyzing talk*. Third Edition. Mahwah, NJ: Lawrence Erlbaum Associates.

Marshall, C.R., & Van der Lely, H.K.J. (2006). A challenge to current models of past tense inflection: the impact of phonotactics. *Cognition*, 100, 302–320. DOI: 10.1016/j.cognition.2005.06.001

Menn, L., & Matthei, E. (1992). The "two-lexicon" approach of child phonology: Looking back, looking ahead. In C.A. Ferguson, L. Menn, & C. Stoel-Gammon (Eds.), *Phonological development: Models, research, implications* (pp. 211–248). Timonium, MD: York Press.

Pinker, S., & Prince, A.S. (1988). On language and connectionism: Analysis of a parallel distributed processing model of language acquisition. *Cognition*, 28, 73–194. DOI: 10.1016/0010-0277(88)90032-7

Pinker, S., & Ullman, M.T. (2002). The past and future of the past tense. *Trends in Cognitive Sciences*, 6, 456–463. DOI: 10.1016/S1364-6613(02)01990-3

Prince, A., & Smolensky, P. (2004). *Optimality theory: Constraint interaction in generative grammar*. Oxford: Blackwell. DOI: 10.1002/9780470756171.ch1

Ramscar, M., & Dye, M. (2010). Learning language from the input: Why innate constraints can't explain noun compounding. *Cognitive Psychology*, 62, 1–40. DOI: 10.1016/j.cogpsych.2010.10.001

Smolensky, P. (1999). Grammar-based connectionist approaches to language. *Cognitive Science*, 23, 589–613. DOI: 10.1207/s15516709cog2304_9

Stemberger, J.P. (1993). Glottal transparency. *Phonology*, 10, 107–138. DOI: 10.1017/S0952675700001755

Stemberger, J.P. (2007). Children's overtensing errors: Phonological and lexical effects on syntax. *Journal of Memory and Language*, 57, 49–64. DOI: 10.1016/j.jml.2007.02.003

Storkel, H.L., Armbrüster, J., & Hogan, T.P. (2006). Differentiating phonotactic probability and neighborhood density in adult word learning. *Journal of Speech, Language, and Hearing Research*, 49, 1175–1192. DOI: 10.1044/1092-4388(2006/085)

Storkel, H.L., & Rogers, M.A. (2000). The effect of probabilistic phonotactics on lexical acquisition. *Clinical Linguistics and Phonetics*, 14, 407–425. DOI: 10.1080/026992000415859

Appendix

This is a list of all the compounds analyzed in the present chapter, listing also the first member of the compound, its adult pronunciation in the dialect in question, and each of the child's pronunciations (with number of tokens). The list of compounds is alphabetical, with three exceptions (*Carebears* after *airport*; *toothpaste* after *birthday*; *toolbox* after *schoolbus*), because these pairs of words have the same set of non-rhyming matched words. Where two or more compounds have the same initial element, the first element and adult pronunciation are listed only once (in a merged cell). When two or more compounds have the same matched independent word(s), the matched word(s) is/are listed only once, in a merged cell. In cases where there is variation in the pronunciation that is not relevant to this paper, the two pronunciations are indicated, but the token count is summed. More-reduced pronunciations are always listed above less-reduced pronunciations.

			Compound		Independent		
Compound	1st element	Adult pronunciation	Child's pronunciation of 1st element	N	Matched noun(s)	Child's pronunciation	N
airplane	air	ɛɹ	ɛ	10	chair hair there square bear	tʃɛ ~ fɛ hɛ ~ ʔɛ dɛ skwɛ bɛɹ ~ bɛə ~ biə	8 2 20 11 7
airport			ɛ	1			
carebears	care	kɛɹ	kɛ	1			
backhoe	back	bæk	bæk	2	back	bæk	6
bathroom	bath	bæθ	bæf	1	bath	bæf	3
birthday	birth	bɹ̩θ	bʊf	2	bath both mouth	bæf boʊf maʊf	3 2 5
toothpaste	tooth	tuθ	tu	1			
blackbirds	black	blæk	bwæk	1	black	bwæk bəwæk	4 1
blueberry	blue	blu	bu	1	blue	bu bwu	13 1
busstop	bus	bʌs	bʌ bʌs	1 1	bus	bʌs	6
charcoal	char	tʃaɹ	tʃa	1	car star	ka ~ kʌ kaɪ sta	12 2 2
dumptruck	dump	dʌmp	dʌ	1	front tent cement drink sink	fwʌn fwʌnt tɛnt sɪmɛnt dwɪŋk sɪŋk	1 1 1 2 2 1

			Compound		Independent		
Compound	**1st element**	**Adult pronunciation**	**Child's pronunciation of 1st element**	**N**	**Matched noun(s)**	**Child's pronunciation**	**N**
fireman	fire	faɪɹ	faɪ.ə	1	fire	faɪ.ə ~ faɪjə	9
fireworks			faɪ.ə	1			
firewhistle			faɪ.ə ~ faɪjə	4			
football	foot	fʊt	fʊ ~ fɔ	8	foot	fʊt	2
frenchfries	french	fɹɛɲtʃ	fwɛs	1	lunch	wʌns	5
friendbear	friend	fɹɛnd	fwɛn	1	sand hand ground round around 	sæn hæn hænd gwaʊn waʊn əwaʊn ~ waʊn əwaʊnd	7 4 1 2 1 8 2
grasshopper	grass	ɡɹæs	gwæs ~ bæs	15	grass	gwæs	8
hamburger	ham	hæm	hæm	1	him worm plum gum	hɪm wʊm pwʌm gʌm	3 4 2 1
haystack	hay	heɪ	heɪ	1	hay	heɪ	2
horsefish	horse	hɔɹs	hɔs	1	horse	hɔɪs	1
horseface			hɔs	1			
hotdog	hot	hɑt	hɑ	2	hot	hɑt	8
lawnmower	lawn	lɔn	wɔ	1	lawn	waʊn	1
mailman	mail	meɪl	mɛ	2	mail	meɪ meɪ.ə ~ meɪ.ʊ	1 2
mailbox			mɛ meɪ	4 1			
nighttime	night	naɪt	naɪ	1	night	naɪt	1
outside	out	aʊt	aʊ	3	shout	saʊt	1
pancake	pan	pæn	pæn	4	pan	pæn	1
pineapple	pine	paɪn	paɪn	2	fine mine nine sign	faɪn maɪn naɪn saɪn	4 3 1 1
pinecone			paɪn	2			
popsickle	pop	pɑp	pɑ pɑp	7 4	pop	pɑ pɑp	1 7
rainbow	rain	ɹeɪn	weɪn	3	rain	weɪn	2
sandbox	sand	sænd	sæ sæn	1 7	sand	sæn	7
sandcastle			sæn	10			

			Compound		Independent		
Compound	**1st element**	**Adult pronunciation**	**Child's pronunciation of 1st element**	**N**	**Matched noun(s)**	**Child's pronunciation**	**N**
schoolbus	school	skul	skʊ	1	pool	pʊ puə ~ pu.ə	1 2
toolbox	tool	tul	tʊ	1			
seatbelt	seat	sit	si	2	seat	sit	3
sidewalk	side	saɪd	saɪ	1	slide	swaɪ swaɪd	1 1
snowman	snow	snoʊ	snoʊ	1	blow go mow no show throw toe	boʊ goʊ ~ doʊ moʊ noʊ soʊ foʊ toʊ	1 15 2 47 1 2 5
strawberry	straw	stɹɔ	stɔ ~ stwɔ	7			
suitcase	suit	sut	su	1	boot	but	1
sunglasses	sun	sʌn	sʌn	2	sun	sʌn	2
sunlotion			sʌn	1			
sunset			sʌ	1			
toybox	toy	tɔɪ	taɪ	2	boy	bɔɪ bɔɪ.ə	1 1
washcloth	wash	waʃ	wæf	1	dish fish brush bush push smash mustache	dɪs ~ dɛs fɪs ~ fɛs bʌs bʊs pʊs smæs mʌstæs	3 14 3 2 1 2 2
wheelbarrow	wheel	wil	wi	4	seal	siə ~ si.ə	11
zookeeper	zoo	zu	zu	1	zoo	zu	1

The locus of the masked onset priming effect

Evidence from Korean

Naoko Witzel[i], Jeffrey Witzel[i], and Yujeong Choi[ii]
[i]University of Texas at Arlington / [ii]University of Toronto

This study investigates the masked onset priming effect (MOPE) in Korean. The results revealed facilitated naming for nonwords written in the alphabetic syllabary *hangul* when primes and targets shared an initial consonant-vowel (CV) syllable as well as when they shared only an initial onset (C) phoneme. However, there was greater priming at the syllable level than at the phoneme level. Taken together with previous research on Korean (Kim & Davis, 2002), these findings indicate that the MOPE reflects facilitated grapheme-to-phoneme conversion processes when the pronunciation of the target is computed through the nonlexical route, and are interpreted to support the Forster and Davis (1991) model of this effect.

Keywords: masked onset priming, naming task, Korean, hangul

The masked onset priming effect (MOPE) refers to the facilitated naming of letter-string targets when they are preceded by a masked prime that has the same initial sound(s) (*basin-BORED*) relative to an all-letter-different prime (*music-BORED*) (Forster & Davis, 1991; Kinoshita, 2000, 2003). This effect has been observed in naming tasks, but not in lexical decision, indicating that it relates to reading targets aloud, and not to visual word recognition processes (Forster & Davis, 1991; Grainger & Ferrand, 1996). As its name suggests, the MOPE has been shown to be serial in nature. It is obtained when the initial sounds overlap between the prime and target, but not when they overlap later in the letter strings (Forster & Davis, 1991; Kinoshita, 2000; Schiller, 2004).

One analysis of the MOPE is that this effect sheds light on the process of computing pronunciation from script (Forster & Davis, 1991; Kinoshita, 2003). Specifically, findings related to this effect have been interpreted within the dual-route framework of reading aloud (Coltheart, Woollams, Kinoshita, & Perry, 1999; Forster & Davis, 1991; Mousikou, Coltheart, Finkbeiner, & Saunders, 2010;

DOI 10.1075/bct.80.04wit

Mousikou, Coltheart, & Saunders, 2010). Under this model, there are two ways of computing the phonology of a visually presented letter string. One is the lexical route, which requires accessing the word in the mental lexicon in order to retrieve its pronunciation. The other is the nonlexical route, which computes pronunciation through grapheme-phoneme correspondence rules (Coltheart, Rastle, Perry, Langdon, & Ziegler, 2001). It has been argued that the MOPE reveals aspects of phonological computation through the nonlexical route. In particular, this effect has been taken to reflect the serial nature of grapheme-to-phoneme conversion (GPC) processes.

Under this dual-route framework, there are in fact two different accounts of the MOPE – the original Forster and Davis (1991; henceforth F&D) account and an account based on the dual-route cascaded (DRC) model of reading aloud (Coltheart et al., 1999; Mousikou et al., 2010). Under both models, GPC processes engaged by the prime facilitate the pronunciation of the target. According to the F&D account, this effect depends on whether the pronunciation of the target is lexically controlled. When pronunciation is not lexically specified – that is, when it can be reliably computed using the nonlexical route – the GPC processes initiated by the prime can be carried over to the processing of the target, and the MOPE can be obtained. However, these nonlexical GPC processes do not facilitate phonological form retrieval when the lexical route is used to pronounce the target. This model explains why the MOPE is observed when all of the targets are regularly spelled words (*MINT*), whose pronunciation can be computed using nonlexical GPC processes, but not when the targets include irregularly spelled words (*PINT*), whose phonological form must be retrieved from the lexical entry (Forster & Davis, 1991; Kinoshita & Woollams, 2002). It also explains why the MOPE is obtained when the targets are nonwords, or letter strings that can only be assigned pronunciations through the nonlexical route (*FENT*; Forster & Davis, 1991).[1] The DRC model, on the other hand, holds that this priming effect is not constrained by properties of the target. Furthermore, this model holds that under masked conditions, the prime is presented for such a short time that nonlexical GPC processes can map only the first letter onto a phoneme by the time the target is displayed (Coltheart et al., 2001; Mousikou et al., 2010). Priming then occurs when the target shares a first phoneme with the prime.

Another interpretation of the MOPE holds that this effect occurs much later in the naming process. Under this view, it is argued that the MOPE reflects facilitated speech planning, which takes place well after GPC processes have been completed (Kinoshita, 2000; Kinoshita & Woollams, 2002; Malouf & Kinoshita, 2007). Support for this model comes from findings that are difficult to handle under the GPC-based accounts discussed above. For instance, Malouf and Kinoshita (2007) found a MOPE for high-frequency words. These results conflict with those of

Forster and Davis (1991), who argued that there should be no MOPE for high-frequency targets because lexically-based phonological form retrieval for such words can be completed before GPC-based phonological computation. Evidence for the speech planning account also comes from results indicating that there is no MOPE when related primes are unpronounceable (Dimitropoulou, Duñabeitia, & Carreiras, 2010). If only the first letter of the prime is converted to sound as the DRC account suggests, the pronounceability of this stimulus should not matter. Further support for this account is provided by picture naming experiments. Schiller (2008), for instance, found that naming latencies were faster when picture targets were preceded by masked primes whose initial sounds overlapped with those of the picture names. Since pictures cannot be named through the nonlexical route, this finding has been taken to show that the MOPE is related to speech planning, and not to GPC processes.

The speech planning account is also supported by recent research on the MOPE in Japanese (Verdonschot, Kiyama, Tamaoka, Kinoshita, La Heij, & Schiller, 2011). In this language, it was found that the MOPE is obtained not at the phoneme level, but at the mora level. The mora is a prosodic unit that has several realizations in Japanese (where 'C' refers to a consonant and 'V' to a vowel): CCV, CV, V, the first part of geminate consonants, and nasal codas. For example, the two syllable Japanese word *Nissan* (日産; the Japanese automaker) can be separated into four morae as *ni.s.sa.n*. These units play an important role in Japanese phonology and in fact are considered the basis of its speech rhythm (Kubozono, 1985, 1989; Kureta, Fushimi, & Tatsumi, 2006; Otake, Hatano, Cutler, & Mehler, 1993; Port, Dalby, & O'Dell, 1987; Warner & Arai, 2001). Verdonschot et al. (2011) interpret this mora-level MOPE in Japanese in terms of the speech planning model and conclude that the mora is the functional phonological unit of speech planning in this language. It is important to note that this mora-level MOPE was obtained when primes and targets were presented in *kana*, a mora-based script, as well as in *romaji*, a script based on the Roman alphabet that is fully phonemically decomposable and in which mora units have no special status. The results for the kana prime-target pairs could of course be explained in terms of facilitated grapheme-to-phoneme conversion whereby only the sound unit represented in the script is able to be primed. Under such an account, mora-based characters would prime morae, but not their component phonemes. The results for romaji, on the other hand, resist explanation under such a model. Because this script represents individual phonemes, a GPC-based model would predict priming at the phoneme level for romaji prime-target pairs.

These Japanese MOPE results, however, do not match well with the findings from Korean (Kim & Davis, 2002), a related East Asian language that can also be written in different scripts. Indeed, the Korean findings to date appear to pose problems for all three models of this priming effect. Korean uses both an alphabetic syllabary called *hangul* and a logographic script based on Chinese characters called *hanja*. In hangul, each character represents a syllable that is composed of separate letters corresponding to its onset, nucleus, and coda. For example, the hangul character 마 represents the syllable /ma/, with its left letter ㅁ standing for the /m/ onset, and its right letter ㅏ for the /a/ nucleus. By contrast, each hanja character represents a morpheme. For instance, the hanja character 馬 means 'horse' and is read as /ma/, but it cannot be decomposed orthographically into its component phonemes. Kim and Davis (2002) tested for the MOPE during the naming of Korean words written in both of these scripts. For hangul, a MOPE was found when prime-target pairs shared a CV onset and nucleus (겨－결 kyŏ-kyŏl) as well as when they shared a complete CVC syllable (결－결 kyŏl-kyŏl). However, when prime-target pairs shared just an onset phoneme (개－결 kae-kyŏl), there was only a statistically unreliable trend towards a priming effect. No such priming effects were found for hanja targets, which revealed only identity (i.e., hanja primes and hanja targets; 江－江 kang-kang) and homophone (i.e., hangul primes and hanja targets; 강－江 kang-kang) priming.

These findings are problematic for current accounts of the MOPE for several reasons. First, the disparity between the priming effects for hangul and hanja targets presents challenges for both the DRC and speech planning models. Under the DRC model, the prime initiates nonlexical GPC processes. These processes then influence the phonological computation of the target, regardless of its characteristics. This model thus predicts a MOPE for both hangul and hanja targets when preceded by related hangul primes. However, as discussed above, Kim and Davis (2002) found a MOPE only for hangul prime-target pairs. The speech planning account also predicts priming for both hangul and hanja targets. According to this account, the MOPE occurs at a stage well after GPC processes and lexically-based phonological form retrieval have been completed, so the script properties of the target should have no influence on this effect. The different pattern of results for hangul and hanja targets, however, indicates that the MOPE is indeed moderated by orthography. It is important to note that the disparity between the priming effects for hanja and hangul words is predicted by the F&D account. Under this model, because the pronunciation of hanja targets must be lexically controlled, the MOPE should not be obtained for words in this script. The pronunciation of hangul words, however, can be reliably computed using the nonlexcial route, so a MOPE is expected.

Kim and Davis' (2002) findings are also problematic for the F&D and DRC accounts of the MOPE because there was no reliable onset priming at the phoneme level. As discussed above, these GPC-based accounts hold that the MOPE reflects nonlexical phonological computation processes. Under both models, this priming effect should be obtained at the smallest unit over which GPC processes can operate. For hangul, this would be the phoneme, the sound unit represented by the letters in this orthography. The lack of a phoneme-level MOPE for hangul targets is especially problematic for the DRC model, which posits that generally only the first letter of a masked prime can be mapped onto a phoneme (Mousikou et al., 2010). This model would thus predict essentially equivalent priming for hangul prime-target pairs that share an onset+nucleus and those that share only an onset phoneme. One possible objection to this analysis is that even though hangul is decomposable into letter units, it is actually read as syllable units. However, this does not appear to be the case. Rather, lexical decision findings showing transposed-letter effects in two-character hangul words indicate that this script is fully decomposed by Korean readers (Lee & Taft, 2009).

There are several possible explanations for the lack of a reliable phoneme-level MOPE in Kim and Davis (2002). One explanation might appeal to a speech planning account of this effect under which the functional phonological unit of production planning is not the phoneme, but rather a larger prosodic unit like the mora or syllable. On such an account, the MOPE should occur only when the prime and target overlap at this higher level of representation. Assume, for instance, that the functional phonological unit of production planning in Korean were the mora, as appears to be the case in Japanese (Verdonschot et al., 2011). If that were the case, as in Kim and Davis (2002), the MOPE should be obtained for prime-target pairs that share at least a CV onset and nucleus, but not for pairs that share only an onset phoneme. This is because under moraic phonology (see e.g., Hayes, 1989), in a syllable beginning CV, generally only the vowel occupies a mora (but see Jun, 1994, for evidence suggesting that Korean aspirated and fortis obstruents have an underlying mora). It is important to note that in order for this to be a plausible analysis, there should be independent evidence suggesting that the mora is a salient level of phonological representation in Korean. Some evidence along these lines comes from a perceptual study in which Korean speakers were asked to discriminate between resynthesized Korean, English, Italian, and Japanese sentences in which only speech rhythm information was retained (Cho, 2004). The resynthesized Korean was able to be reliably distinguished from both English (a stress-timed language) and Italian (a syllable-timed language), but not from Japanese (a mora-timed language). This was interpreted to indicate that speech rhythm in both Korean and Japanese is based on the mora (but see Han, 1964). Although this mora-based production planning account would provide a unified model for the MOPE results in both Japanese and Korean, it is certainly not the only possibility. Alternatively, it could be that the functional phonological unit of production in Korean is the syllable and that overlap at this level is required for the MOPE in this language. Again, this account would explain why

Kim and Davis (2002) obtained a MOPE for prime-target pairs that shared at least a minimal syllable ((C)V), but not for pairs that shared only an onset phoneme.

Another, perhaps simpler, explanation for why the Kim and Davis (2002) study might have failed to find a MOPE at the phoneme level is that it used words, not nonwords, as primes and targets. This raises the possibility that for at least for some of the targets, the lexical route was used to assign pronunciation, rather than the nonlexical route. This is problematic because, as discussed above, the F&D account holds that the MOPE is obtained only when the pronunciation of the target is computed using nonlexical GPC processes. The use of the lexical route to pronounce even a subset of these words might explain why there was only a trend toward a MOPE when prime-target pairs overlapped by a single initial C phoneme.

The present study attempted to address these problematic findings for the MOPE in Korean by examining the locus (or scope) of this priming effect when readers were forced to use the nonlexical route to pronounce targets. This was done by investigating the MOPE with hangul nonwords. Specifically, prime-target pairs of two-syllable hangul nonwords were tested. Related primes overlapped with targets in terms of their first CV syllable (피추-피토 p'ich'u-p'it'o) or initial onset (C) phoneme (페추-피토 p'ech'u-p'it'o). According to GPC-based models of the MOPE, this effect should be obtained at the smallest unit over which orthography-to-phonology computation processes can operate. The MOPE should therefore be obtained at both the syllable and phoneme levels. The F&D and DRC models, however, make different predictions about the relative strength of these effects. Recall that under the DRC model, GPC processes engaged by the masked prime allow for only its first letter to be mapped onto a phoneme before the target is displayed. Because the first letter is the same in both the syllable- and phoneme-overlap conditions, this model would predict essentially equivalent priming effects for these conditions. Under the F&D account, a larger priming effect for the syllable-overlap condition is possible because more of the GPC processes relevant to the prime can be carried over when assigning a pronunciation to the target. Finally, assuming that a prosodic unit above the level of the phoneme is the functional phonological unit of production planning in Korean, the speech planning account would predict priming at the syllable level, but not at the phoneme level, as in Kim and Davis (2002).

Method

Participants

Twenty-four native Korean speakers participated in the experiment. All participants were affiliated with the University of Texas at Arlington at the time of the experiment. All reported that Korean was their native and dominant language. They were remunerated for their time.

Materials and design

There were 144 targets, all of which were bi-syllabic nonwords presented in hangul (피토 p'it'o). Each was preceded by three prime types, which were also bi-syllabic hangul nonwords: syllable, phoneme, and all-letter-different (ALD) primes (see the Appendix for a complete list of the prime-target pairs). These primes differed in the amount of overlap they had with the target. Syllable primes had the same initial character as the target (피추–피토 p'ich'u-p'it'o), which corresponded to the same first mora/syllable. Phoneme primes shared the same initial letter with the target (페추–피토 p'ech'u-p'it'o), which corresponded to the same first onset phoneme. The ALD primes served as controls, and did not overlap at all with the target (카추–피토 k'ach'u-p'it'o). In order to ensure consistency among the primes, the second syllable was the same across all three conditions. Three counterbalanced lists of items were constructed such that each target appeared in all three conditions across lists. The study thus employed a 3x3 design, with list as a non-repeated measure and prime type (syllable, phoneme, ALD) as a repeated measure.

Procedure

The experiment was controlled using DMDX software (Forster & Forster, 2003). Primes were presented in Batang 11 pt font, and targets were presented in Dotum 12 pt font using a color monitor with a 16.67 ms refresh rate. A standard three-field masked priming procedure was used (Forster & Davis, 1984), in which each trial consisted of a 500 ms forward mask (#####), a 50 ms prime, and a 500 ms target, all presented in the center of the screen. Participants read each target aloud as quickly and accurately as possible. All instructions were given in Korean. Before the experimental items, there were 8 practice trials, none of which were repeated as experimental items.

Table 1. Naming latency/reaction time (RT) means and standard deviations (in milliseconds), priming effects, and percent error rates (%ER) for *hangul* nonword targets.

Prime type	Example	RT (ms)			%ER
		M	SD	Priming	
Syllable	피추-피토	581	81	16***	5.99
Phoneme	페추-피토	588	82	9*	6.34
ALD control	카추 피토	597	79		5.56

*** $p < .001$, * $p < .05$

Results

Vocal responses were hand-marked using CheckVocal (Protopapas, 2007). Incorrect responses (i.e., responses that did not match the target or that involved some disfluency) were not included in the analyses of the naming latencies/reaction times (RTs). Outlier data points were adjusted to two SD units above and below the mean for each participant (affecting 0.49% of the data). RTs and error rates (ERs) were analyzed using an F1.F2 analysis procedure, in which data were aggregated across items for the subject analysis (*F*1), and across subjects for the item analysis (*F*2). The mean RTs and ERs for each condition are presented in Table 1.

In the RT analyses, the effect of prime type was significant ($F1(2,42) = 9.72$, $p < .001$; $F2(2,282) = 9.13$, $p < .001$). Planned comparisons showed that consistent with a MOPE at the syllable level, there was a statistically reliable priming effect with syllable primes (16 ms) ($F1(1,21) = 14.59$, $p < .001$; $F2(1,141) = 19.29$, $p < .001$). The priming effect with phoneme primes (9 ms) was also significant ($F1(1,21) = 6.67$, $p < .05$; $F2(1,141) = 4.71$, $p < .05$), indicating that a MOPE at the phoneme level as well. A comparison of the related conditions also showed that targets were named more quickly with syllable primes than with phoneme primes ($F1(1,21) = 5.07$, $p < .05$; $F2(1,141) = 4.18$, $p < .05$). There were no significant ER differences among the conditions (all *F*'s < 1.06).[2]

Discussion

The present study shows that in the naming of Korean hangul nonwords, a MOPE is obtained when primes and targets share an initial CV syllable as well as when they share only an initial onset (C) phoneme, with greater priming at the syllable level than at the phoneme level. With respect to Korean script processing in general, these findings indicate that although each hangul character represents a syllable, this script is nevertheless (automatically) decomposed into independent letter/phoneme units (see also Lee & Taft, 2009). Furthermore, with regard to teasing between competing models of the MOPE, these findings are most consistent with the predictions of the F&D account. This model holds that the MOPE reflects facilitated grapheme-to-phoneme conversion when the pronunciation of a target is computed through the nonlexical route. As discussed above, this account predicts a MOPE at the smallest orthographic unit over which GPC processes can operate. In the case of the alphabetic syllabary hangul, this is the letter/phoneme. The F&D model also predicts a larger priming effect at the syllable level than at the phoneme level. This is because more of the GPC processes initiated by the syllable prime can be applied when computing the pronunciation of its related target. Again, both of these predictions were borne out by the results of this experiment.

The DRC and speech planning accounts of the MOPE do not fare as well. Like the F&D model, the DRC account posits that the MOPE reflects facilitated grapheme-to-phoneme conversion. Under this model, the masked prime engages nonlexical GPC processes, which can map only the first letter onto a phoneme by the time the target is displayed (Coltheart et al., 2001; Mousikou et al., 2010). In the present experiment, because the first letter was the same in both the syllable and phoneme primes, this model predicts roughly equivalent priming effects for these conditions. Contrary to this prediction, however, the results revealed a larger priming effect at the syllable level. For its part, the speech planning account holds that the MOPE reflects relative processing ease as sounds are slotted into the production plan for a letter string. Recall that in order for this model to account for the lack of a phoneme-level MOPE in Kim and Davis (2002), it would appear necessary to assume that the functional phonological unit of production planning in Korean is not the phoneme, but a larger prosodic unit like the mora or syllable. In the present study, this account therefore predicts priming at the syllable level, but not at the phoneme level. The results, however, revealed priming at both levels.

It is also important to note that the F&D model appears to provide the best account not only for the findings of the present study, but for the complete set of findings related to the MOPE in Korean. Recall that Kim and Davis (2002) found facilitated naming for Korean prime-target pairs that shared a CV onset and nucleus when the words were presented in the alphabetic syllabary hangul. However, they found no such effect for words presented in the logographic script hanja. As discussed above, the disparity in the results for hangul and hanja targets is problematic for both the DRC and speech planning models. Under both of these models, the script properties of the target should not influence this priming effect.

In the DRC model, the nonlexical GPC processes engaged by the prime can facilitate the naming of the target regardless of its script properties. And according to the speech planning model, because the MOPE facilitates production planning, at a stage well after GPC processes have been completed, the script properties of the target should be irrelevant to this effect. Only the F&D account correctly predicts a MOPE for hangul words, whose pronunciations can be computed using the nonlexical route, but not for hanja words, whose pronunciations can only be retrieved through the lexical route.

One possible objection to the predictions for the speech planning model presented above is that the functional phonological unit of production planning in Korean may not be a larger prosodic unit like the mora or syllable. Rather, as in English and other languages that have shown phoneme-level MOPEs, the phoneme may be the relevant production planning unit in Korean. If this is the case, consistent with the results of the present experiment, the MOPE should be obtained at the level of the phoneme, and there should be more priming with greater prime-target overlap. Although such an account might explain the results of the present experiment, it would not offer a straightforward explanation (i) for the lack of a phoneme-level effect in Kim and Davis (2002) or (ii) for the disparity between the priming effects for hangul and hanja targets in this earlier study. In short, whether the functional phonological unit of production planning in Korean is the phoneme or a larger prosodic unit, the speech planning model cannot account for the complete set of MOPE results for this language.

It is important to emphasize that much hinges on determining the correct account and the precise locus of this priming effect. Indeed, if the MOPE reflects processes involved in grapheme-to-phoneme conversion, as posited under both the F&D and DRC accounts, this effect has important implications for computational models of reading aloud. In particular, this effect could be taken as strong evidence that the nonlexical route does not compute phonology for letters in parallel, but rather that grapheme-to-phoneme conversion processes occur serially across the letter string (see e.g., Coltheart et al., 2001; Coltheart et al., 1999). If, on the other hand, the MOPE relates to speech planning processes, this priming effect would have no bearing on whether grapheme-to-phoneme computation is serial or parallel in nature (Kinoshita, 2003). Instead, this effect could be used only to investigate issues related specifically to production processes, such as questions related to the functional unit(s) of production planning in a given language (e.g., Ferrand, Segui, & Grainger, 1996; Schiller, 1998, 1999, 2000; Verdonschot et al., 2011; but see also Brand, Rey, & Peereman, 2003). As discussed above, taken together with previous work on the MOPE in Korean (Kim & Davis, 2002), the results of the present study come down relatively firmly in support of a GPC-based model of this priming effect, and specifically, of the F&D

account. Under this model, the MOPE occurs because the prime engages nonlexical GPC processes that can be carried over when computing the pronunciation of the target through the nonlexical route. Whether nonlexical GPC processes are used to pronounce the target is in turn determined by the properties of the target itself as well as by the extent to which other items in the experiment encourage or demand (as in the case of nonwords) the use of the nonlexical route.

In closing, it is important to note that the present study might also suggest a framework for future investigations into the MOPE. Indeed, more research is necessary in order to determine the precise nature of this effect as well as to account for the conflicting results that have been obtained across studies and languages. Answers to these questions might be provided by more extensive research into languages with different scripts and into languages like Korean and Japanese in particular – that is, languages with multiple scripts, each of which encodes a different level of phonological information.

Notes

1. Similar form priming for nonwords is generally not found in lexical decision tasks (for discussion and review, see Forster, Mohan, & Hector, 2003).

2. This pattern of results was confirmed with linear mixed-effects modelling analyses. F1.F2 analyses are reported in this study to allow for straightforward comparisons with Kim and Davis (2002).

References

Brand, M., Rey, A., & Peereman, R. (2003). Where is the syllable priming effect in visual word recognition? *Journal of Memory and Language*, 48, 435–443. DOI: 10.1016/S0749-596X(02)00522-3

Cho, M.-H. (2004). Rhythm typology of Korean speech. *Cognitive Processing*, 5, 249–253. DOI: 10.1007/s10339-004-0023-1

Coltheart, M., Rastle, K., Perry, C., Langdon, R., & Ziegler, J. (2001). DRC: A dual route cascaded model of visual word recognition and reading aloud. *Psychological Review*, 108, 204–256. DOI: 10.1037/0033-295X.108.1.204

Coltheart, M., Woollams, A., Kinoshita, S., & Perry, C. (1999). A position-sensitive Stroop effect: Further evidence for a left-to-right component in print-to-speech conversion. *Psychonomic Bulletin & Review*, 6, 456–463. DOI: 10.3758/BF03210835

Dimitropoulou, M., Duñabeitia, J. A., & Carreiras, M. (2010). Influence of prime lexicality, frequency, and pronounceability on the masked onset priming effect. *The Quarterly Journal of Experimental Psychology*, 63, 1813–1837. DOI: 10.1080/17470210903540763

Ferrand, L., Segui, J., & Grainger, J. (1996). Masked priming of word and picture naming: The role of syllabic units. *Journal of Memory and Language*, 35, 708–723. DOI: 10.1006/jmla.1996.0037

Forster, K. I., & Davis, C. (1984). Repetition priming and frequency attenuation in lexical access. *Journal of Experimental Psychology: Learning, Memory, and Cognition*, 10, 680–698. DOI: 10.1037/0278-7393.10.4.680

Forster, K. I., & Davis, C. (1991). The density constraint on form-priming in the naming task: Interference effects from a masked prime. *Journal of Memory and Language*, 30, 1–25. DOI: 10.1016/0749-596X(91)90008-8

Forster, K. I., & Forster, J. C. (2003). DMDX: A Windows display program with millisecond accuracy. *Behavior Research Methods, Instruments & Computers*, 35, 116–124. DOI: 10.3758/BF03195503

Forster, K. I., Mohan, K., & Hector, J. (2003). The mechanics of masked priming. In S. Kinoshita & S. J. Lupker (Eds.), *Masked priming: The state of the art* (pp. 3–37). Hove, England: Psychology Press.

Grainger, J., & Ferrand, L. (1996). Masked orthographic and phonological priming in visual word recognition and naming: Cross-task comparisons. *Journal of Memory and Language*, 33, 623–647. DOI: 10.1006/jmla.1996.0033

Han, M. (1964). Duration of Korean vowels. *Studies in the Phonology of Asian Languages II*. Acoustic Phonetics Research Laboratory, University of Southern California.

Hayes, B. (1989). Compensatory lengthening in moraic phonology. *Linguistic Inquiry*, 20, 253–306.

Jun, J. (1994). Metrical weight consistency in Korean partial reduplication. *Phonology*, 11, 69–88. DOI: 10.1017/S0952675700001846

Kim, J., & Davis, C. (2002). Using Korean to investigate phonological priming effects without the influence of orthography. *Language and Cognitive Processes*, 17, 569–591. DOI: 10.1080/01690960143000281

Kinoshita, S. (2000). The left-to-right nature of the masked onset priming effect in naming. *Psychonomic Bulletin & Review*, 7, 133–141. DOI: 10.3758/BF03210732

Kinoshita, S. (2003). The nature of masked onset priming effects in naming: A review. In S. Kinoshita & S. J. Lupker (Eds.), *Masked priming: The state of the art* (pp. 223–238). Hove, England: Psychology Press.

Kinoshita, S., & Woollams, A. (2002). The masked onset priming effect in naming: Computation of phonology or speech planning? *Memory and Cognition*, 30, 237–245. DOI: 10.3758/BF03195284

Kubozono, H. (1985). Speech errors and syllable structure. *Linguistics and Philology*, 6, 220– 243.

Kubozono, H. (1989). The mora and syllable structure in Japanese: Evidence from speech errors. *Language and Speech*, 32, 249–278.

Kureta, Y., Fushimi, T., & Tatsumi, I. F. (2006). The functional unit of phonological encoding:Evidence for moraic representation in native Japanese speakers. *Journal of Experimental Psychology: Learning, Memory, and Cognition*, 32, 1102–1119. DOI: 10.1037/0278-7393.32.5.1102

Lee, C. H., & Taft, M. (2009). Are onsets and codas important in processing letter position? A comparison of TL effects in English and Korean. *Journal of Memory and Language*, 60, 530–542. DOI: 10.1016/j.jml.2009.01.002

Malouf, T., & Kinoshita, S. (2007). Masked onset priming effect for high-frequency words: Further support for the speech-planning account. *The Quarterly Journal of Experimental Psychology*, 60, 1155–1167. DOI: 10.1080/17470210600964035

Mousikou, P., Coltheart, M., Finkbeiner, M., & Saunders, S. (2010). Can the dual-route cascaded computational model of reading offer a valid account of the masked onset priming effect? *Quarterly Journal of Experimental Psychology*, 63, 984–1003. DOI: 10.1080/17470210903156586

Mousikou, P., Coltheart, M., & Saunders, S. (2010). Computational modelling of the masked onset priming effect in reading aloud. *European Journal of Cognitive Psychology*, 22, 725–763. DOI: 10.1080/09541440903052798

Otake, T., Hatano, G., Cutler, A., & Mehler, J. (1993). Mora or syllable? Speech segmentation in Japanese. *Journal of Memory and Language*, 32, 258–278. DOI: 10.1006/jmla.1993.1014

Port, R. F., Dalby, J., & O'Dell, M. (1987). Evidence for mora-timing in Japanese. *Journal of the Acoustical Society of America*, 81, 1574–1585. DOI: 10.1121/1.394510

Protopapas, A. (2007). CheckVocal: A program to facilitate checking the accuracy and response times of vocal responses from DMDX. *Behavior Research Methods*, 39, 859–862. DOI: 10.3758/BF03192979

Schiller, N. O. (1998). The effect of visually masked syllable primes on the naming latencies of words and pictures. *Journal of Memory and Language*, 39, 484–507. DOI: 10.1006/jmla.1998.2577

Schiller, N. O. (1999). Masked syllable priming in English nouns. *Brain and Language*, 68, 300–305. DOI: 10.1006/brln.1999.2109

Schiller, N. O. (2000). Single word production in English: The role of subsyllabic units during phonological encoding. *Journal of Experimental Psychology: Learning, Memory, and Cognition*, 26, 512–528. DOI: 10.1037/0278-7393.26.2.512

Schiller, N. O. (2004). The onset effect in word naming. *Journal of Memory and Language*, 50, 477–490. DOI: 10.1016/j.jml.2004.02.004

Schiller, N. O. (2008). The masked onset priming effect in picture naming. *Cognition*, 106, 952–962. DOI: 10.1016/j.cognition.2007.03.007

Verdonschot, R. G., Kiyama, S., Tamaoka, K., Kinoshita, S., La Heij, W., & Schiller, N. O. (2011). The functional unit of Japanese word naming: Evidence from masked priming. *Journal of Experimental Psychology: Learning, Memory, and Cognition*, 37, 1458–1473. DOI: 10.1037/a0024491

Warner, N., & Arai, T. (2001). Japanese mora-timing: A review. *Phonetica*, 58, 1–25. DOI: 10.1159/000028486

Appendix
Items used in the experiment

Items are separated by semicolons. The entry for each item contains the syllable prime, phoneme prime, ALD control prime, and finally the target (in bold).

피추, 페추, 카추, **피토**; 테무, 토무, 흐무, **테차**; 체테, 치테, 쿠테, **체호**; 커패, 코패, 짜패, **커무**; 매히, 무히, 프히, **매타**; 헤타, 호타, 커타, **헤추**; 배토, 부토, 허토, **배카**; 빼코, 뿌코, 피코, **빼저**; 대메, 드메, 푸메, **대스**; 따저, 떼저, 츠저, **따수**; 기캐, 가캐, 추캐, **기쏘**; 깨수, 끼수, 트수, **깨로**; 즈끼, 자끼, 너끼, **즈케**; 쩨토, 찌토, 카토, **쩨푸**; 사베, 스베, 투베, **사너**; 쑤매, 써매, 니매, **쑤하**; 내카, 누카, 소카, **내메**; 러마, 래마, 티마, **러소**; 페너, 푸너, 해너, **페카**; 투치, 태치, 커치, **투파**; 초쿠, 치쿠, 머쿠, **초타**; 크호, 캐호, 메호, **크추**; 모츠, 마츠, 헤츠, **모패**; 호채, 하채, 페채, **호트**; 바러, 비러, 포러, **바수**; 빠키, 뿌키, 데키, **빠해**; 드서, 디서, 캐서, **드푸**; 떠재, 또재, 카재, **떠추**; 구뻬, 가뻬, 미뻬, **구쌔**; 꼬터, 깨터, 니터, **꼬바**; 주꼬, 지꼬, 세꼬, **주러**; 째히, 쩌히, 루히, **째토**; 새카, 서카, 리카, **새버**; 씨매, 쎄매, 바매, **씨노**; 노찌, 너찌, 스찌, **노따**; 라베, 루베, 초베, **라티**; 패후, 피후, 초후, **패타**; 트푸, 타푸, 키푸, **트채**; 차매, 츠매, 키매, **차허**; 캐터, 쿠터, 하터, **캐무**; 므터, 머터, 헤터, **므치**; 허타, 후타, 채타, **허쿠**; 비쿠, 버쿠, 포쿠, **비헤**; 뽀재, 빠재, 니재, **뽀세**; 도네, 대네, 히네, **도짜**; 떼카, 뚜카, 흐카, **떼비**; 가더, 고더, 히더, **가뚜**; 꺼노, 꾸노, 세노, **꺼자**; 자너, 지너, 메너, **자쓰**; 쪼후, 쩌후, 테후, **쪼키**; 세카, 수카, 미카, **세버**; 써키, 쑤키, 해키, **써모**; 네쯔, 나쯔, 커쯔, **네후**; 로쿠, 리쿠, 헤쿠, **로꺼**; 프무, 퍼무, 키무, **프채**; 태카, 토카, 헤카, **태피**; 치퍼, 체퍼, 캐퍼, **치후**; 코후, 커후, 새후, **코체**; 마해, 미해, 커해, **마푸**; 하츠, 허츠, 미츠, **하패**; 브추, 버추, 파추, **브래**; 삐마, 뿌마, 체마, **삐쌔**; 데초, 다초, 히초, **데수**; 뜨추, 떼추, 키추, **뜨저**; 개누, 기누, 저누, **개싸**; 끄하, 꺼하, 새하, **끄피**; 재카, 지카, 머카, **재누**; 쩌코, 짜코, 히코, **쩌그**; 시까, 서까, 노까, **시래**; 쏘카, 쑤카, 너카, **쏘재**; 너추, 네추, 리추, **너해**; 레코, 라코, 시코, **레누**; 파키, 패키, 초키, **파후**; 타키, 테키, 무키, **타해**; 츠해, 차해, 티해, **츠메**; 케미, 쿠미, 츠미, **케타**; 미패, 므패, 타패, **미허**; 해티, 호티, 차티, **해푸**; 버체, 바체, 꼬체, **버루**; 쁘재, 빼재, 쭈재, **쁘나**; 더모, 두모, 까모, **더세**; 때피, 따피, 너피, **때호**; 그무, 게무, 러무, **그차**; 께포, 까포, 너포, **께수**; 저꼬, 제꼬, 무꼬, **저파**; 쭈포, 쩌포, 니포, **쭈베**; 소커, 수커, 피커, **소베**; 싸피, 써피, 투피, **싸므**; 나캐, 너캐, 히캐, **나스**; 리차, 러차, 뿌차, **리메**; 퍼토, 푸토, 히토, **퍼츠**; 터해, 투해, 프해, **터마**; 채머, 차머, 티머, **채쿠**; 카무, 케무, 때무, **카치**; 무허, 마허, 때허, **무피**; 후코, 헤코, 치코, **후마**; 베키, 버키, 라키, **베모**; 뿌매, 삐매, 로매, **뿌커**; 디노, 다노, 무노, **디채**; 띠메, 또메, 나메, **띠구**; 고네, 거네, 스네, **고찌**; 까너, 끄너, 리너, **까소**; 지뿌, 조뿌, 나뿌, **지깨**; 짜티, 쯔티, 쎄티, **짜포**; 서티, 소티, 자티, **서내**; 쌔마, 쑤마, 키마, **쌔추**; 니파, 누파, 제파, **니호**; 루초, 레초, 키초, **루파**; 푸모, 퍼모, 키모, **푸해**; 토허, 테허, 캐허, **토차**; 추코, 처코, 테코, **추머**; 키하, 코하, 므하, **키태**; 머키, 모키, 페키, **머후**; 히머, 하머, 캐머, **히추**; 부코, 비코, 재코, **부짜**; 빼피, 빼피, 쿠피, **빼고**; 다찌, 대찌, 허찌, **다쎄**; 또미, 떠미, 째미, **또사**; 게티, 구티, 주티, **게소**; 끼하, 꼬하, 메하, **끼모**; 조테, 지테, 후테, **조싸**; 찌퍼, 쪼퍼, 채퍼, **찌하**; 수짜, 시짜, 채짜, **수꼬**; 쎄마, 씨마, 허마, **쎄투**; 느패, 니패, 루패, **느가**; 래초, 러초, 게초, **래피**; 포캐, 피캐, 허캐, **포무**; 티카, 투카, 해카, **티페**; 처푸, 치푸, 코푸, **처타**; 쿠모, 커모, 츠모, **쿠티**; 메퍼, 모퍼, 트퍼, **메히**; 흐코, 해코, 터코, **흐차**; 보까, 버까, 누까, **보째**; 빼루, 뽀루, 메루, **빼키**; 두카, 더카, 네카, **두새**; 뚜히, 따히, 께히, **뚜초**; 거헤, 가헤, 치헤, **거노**; 꾸조, 깨조, 라조, **꾸치**; 제디, 자디, 너디, **제카**; 쯔초, 째초, 리초, **쯔사**; 스쿠, 세쿠, 지쿠, **스라**; 쓰쿠, 싸쿠, 조쿠, **쓰치**; 누채, 너채, 히채, **누바**; 르찌, 레찌, 투찌, **르바**

The reversal of the BÄREN–BEEREN merger in Austrian Standard German

Marjoleine Sloos
Interacting Minds Centre, Aarhus University

In language change, a reversal of a merger is generally considered to be impossible, since after two sounds have become fully merged, they are no longer distinct, so no phonetic or phonological cues exist that could reverse this process. This article investigates such an 'impossible' merger reversal: the split of the BÄREN vowel (orthographically represented by <ä> or <äh>) and the BEEREN vowel (orthographically represented by <e>, <ee> or <eh> in Austrian Standard German. We investigated a corpus of spoken data, measured the acoustic properties of the vowels, and determined the degree of the merger (by computing Pillai scores) for younger and older speakers. It turns out that the two sounds were formerly merged, but currently a split can be observed as an ongoing process. This paper argues that language contact with Standard German as it is spoken in Germany motivates the ongoing reversal. Since the BÄREN vowel is also subject to substantial variation in German Standard German, in order to get the split right, Austrian speakers are likely to invoke orthographical knowledge. We will consider the mental representations of this sound, including the graphemic representations from an Exemplar-theoretical viewpoint.

Keywords: Austrian Standard German, BÄREN vowel, Exemplar Theory, merger, orthography, reversal, unmerger

Reversal of a merger

In a merger, two different sounds converge on a single sound. It is usually assumed that a merger, if completed, cannot be reversed for the logical reason that after merging no phonetic or phonological cues exist that can serve as a means for reversal. Even in dialect contact, in which dialect M has the merger and dialect S has the split, M speakers will not learn the split, for they are not able to perceive the categorical distinction; if speakers try to reverse a merger, they will not get it

DOI 10.1075/bct.80.05slo

right (Labov, 1994). However, a few cases have been reported in which unmerging does seem to occur. Labov (1994) attributes this reversal to the occurrence of lexical loanword strata – explicitly excluding other potential reasons, such as orthography. There seem to be alternative circumstances in which a reversal of a merger could occur, however. Maguire (2008: 332, 333, 357) claims that reversals can occur "given the right social context", that is, under pressure of e.g. orthography, dialect contact and/or dialect levelling, and hypercorrection. In fact, under these circumstances, vowel mergers may be considered as incomplete, i.e. as near-mergers. In case of such a near-merger, some speakers merge two vowels and other speakers don't. It is also possible that vowels are still phonologically distinct, but that the speakers do not perceive the difference (Trudgill & Foxcroft, 1978). It may even be the case that speakers merge in production, but still perceive a split in the speech of others (Hay, Warren, & Drager, 2006). Whether vowels are completely merged or not is difficult to establish, and subtle differences which might not be apparent first, may turn out to be cues for perceptual distinction on closer inspection (Watt, 1998).

This article investigates the BÄREN-BEEREN merger in Austrian Standard German. The BÄREN-BEEREN merger is a well-known merger in Standard German studies (Hove, 2002; Kleiner & Knöbl, 2011; König, 1989; Sloos, 2013; Spiekermann, 2008) and most pervasive in Austria and the Low-German area. Austrian speakers not only produce a merger, they also perceive it to the extent that even in linguistic research by Austrian linguists, the BÄREN and the BEEREN vowels are not investigated individually, since they are presumed to be fully merged (like Ehrlich, 2010; Moosmüller, 2007). The BÄREN vowel as such does not occur in the Austrian dialects either, and (unlike in Germany), a stylistic difference does not exist (cf. Muhr, 2007). Still, an orthographical difference is maintained for the two vowels. The present article observes a current reversal of this merger. This indicates that (1) speakers are aware of the difference between the vowels and (2) they know how the split should be made (provided they do it correctly, which is the case). But do speakers make the split on the basis of orthography only? Or do they rely on other – unknown – cues as well? And what is the motivation for the current reversal?

There are three aspects in the reversal to consider: (1) speakers have to be aware of the phonemic distinction between the BÄREN and the BEEREN vowels, (2) speakers have to be motivated to undo the merger, and (3) speakers have to know how to make the distinction. I will argue that speakers know the phonemic distinction through orthography as well as the local dialects in Austria, although in the dialects, the pronunciation of the BÄREN vowel differs from that in the standard variety. Second, the motivation for the unmerger is most plausibly the distinction that exists in the Northern Standard varieties (as spoken in

Germany) – which is broadcasted through the media in Austria – and which most likely functions as the prestige variety. Crucially, however, in these northern varieties, much variation occurs as well. That is, in order to get the split right, Austrian speakers can neither fully rely on the distinction in their local dialects, nor on the distinction in the prestige varieties to which they orient themselves. Although the distribution in those varieties certainly play an important role in the current reversal of the merger, orthography is the clearest cue for getting the split right.

If it is indeed the case that spelling and contact with other varieties play a role in the change of a phonological system, phonological models should incorporate this information. Phonological feed-forward models do not allow for the influence of e.g. orthography. However, such non-grammatical information can be contained in the lexicon, as usage-based models and psycholinguistic models suggest. The way to model non-grammatical information in the lexicon, though, is also not straightforward. For instance, contact between different varieties does not *necessarily* influence the pronunciation of the standard variety. So, the question is which information is contained in the lexicon. Or, more specifically, is orthographic information stored in the lexicon? And why does this information make a difference only in particular cases (given that some sounds are represented by different spellings)? By examining the ongoing reversal of a merger (the BÄREN–BEEREN merger in the Austrian variety of Standard German) we will address these questions.

This article is structured as follows. The next section "From Distinction to Merger", outlines the historical development of the BÄREN–BEEREN merger in Standard German and Austrian Standard German. The third section "The Polycentric Character of German" provides some background information about the different standard varieties in German. The fourth section presents the procedure used to investigate the current variation in the BÄREN–BEEREN merger. The fifth section contains the results. The final section contains the overall discussion and conclusion and considers the results within the Exemplar-theoretical framework.

From distinction to merger

This section considers the contrast between and merger of the BÄREN and BEEREN vowels through the ages, showing that a (near-) merger occurred in Standard German. Generally speaking, in Standard German, the pronunciation of the BÄREN vowel is subject to extensive variation. The vowel – orthographically represented by <ä> or <äh> – may be pronounced as a long *higher-mid* unrounded front vowel [eː], or as a long *lower-mid* unrounded front vowel [ɛː], or any realization in between. We thus find the following variation (all forms here are Standard German):

(1) Bäder b[eː]der ~ b[ɛː]der 'bath.PLUR'
Bären b[eː]ren ~ b[ɛː]ren 'bear.PLUR'

In case the pronunciation is the higher-mid vowel [eː], neutralization may occur with the BEEREN vowel (b[eː]ren 'berry.PLUR'), which is orthographically represented by <e>, <ee> or <eh>. The pronunciation of the BÄREN vowel has been investigated in a number of studies (Hove, 2002; Kleiner & Knöbl, 2011; König, 1989; Sloos, 2013; Spiekermann, 2008), which implicitly assume that the pronunciation of the BÄREN vowel as [eː] indicates a merger with the BEEREN vowel. However, this is not necessarily the case: it is possible that both vowels are raised and a distinction is still made, and it is also possible that both vowels are pronounced lower and a distinction is still maintained. Theoretically speaking, it is even possible that the vowels are reversed, which is certainly not the case in the Standard variety, but possibly is in some dialects. This is beyond the scope of this paper and left for future investigation. This paper focuses on the conditions under which a merger or a split is made, in particular in the Austrian variety of Standard German.

It should be noted at this point that Standard German also has a short vowel [ɛ], which can be orthographically represented by either <ä> or <e>. This vowel is found in *hält* 'hold.3SG' and *Held* 'hero'. Interestingly, *hält* and *Held* are perfect homonyms (pronounced as [hɛlt]) and as far as I know, no variation has been observed. This is the first indication that orthography can never be the only factor that drives the split of the BÄREN–BEEREN merger.

The BÄREN and BEEREN vowels were distinct phonemes in Old High German (OHG) with different sources and also different paths of development. We know that in OHG <ä> and <e> were pronounced differently since in poetry of that period <e> never rhymed with <ä> (Fourquet (1952: 518) in Voyles (1991: 171)). An important characteristic of a merger is generally a long period of confusion, or rather variation, between two sounds (Labov, 1994) and many current variation patterns seem to have a long sociolinguistic history (Milroy, 2004). Such long-term indecisiveness also arose in the BÄREN–BEEREN merger after the OHG period, when the distinction between the vowels gradually declined. This is reflected by the variation in the spelling. From 1350 until 1700, the usage of the grapheme <ä>[1] increased and spread from Upper German across the whole German-speaking area (Moser et al., 1987: 220). This spreading of the spelling <ä> for the BÄREN vowel in itself is, of course, not a sign that the vowel was pronounced as a low vowel in those cases. Rather, it could be the case that the former spelling

<e> indicated a pronunciation with a high vowel ([eː]) and the subsequent change to the grapheme <ä> indicated a *prescriptive* use of [ɛː]. This change in spelling occurred most frequently in the sixteenth century. During the seventeenth century, the opposite tendency set in: the grapheme <ä> was again gradually replaced by <e> (Moser, 1929: 150). This sudden reversal suggests that the pronunciation either went into the direction of [eː] or that it was already pronounced as an [eː] (and possibly did not change under the influence of the grapheme <ä> at all). During the eighteenth century, confusion about the pronunciation was greatest. In an overview of the pronunciation of Standard German in the eighteenth century, Tritschler (1913) reports not only that written <e> was sometimes pronounced as [ɛː], but also that written <ä> was sometimes pronounced as [eː]. In the beginning of the twentieth century, Viëtor (1909) notes the decline of the BÄREN–BEEREN distinction and predicted that a full merger would take place in favour of the BEEREN vowel. In the following section we will see that this prediction was not borne out.

Summarizing, after the OHG distinction between the BÄREN and the BEEREN vowel, an increasing tendency towards a merger set in, which could not be stopped by (prescriptive) spellings in the sixteenth century.

The polycentric character of German

Standard German is spoken in Germany, Austria, and Switzerland. Clear differences, both in pronunciation and lexicon, have been observed between the standard varieties in these three countries, and therefore German is traditionally considered as a polycentric language (Ammon, 1996; Clyne, 1991), or a language with different nationalects. One of the features that is clearly distinct in these nationalects is the pronunciation of the BÄREN vowel. This vowel has been investigated in a number of studies on Standard German in Germany and in Switzerland which reveal much variation: mergers do occur in the northern areas, but distinction is more common in the southern varieties including Switzerland (Hove, 2002; Kleiner & Knöbl, 2011; König, 1989; Sloos, 2013; Spiekermann, 2008; Stearns & Voge, 1979). Stylistic variation also occurs: in higher registers, [ɛː] is more common (Mangold, 1994; Stearns & Voge, 1979). Moreover, extensive variation is observed in the local dialects (Schmidt & Herrgen, 2008, 2011).

As for Austrian Standard German, on the other hand, it is generally hold that the BÄREN and BEEREN vowels are completely merged at the sound level (the orthographical distinction is also maintained in Austria). In an early paper, Abraham (1971: 95) observes:

> "Zur Stützung des postulierten phonemischen Unterschieds zwischen /ä/ und /e/ werden Wortpaare wie *wären/wehren* angeführt; daneben wird sogar langes ä in *Mänade* und *Präsenz* gegenüber kurzem *ä* in *Dämonen* und *Präsent* beobachtet. Dieser Laut is jedenfalls für unsere Umgangssprache (auch sozial gehobener Klassen) phonemisch irrelevant..."
> *In support of the postulated phonemic distinction between /ä/ and /e/, word pairs such as* wären/wehren *are provided, moreover, even a short-long opposition is observed in* 'Mänade' *and* 'Präsenz'. *In any case, this sound is phonemically irrelevant for our variety (viz. Austrian Standard German, author) (also for the socially upper classes) ...*

Also Wiesinger (1996:156) postulates that a closed pronunciation (i.e. [eː]) is common for the written long <ä> in Austrian German. Similarly, the Austrian Pronunciation Database and Austrian Dictionary (Muhr, 2007) provides the transcription [eː] for the BÄREN vowels in Austrian Standard German, whereas it transcribes the vowels as [ɛː] in German Standard German. The latter transcription respects the stylistic difference in pronunciation in German Standard German (the dictionary is based on formal speech style), hence [ɛː] in German Standard German. The fact that the vowel is transcribed as [eː] in Austrian Standard German is consistent with the viewpoint that no stylistic differentiation in Standard Austrian German occurs.

The BÄREN–BEEREN merger in Austrian Standard German occurs across the board – in all speech varieties – such that the BÄREN vowel is considered the same as the BEEREN vowel; therefore, pronunciation studies (like Ehrlich, 2010; Moosmüller, 2007) do not even investigate them separately. Is the distinction made in the dialects? As for the Austrian dialects, the BÄREN vowel sometimes appears to be realized as /aː/ (e.g. Šubrt (2010) on the Vienna dialect, Abraham (1971) on Montafon):

(2)	*Austrian Standard German*	*German Standard German*	*gloss*
	Rad-l	Räd-chen	wheel.DIM
	wa	wär	be.SUBJ

So in the dialects, a phonemic distinction between the BÄREN and BEEREN vowels does occur, which may contribute to the awareness that these vowels are underlyingly distinct. However, the deviant pronunciation as a low vowel must lead to the conclusion that dialect levelling, if it would occur, is highly unlikely to directly affect the pronunciation of the BÄREN–BEEREN merger and reversal in Austrian Standard German, since other realizations are involved.

So for Austrian Standard German, the awareness of a phonemic distinction between the BÄREN and BEEREN vowels may be enhanced by the phonemic distinction in the dialects as well as the graphemic distinction. However, the realization in the dialects does not correspond to that in other varieties of German, so it probably does not form a cue for a correct reversal of the merger. In order to get insight into the true nature of the merger and split of the BÄREN and BEEREN vowels in Austrian Standard German, the following sections present an acoustic analysis of corpus data of spontaneous speech.

Procedure

This section provides background information about the data, and explains the methodology of the acoustic measurements and the statistical procedure that provides insight into the degree of merger of the BÄREN and BEEREN vowel. We will successively discuss the data, the measurement of the vowels in Praat, the normalization procedure, and the statistical procedure to obtain the speaker means in the degree of their merger (Pillai scores).

The data

We investigated the current pronunciation of the BÄREN and BEEREN vowel in colloquial Standard German in Austria. The data for this study are part of the corpus of spoken Standard German, *Deutsch Heute* 'German Today', which has been collected at the *Institut für Deutsche Sprache* in Mannheim (IDS, Project *Variation des gesprochenen Deutsch* 'Variation in spoken German' (Brinckmann, Kleiner, Knöbl, & Berend, 2008). The recordings of the corpus were made between 2006 and 2009. For this study, we investigated all locations in Austria for which older and younger speakers were recorded, namely, six sites (Bludenz, Eisenstad, Leoben, Lienz, Linz, Vienna). Per location, four students at a local secondary school were interviewed, two females and two males, aged between sixteen and nineteen. In addition, one female and one male speaker aged between fifty and sixty were recorded. In total, 33 speakers were analysed. Only biographic interviews were used with spontaneous speech data on fixed topics, such as dialect preferences, occupational background (older speakers), and leisure time (younger speakers). Each interview lasted for 30–45 minutes and was annotated in standard spelling in Praat (Boersma & Weenink, 2010). In sum, the data contained 393 unambiguous cases of the BÄREN vowel, which were analysed for the present study (an average of 11.2 per speaker).[2] Another six BEEREN vowels per speaker were analysed.

Measuring the BÄREN and the BEEREN vowel

In order to be able to compare the pronunciation of the vowels, their pronunciation have to be quantified in a unified way. The vowels [eː] and [ɛː] differ from each other in height, viz. [eː] is higher than [ɛː]. A small difference in frontness also occurs: [eː] is slightly more fronted than [ɛː]. Differences in the high-low dimension are reflected in the first formant (*F*1) of the vowels, whereas differences in the front-back dimension correspond to the value of the second formant (*F*2). This is shown in Figure 1, where the values of *F*1 and *F*2 are provided in Hertz (Hz).

The Praat speech processing software (Boersma & Weenink, 2010) was used to create spectrograms and the steady state of the vowels was manually segmented. The steady state is defined as the period in which *F*1 and *F*2 are stable, i.e. are not in a transition phase with an adjacent sound or, in other words, do not show coarticulation (note that neither the BÄREN vowel nor the BEEREN vowel diphthongizes). Formant tracks were automatically computed by using the Burg LPC algorithm in Praat. The tracks were manually corrected if a visual mismatch between the formant tracks and the formant bands in the spectrogram was observed. Since the vowels that were measured almost always had a clear steady state (i.e. stable *F*1 and *F*2), that is, they were truly monophthongs, it sufficed to measure the temporal midpoint of the vowels. This temporal midpoint and the *F*1 and

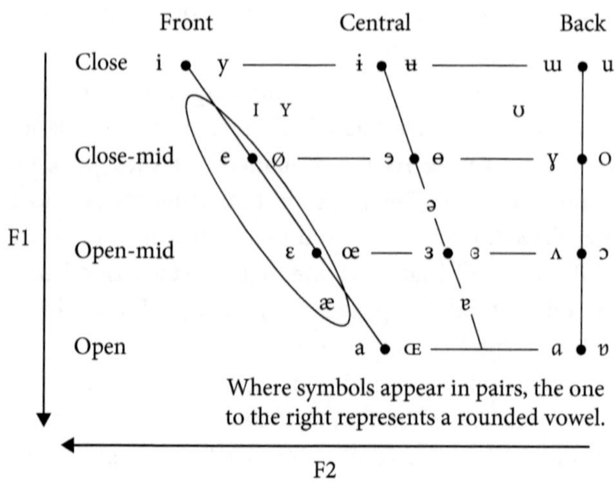

Figure 1. Vowel space diagram. F1 corresponds to the vowel height and F2 corresponds to the frontness of the vowel.

F2 were measured by using a Praat script.[3] To compare the BÄREN vowel with the BEEREN vowel, three prototypical realizations of the BEEREN vowel (i.e. accented vowels in content words that do not undergo raising or lowering due to context) were measured for each speaker. Since German mid front vowels are often lowered before -r (Hall, 1993; König, 1989; Sloos, 2013), three more realizations per speaker of the BEEREN vowel were measured in pre-r context.[4]

Vowel normalization

The vowels in the data show much variation, caused by different factors: physiological differences between the speakers, phonological merger and distinction, and sociolinguistic and dialectal influences. In order to eliminate the physiological differences, but maintain the phonological and sociolinguistic differences, a normalization procedure is common in studies of this type. Here we used the Fabricius and Watt normalization technique, conducted with the package {vowels} in the R statistical analysis environment (Fabricius, Watt, & Johnson, 2009; Thomas & Kendall, 2007; Watt & Fabricius, 2002). On the basis of the maximal vowel space of each speaker, this normalization procedure calculates the individual centre of gravity in the oral cavity and transforms the *F1* and *F2* for each token accordingly. The interested reader is referred to Fabricius et al. (2009) and Watt & Fabricius (2002) for details about this procedure.

Pillai-scores as a degree of merger

Subsequently, to obtain a value for the degree of merger, the data were analysed for their Pillai score, which is a measure for the degree of merger (Hall-Lew, 2010). The Pillai score is the result of a MANOVA test on the difference between the normalized tokens of two vowel types, providing a score for each speaker. In the Pillai score, information about the difference between the two vowels is maintained. The Pillai score can also neutralize for phonological context. Moreover, the Pillai score allows for the use of unbalanced (interview/conversation) data (Hall-Lew, 2010). The higher the Pillai score, the larger the distinction between the two vowels for the speaker. Significant scores ($p \leq 0.05$) were taken as evidence for a distinction. In the computation of the Pillai score, the phonological environment was taken into account (i.e. the sound following the vowels). Thus, the Pillai score is used as an indication for the degree of merger and distinction.

Results

All Pillai scores are contained in the Appendix. Among the 34 speakers, only six made a distinction. Five of them belonged to the younger generation. The only older speaker who made the split was from Bludenz, close to the Swiss border, where the Alemannic dialect is spoken, in which a low BÄREN vowel is common and which sometimes influences the pronunciation in the standard variety (see Sloos, 2013: 109–126). After we obtained the Pillai scores, we used them for cartographical purposes. In order to investigate change in progress, separate analyses were made for older and younger speakers (since we assume that younger speakers are more inclined to use the innovative sounds and older speakers retain the pronunciation to which they are used (e.g. Labov 2001; Milroy & Milroy 1985)).

For each speaker, the Pillai score indicates whether a merger or a distinction was made: the value 1 was assigned if she merged the BÄREN and BEEREN vowel and the value 2 was assigned if she made a distinction between the BÄREN and BEEREN vowel. Subsequently, for each location, these scores were averaged for the older speakers and the younger speakers separately. To visualize the areal distribution of merger and distinction, maps were produced, using the R packages *maps* (Becker & Wilks, 2011b), *mapdata* (Becker & Wilks, 2011a), and *geoR* (Ribeiro Jr & Diggle, 2001). Isoglosses were estimated by the software and indicate the proportion of speakers who merge the vowels vs. speakers who distinguish the vowels on a scale of 1 (only merged, relatively dark) to 2 (only distinction, relatively light).

Figure 2. Neutralization and distinction within the older speakers: dark areas correspond with relatively many speakers who merge the BÄREN and BEEREN vowels and the light areas correspond with relatively many speakers who distinguish in the production of the BÄREN and BEEREN vowels. Further see text.

Figure 3. Neutralization and distinction within the younger speakers: dark areas correspond with relatively many speakers who merge the BÄREN and BEEREN vowels and the light areas correspond with relatively many speakers who distinguish in the production of the BÄREN and BEEREN vowels. Further see text.

Figure 2 shows the results for the older speakers. As expected, the map displays a merger in Austrian Standard German (relatively dark). Figure 3 shows the results for the younger speakers, which displays more of a split in the younger speakers. So the younger speakers make a split more often than the older speakers do, thus it appears that an ongoing split, or reversal of the merger, occurs.

General discussion and conclusions

We investigated the pronunciation of the BÄREN and the BEEREN vowel in Standard German in terms of merger and split. In OHG, these vowels were distinctive, which was followed by a long period of ongoing merger. The results of this paper revealed an ongoing reversal of that merger in Austria. This is remarkable, since it is commonly assumed that no distinction in the pronunciation occurred in Austrian. Although awareness of the phonemic distinction may exist on the basis of a distinction in the dialects and in orthography, this is certainly not enough for a reversal to occur. Which could be the motivation for the merger reversal? Whatever the answer is, it must be unrelated from the distinction in the dialects and orthography, since (1) the distinction in the dialects involves other vowels than the ongoing reversal observed in the standard variety and (2) the short vowels with the same orthographic representations in the homophonous *hält/Held* pair do not undergo the split.

The answer has to be sought in the pluricentric character of German, discussed above. In a pragmatic study on the influence of German Standard German on Austrian Standard German through television broadcasting, Muhr (1995, 2003) argues that Austrians are gradually more and more inclined to orient themselves to the standard variety as it is spoken in Germany. Austrian-German language contact occurs under the influence of tourism, mass media, and economical co-operation, and shows a lexical and grammatical shift in Standard Austrian German towards Standard German as spoken in Germany. I am not aware of pronunciation studies regarding the accommodation of the Austrians towards the standard variety in Germany. But in general, grammatical changes occur relatively late in contact situations, pronunciation being affected earlier. Adaptation of the pronunciation in Austrian Standard German is therefore expected. This idea is supported by the findings of Hove (2002), who demonstrates that younger speakers in Switzerland, under the influence of the media, adopt a pronunciation that is more like German Standard German. Hove (2002) found a more positive attitude toward the variety in Germany among younger Swiss speakers than to their own Standard Swiss German variety, which they tend to regard as inferior. Similarly, I would suppose that the pronunciation in Austrian Standard German among younger speakers is influenced by German Standard German, which they consider to be the prestige variety.

Since, as has been shown in previous studies about the BÄREN vowel (Hove, 2002; Kleiner & Knöbl, 2011; König, 1989; Sloos, 2013; Spiekermann, 2008; Stearns & Voge, 1979), a BÄREN–BEEREN distinction does occur in formal registers in German Standard German and to a lesser extent in the colloquial standard variety, here we may find a motivation for the Austrian speakers to reverse the BÄREN–BEEREN merger. So, since German Standard German functions as the prestige variety, we may expect the Austrian speakers to orient themselves toward that variety in their pronunciation of the BÄREN vowel as well. This motivation in itself, however, does not guarantee the correct reversal of the BÄREN–BEEREN merger in Standard Austrian German. As the previous studies have shown, the pronunciation of the BÄREN vowel, in Germany, is subject to extensive variation. Thus the Austrian speakers get a variable input for the BÄREN vowel: sometimes it is merged with the BEEREN vowel, sometimes it is not. On the basis of this variable input – which hinges on style, lexical frequency, pre-r context, regiolectal variation, and a more general tendency to unmerge (see Sloos, 2013) – it is not easy for the Austrian listener to figure out the correct pronunciation of the BÄREN–BEEREN vowels. Thus, although the pronunciation in German Standard German can function as a motivation for reversal, in order to get the split right, the German Standard variety itself is not a very reliable source.[5]

Summarizing so far, we conclude that younger speakers of Austrian Standard German orient themselves toward the German Standard German variety and we suppose that, under the influence of that prestige variety, they make a distinction between the BÄREN and BEEREN vowels which were previously merged in their native variety (as the older speakers' data showed, recall Figure 2). However, since the BÄREN vowel is variable in German Standard German, it is rather unlikely that Austrian speakers get the split right on the basis of this language contact. The correct distribution of the BÄREN and the BEEREN vowels may be based on the phonemic distinction in the dialects, but note that the dialectal pronunciation differs from that in the standard variety. Phonemic awareness may be strengthened by the distinction maintained in the orthography. This is the only consistent source for the distinction. However, orthography alone cannot be the cause of the reversal either (since no distinction is made between the graphemes <ä> and <e> where they represent the short vowel); therefore, I suppose that the combination of contact with the prestige variety together with orthography are responsible for the BÄREN–BEEREN reversal.

One of the questions posed in the first section addressed the lexical storage of the sounds that are involved in the reversal of a merger. Sound change is not part of the phonological grammar proper (although sound change may eventually lead to grammatical change, which can be modelled in generative grammar). The results can probably best be modelled in Exemplar Theory (ET), which can account for the sound change and also the mental representations of the words (Bybee, 1999; Johnson, 1997). In ET, each instantiation of a word is stored in the mental lexicon as an exemplar. Storage occurs on the basis of similarity, such that more similar exemplars are stored in exemplar categories. Categorization is word-based. Different categories are connected on the basis of analogical relations between words.

In ET, production depends on neural activation, that is, the most highly activated exemplars are selected for pronunciation. In variation, similar exemplars or exemplar categories may compete with each other and the strongest is selected for production. If no decision can be made on the basis of purely linguistic information, other information may be invoked. Hay et al. (2006) suggest that in case of equal competition between different exemplars – but not otherwise – speakers may rely on other cues; for instance, social information. This implies that sociolinguistic information is stored alongside the pronunciation of the word. I would like to suggest that if social cues are lacking, or if social cues also do not lead to a decision, speakers may in addition rely on orthographic information. Consequently, information about spelling must also be stored in exemplars. Orthographical information becomes available as a cue for pronunciation if, and only if, linguistic as well as social information fall short in the selection process. The latter assumption is necessary since orthographical information alone cannot warrant a certain pronunciation: recall that notwithstanding the orthographic difference between <ä> and <e> where it represents a short vowel, no variation occurs; and despite the former (prescriptive) use of the grapheme <ä>, especially in the sixteenth century, the BÄREN–BEEREN merger still proceeded. Orthography therefore only seems to be invoked by more or less conscious intervention. I would therefore suggest that orthography – also because it is learned separately and memorized consciously, unlike auditory information – is stored at another category level, which is, of course, connected to the auditory level. Like the other parts of the lexicon, the categories at the orthographic level must be formed on the basis of words and connected to the auditory level on a word-by-word basis. The viewpoint that there is a direct connection between the auditory and visual representations of words is supported by cross-modal priming studies, which reveal that auditory perception primes visual activation and visual priming leads to auditory activation (Swinney, 1979 and much subsequent work).

The findings in this article are also perfectly in line with recent psycholinguistic results in which an independent effect of orthography cannot be found, but in which spelling seems to have an influence on pronunciation *in combination with other factors*. In a lexical decision task, Cutler, Treiman and van Ooijen (2010) found that reaction times of non-words are longer if they contain sounds that can be spelled in multiple ways. Crucially, the effect only occurs if filler words also contain phonemes that can be spelled in multiple ways, but it disappears if fillers consist of only unambiguous spellings. Also in production experiments, orthographical influence on pronunciation has been reported. Again, if orthography is the only factor that could influence the pronunciation, a null effect is found, but if memorization also plays a role in the task, orthographical influence may occur (Alario, Perre, Castel, & Ziegler, 2007). These results show, similar to the corpus study reported in this paper, that orthographical influence on pronunciation combines with other factors and cannot be the only factor that drives pronunciation into a particular direction. This supports the viewpoint that orthographical information is stored in the lexicon, but in a different way than auditory information, that the visual and auditory representations are connected on a word-by word basis, and that orthographic information is only retrieved if other cues are lacking.

To conclude, this paper showed that a reversal of a merger can occur if there is a sociolinguistic motivation for the reversal and that speakers get the split right if they can rely on a distinction in the orthography. This has some implications for Exemplar Theoretical modelling, but more research on the influence of orthography and sociolinguistic factors on the pronunciation is certainly warranted to optimize the model. Also, the exact pronunciation of the BEEREN and BÄREN vowels in Austrian Standard German among younger speakers is left for further research. An intriguing question that requires more investigation concerns the orientation of the Austrian and Swiss speakers toward the prestige variety in Germany in relation to the pronunciation of the BEEREN and BÄREN vowels. The same orientation works out into different directions. Whereas in Austrian Standard German, the old situation was a merger and a current reversal is observed, Swiss Standard German shows the opposite: a former distinction is currently merged. We will investigate this in the near future.

Acknowledgements

This research was made possible by a DFG grant, project 1624/1 'Frequency Effects in Language'. The corpus material was made available to the author by Stefan Kleiner of the *Institut für deutsche Sprache*, Mannheim, which is gratefully acknowledged. This paper benefitted much from the comments on an earlier version of Jeroen van de Weijer and two anonymous reviewers of *The Mental Lexicon*.

Notes

1. Originally, the grapheme consisted of an <a> with a small <e> on top of it, which later developed into <ä>.

2. In general, vowel length is unambiguous, except in *Städte* 'town.PLUR' and *nächst* 'next'. Therefore the respective lemmas are excluded from analysis.

3. I am grateful to Jos Pacilly (Leiden University) for providing the Praat script to me.

4. Six BEEREN vowels per speaker might seem not enough, compared to the number of BÄREN vowels, but the reader should keep in mind that the BÄREN vowel is subject to extensive variation, which is not the case for the BEEREN vowel.

5. One might wonder whether hypercorrection does occur in the sense that the BEEREN vowel also lowers to [ɛː]. The data do not provide evidence for that.

References

Abraham, W. (1971). Das Vokalsystem der Mundart des Montafons. *Zeitschrift Für Dialektologie Und Linguistik*, 38(1), 95–120.

Alario, F.X., Perre, L., Castel, C., & Ziegler, J.C. (2007). The role of orthography in speech production revisited. *Cognition*, 102(3), 464–475. DOI: 10.1016/j.cognition.2006.02.002

Ammon, U. (1996). On comparing the centers of plurinational languages: The example of German. In M. Hellinger & U. Ammon (Eds.), *Contributions to the sociology of language* (pp. 17–36). Berlin: Walter de Gruyter.

Becker, R. A., & Wilks, A. R. (1993). Maps in S. *AT\&T Bell Laboratories Statistics Research Report*, 93(2).

Becker, R. A., & Wilks, A. R. (1995). Constructing a geographical database. *AT\&T Bell Laboratories Statistics Research Report*, 95(2).

Boersma, P., & Weenink, D. (2010). *Praat: Doing phonetics by computer. [computer program].*

Brinckmann, C., Kleiner, S., Knöbl, R., & Berend, N. (2008). German today: An areally extensive corpus of spoken Standard German. *Proceedings of the Sixth International Conference on Language Resources and Evaluation*, Marrakech, Marocco, 3185–3191.

Bybee, J. L. (1999). Usage-based phonology. *Functionalism and Formalism in Linguistics*, 1, 211–242. DOI: 10.1075/slcs.41.12byb

Clyne, M. (1991). German as a pluricentric language. In M. Clyne (Ed.), *Pluricentral languages. Differing norms in different nations* (pp. 117–148). Berlin: Mouton de Gruyter. DOI: 10.1515/9783110888140

Cutler, A., Treiman, R., & van Ooijen, B. (2010). Strategic deployment of orthographic knowledge in phoneme detection. *Language and Speech*, 53(3), 307–320. DOI: 10.1177/0023830910371445

Ehrlich, K. (2010). Die Aussprache des österreichischen Standarddeutsch: *Umfassende Sprech-und Sprachstandserhebung der österreichischen Orthoepie*. PhD dissertation, Universität Wien.

Fabricius, A., Watt, D., & Johnson, D. E. (2009). A comparison of three speaker-intrinsic vowel formant frequency normalization algorithms for sociophonetics. *Language Variation and Change*, 21, 413–435. DOI: 10.1017/S0954394509990160

Hall, T. A. (1993). The phonology of German /R/. *Phonology*, 10(1), 83–105. DOI: 10.1017/S0952675700001743

Hall-Lew, L. (2010). Improved representation of variance in measures of vowel merger. *Proceedings of Meetings on Acoustics*, Baltimore: Maryland, 127(3), 060002–060012.

Hay, J., Warren, P., & Drager, K. (2006). Factors influencing speech perception in the context of a merger-in-progress. *Journal of Phonetics*, 34(4), 458–484. DOI: 10.1016/j.wocn.2005.10.001

Hove, I. (2002). *Die Aussprache der Standardsprache in der deutschen Schweiz*. Tübingen: Niemeyer. DOI: 10.1515/9783110919936

Johnson, K. (1997). Speech perception without speaker normalization: An exemplar model. In K. Johnson & J. W. Mullennix (Eds.), *Talker variability in speech processing* (pp. 145–165). San Diego: Academic Press.

Kleiner, S., & Knöbl, R. (2011). *Hochdeutsch und Hochdeutsch: Regionale Gebrauchsstandards imgesprochenem Deutsch* (No. Sprachreport 2). Mannheim: Institut für Deutsche Sprache.

König, W. (1989). *Atlas zur Aussprache des Schriftdeutschen in der Bundesrepublik Deutschland*. Ismaening: Max Hueber Verlag.

Labov, W. (1994). *Principles of linguistic change: Internal factors*. Massachusetts and Oxford: Wiley-Blackwell.

Labov, W. (2001). *Principles of linguistic change: Social factors*. Malden and Oxford: Blackwell.

Maguire, W. N. (2008). What is a merger, and can it be reversed? *The origin, status and reversal of the 'NURSE-NORTH Merger' in Tyneside English*. PhD dissertation, Newcastle University.

Mangold, M. (1994). *Duden Aussprachewörterbuch*. Mannheim: Duden Verlag.

Milroy, L. (2004). An essay in historical sociolinguistics?: On Donka Minkova's "Philology, linguistics, and the history of [hw]~[w]. *Studies in the History of the English Language II: Unfolding Conversations*, 2, 47.

Milroy, J., & Milroy, L. (1985). Linguistic change, social network and speaker innovation. *Journal of Linguistics*, 21(2), 339–384. DOI: 10.1017/S0022226700010306

Moosmüller, S. (2007). *Vowels in standard Austrian German*. Unpublished habilitation, University of Vienna.

Muhr, R. (1995). Zur Sprachsituation in Österreich und zum Begriff "Standardsprache" in plurizentrischen Sprachen. Sprache und Identität in Österreich. In R. Muhr, R. Schrodt & P. Wiesinger (Eds.), *Österreichisches Deutsch. Linguistische, sozialpsychologische und sprachpolitische Aspekte einer nationalen Variante des Deutschen* (pp. 75–110). Wien: Verlag Hölder-Pichler-Tempsky.

Muhr, R. (2003). Language change via satellite: The influence of German television broadcasting on Austrian German. *Journal of Historical Pragmatics*, 4(1), 103–127. DOI: 10.1075/jhp.4.1.06muh

Muhr, R. (Ed.). (2007). *Österreichisches Aussprachewörterbuch und Österrreichische Aussprachedatenbank*. Frankfurt/M. / Wien: Peter Lang Verlag.

Ribeiro, P.J. Jr., & Diggle, P.J. (2001). GeoR: A package for geostatistical analysis. *R-NEWS, R-NEWS*, 1(2), 15–18.

Schmidt, J.E., & Herrgen, J. (2008). *Digitaler Wenker-Atlas (DiWA)*. http://www.diwa.info/

Schmidt, J.E., & Herrgen, J. (2011). *Sprachdynamik: Eine Einführung in die moderne Regionalsprachenforschung*. Berlin: Erich Schmidt Verlag.

Sloos, M. (2013). *Frequency and phonological grammar: An integrated approach. Evidence from German, Indonesian, and Japanese*. PhD dissertation, University of Groningen.

Spiekermann, H. (2008). *Sprache in Baden-Württemberg: Merkmale des regionalen Standards*. Tübingen: Max Niemeyer Verlag. DOI: 10.1515/9783484971028

Stearns, M.J., & Voge, W. (1979). The contemporary pronunciation of long <ä> in Modern Standard German: A data-based, computer-assisted analysis. In J. Köster (Ed.), *Hamburger Phonetische Beiträge. Untersuchungen zur Phonetik und Linguistik. Miszellen VI* (pp. 127–181). Hamburg: Helmut Buske Verlag.

Šubrt, P. (2010). *Wiener Dialekt*. Unpublished MA thesis, Masaryk University of Brünn.

Swinney, D.A. (1979). Lexical access during sentence comprehension: (Re) consideration of context effects. *Journal of Verbal Learning and Verbal Behavior*, 18(6), 645–659. DOI: 10.1016/S0022-5371(79)90355-4

Thomas, E.R., & Kendall, T. (2007). *NORM: The vowel normalization and plotting suite*. An online tool for sociophonetic vowel normalization. http://ncslaap.lib.ncsu.edu/tools/norm/.

Tritschler, A. (1913). Aussprache des Neuhochdeutschen im 18. *Jahrhundert. Beiträge zur Geschichte der deutschen Sprache und Literatur (PBB)*, 38, 373–458.

Trudgill, P., & Foxcroft, T. (1978). On the sociolinguistics of vocalic mergers: Transfer and approximation in East Anglia. *Sociolinguistic Patterns in British English*, 69–79.

Viëtor, W. (1909). *Die Aussprache des Schriftdeutschen. Mit dem Wörterverzeichnis der amtlichen "Regels für die deutsche Rechtschreibung in phonetischer Umschrift sowie phonetischen Texten"*. Wien: Edition Praesens.

Voyles, J. (1991). A history of OHG i-umlaut. In K. Grubmüller, M. Reis, & B. Wachinger (Eds.), *Beiträge zur Geschichte der deutschen Sprache und Literatur* (pp. 159–194). Tübingen: Max Niemeyer Verlag.

Watt, D., & Fabricius, A. (2002). Evaluation of a technique for improving the mapping of multiple speakers' vowel spaces in the F1 ~ F2 plane. In D. Nelson (Ed.), *Leeds Working Papers in Linguistics and Phonetics* (pp. 159–173). Leeds: University of Leeds.

Wiesinger, P. (1996). Das österreichische Deutsch als eine Varietät der deutschen Sprache. *Die Unterrichtspraxis/Teaching German*, 29(2), 154–164. DOI: 10.2307/3531825

Appendix

Pillai scores and their significance value for all speakers. Pillai scores with a significance value > 0.05 are treated as a distinction and Pillai scores with a significance value < 0.05 are treated as a neutralization.

Location	Speaker	Age	Merger/Split	Pillai	Significance
Bludenz	1	young	NEUTRALIZATION	0.007	0.979
	2	young	DISTINCTION	0.749	0.004
	3	young	NEUTRALIZATION	0.187	0.661
	4	young	NEUTRALIZATION	0.320	0.260
	5	older	DISTINCTION	0.530	0.011
	6	older	NEUTRALIZATION	0.507	0.020
Eisenstadt	1	young	NEUTRALIZATION	0.110	0.498
	2	young	NEUTRALIZATION	0.047	0.563
	3	young	NEUTRALIZATION	0.039	0.684
	4	young	NEUTRALIZATION	0.157	0.278
	5	older	NEUTRALIZATION	0.396	0.133
	6	older	NEUTRALIZATION	0.199	0.514
Leoben/Liezen	1	young	DISTINCTION	0.340	0.016
	2	young	NEUTRALIZATION	0.073	0.527
	3	young	DISTINCTION	0.354	0.030
	4	older	NEUTRALIZATION	0.121	0.773
	5	older	NEUTRALIZATION	0.082	0.741
Lienz	1	young	DISTINCTION	0.653	0.025
	2	young	DISTINCTION	0.458	0.034
	3	young	NEUTRALIZATION	0.306	0.193
	4	older	NEUTRALIZATION	0.006	0.972
	5	older	NEUTRALIZATION	0.029	0.877
Linz	6	young	NEUTRALIZATION	0.006	0.948
	1	young	NEUTRALIZATION	0.061	0.778
	2	young	NEUTRALIZATION	0.427	0.188
	3	young	NEUTRALIZATION	0.436	0.057
	4	older	NEUTRALIZATION	0.084	0.347
	5	older	NEUTRALIZATION	0.511	0.117
Wien	1	young	NEUTRALIZATION	0.016	0.845
	2	young	NEUTRALIZATION	0.189	0.351
	3	young	NEUTRALIZATION	0.025	0.939
	4	older	NEUTRALIZATION	0.374	0.060
	5	older	NEUTRALIZATION	0.228	0.144
	6	older	NEUTRALIZATION	0.216	0.334

Asymmetric lexical access and fuzzy lexical representations in second language learners

Isabelle Darcy, Danielle Daidone, and Chisato Kojima
Indiana University

For L2 learners, confusable phonemic categories lead to ambiguous lexical representations. Yet, learners can establish separate lexical representations for confusable categories, as shown by asymmetric patterns of lexical access, but the source of this asymmetry is not clear (Cutler, Weber, & Otake, 2006). Two hypotheses compete, situating its source either at the lexical coding level or at the phonetic categorization level. The lexical coding deficiency hypothesis suggests that learners' encoding of an unfamiliar category is not target-like but makes reference to a familiar L1 category (encoded as a poor exemplar of that L1 category). Four experiments examined how learners lexically encode confusable phonemic categories. American English learners of Japanese and of German were tested on phonetic categorization and lexical decision for geminate/singleton contrasts and front/back rounded vowel contrasts. Results showed the same asymmetrical patterns as Cutler et al.'s (2006), indicating that learners encode a lexical *distinction* between difficult categories. Results also clarify that the source of the asymmetry is located at the lexical coding level and does not emerge during input categorization: the distinction is not target-like, and makes reference to L1 categories. We further provide new evidence that asymmetries can be resolved over time: advanced learners are establishing more native-like lexical representations.

Keywords: lexical representations in a second language, Japanese, German, phonetic categorization, lexical encoding

In recent years, there has been a growing interest in understanding the way spoken words are stored and accessed in the mental lexicon of bilingual language users (e.g. Broersma, 2012; Cutler, Weber, & Otake, 2006; Darcy, Dekydtspotter, Sprouse, et al., 2012; Dupoux, Sebastián-Gallés, Navarrete, & Peperkamp, 2008; Ju & Luce, 2004; Marian & Spivey, 2003; Ota, Hartsuiker, & Haywood, 2009;

DOI 10.1075/bct.80.07dar

Pallier, Colomé, & Sebastián-Gallés, 2001; Sebastián-Gallés, Rodríguez-Fornells, de Diego-Balaguer, & Díaz, 2006; Spivey & Marian, 1999; Weber & Cutler, 2004).

When recognizing words spoken in their native language, adult listeners activate multiple word candidates (i.e. *a cohort*) that match at least part of the acoustic input. As the input unfolds, the candidate that offers the best match wins the competition (Marslen-Wilson, 1987) and is selected. This process is usually fast and largely error-free. Under normal circumstances, native listeners' perception of the acoustic input is rather faithful, and activation of candidates is straightforward because lexical representations are accurate. Native listeners are also able to exploit phonetic detail bottom-up during on-line word recognition to reduce the number of activated competitors, and make the competition process more selective (Ju & Luce, 2006; McMurray, Tanenhaus & Aslin, 2002; Sumner & Samuel, 2009). Conversely, ambiguous input will lead to a larger number of activated competitors (e.g. Gaskell & Marslen-Wilson, 2001), and slow down recognition.

Recognizing words in a second language (L2) is a much more complicated affair because lexical items from both languages can enter lexical competition under certain conditions. There is strong evidence that bilinguals experience parallel competition from both their languages even in a monolingual mode, both in the auditory modality (Ju & Luce, 2004; Marian & Spivey, 2003; Spivey & Marian, 1999; Weber & Cutler, 2004) and in the visual modality (Dijkstra & van Heuven, 1998; Jared & Szucs, 2002). For instance, in an eye-tracking paradigm, when instructed to click on the picture of a marker, Russian-English bilinguals often looked briefly at the picture of a stamp as well, because its Russian name 'marka' phonologically overlaps with the English word *marker* (Spivey & Marian, 1999; Marian & Spivey, 2003). This effect indicates that the Russian word was at least temporarily part of the cohort. To complicate matters further, not only is the number of competitors to choose from larger, but L2 listeners' perception of the spoken input is often unreliable (see Strange & Shafer, 2008, and Sebastián-Gallés, 2005, for reviews). If the input is less reliable, it is also less efficient in constraining the number of competitors activated (Broersma, 2012; Broersma & Cutler, 2011; Dupoux et al., 2008; Weber & Cutler, 2004). For example, Broersma and Cutler (2011) found in a cross-modal priming study that Dutch listeners' difficulty with the English /ɛ-æ/ contrast led them to activate real words like *deaf* [dɛf] and *lamp* [læmp] more often than native English listeners upon hearing near-word fragments such as [dæf] and [lɛmp] extracted from the words DAFfodil and eviL EMPire.

A further problem is that non-native listeners cannot always rely on fully accurate lexical representations in the first place. The goal of this study is to evaluate whether the less efficient word recognition often observed in L2 learners is due to inaccurate input perception or to fuzzy lexical representations. We now turn to the previous studies more specifically examining the form of lexical representations as the basis for our study.

Background

One of the potential reasons for L2 learners' less efficient word recognition is that L2 learners do not always encode new, L2-specific contrasts accurately for lexical processing (Darcy et al., 2012; Dupoux et al., 2008; Ota, Hartsuiker, & Haywood, 2009; Pallier, Colomé, & Sebastián-Gallés, 2001; Sebastián-Gallés, Rodríguez-Fornells, de Diego-Balaguer, & Díaz, 2006). One possible explanation for less accurate encoding is that confusable L2 phonemic categories lead to imprecise, or fuzzy, lexical representations, and/or less effective mismatch from competitors during on-line lexical access (Broersma, 2012; Ota et al., 2009). For example, it is not rare for Japanese learners of English to confuse words such as *rock* and *lock*, an observation explained by the difficulty that Japanese native speakers have in distinguishing the two English sounds /l/ vs. /r/. As a result, these two words might be either perceived as one another, or encoded in long-term representations as homophones, or both.

Previous studies have shown that L2 learners exhibit repetition priming for minimal pairs in lexical decision, where no such priming was found for native listeners (Darcy et al., 2012; Pallier et al., 2001). Similarly, L2 learners experienced false-alarm recognition of non-words as words (Broersma & Cutler, 2008; Sebastián-Gallés, Echeverría, & Bosch, 2005). In online tasks, abstract encoding of certain non-native dimensions "can remain unavailable even to advanced learners of a second language" (Dupoux et al., 2008, p. 699). These data (see also Trofimovich & John, 2011) suggest that learners might have conflated, fragmentary and imprecise lexical representations for words of their second language. Taken together, these findings suggest that L2 learners' lexical encoding and/or lexical access does not always make use of the necessary linguistic dimensions, and is therefore less efficient than for native listeners.

For instance, Pallier, Bosch, and Sebastián-Gallés (1997), observing unreliable discrimination of Catalan items containing /ɛ/ from minimally different items containing /e/ in Spanish-dominant early bilinguals, argue that these bilinguals did not generally establish a new category for Catalan /ɛ/, despite exposure from an early age. Pallier et al. (2001) then observed repetition priming for Catalan /e/-/ɛ/ minimal pairs, which they interpreted as evidence that Spanish-dominant bilinguals treated such word pairs as homophones (that is, lexical entries are merged), unlike Catalan native speakers. Even though the lexical homophony interpretation is not the only one possible (the same results could be due to the listeners' inability to auditorily *distinguish* the minimal pairs in the first place), these authors attribute the lack of lexical distinction to the bilinguals not having established a distinct phonological category for the Catalan-specific vowel.

However, other researchers have also found cases where L2 learners seem to have separate lexical entries for minimal pairs despite "inadequacies in phonetic perception" (Cutler, Weber, & Otake, 2006, p. 280; see also Escudero, Hayes-Harb, & Mitterer, 2008; Hayes-Harb & Masuda, 2008; Weber & Cutler, 2004). Weber and Cutler (2004) and Cutler et al. (2006) examined pairs of L2 sounds that are both mapped onto one L1 category (and are therefore confusable). They suggest that perceptual mappings, based on acoustic phonetic similarity between the L2 sounds and the corresponding L1 category, establish the most similar one as the dominant category. In the case of English /ɛ/ and /æ/, both mapping onto Dutch /ɛ/, the dominant category is English /ɛ/ because it exhibits a greater acoustic phonetic similarity to Dutch /ɛ/ than English /æ/. In Weber and Cutler's (2004) eye-tracking study, they asked native English listeners and Dutch-English bilinguals to click on pictures of words that they heard, while their eye movements were recorded (visual world paradigm). For example, participants were instructed to click on the picture of a target word (e.g. *panda*, /pænda/), while a phonetically confusable competitor (e.g. *pencil*, /pɛnsɪl/) was also displayed on the screen. For Dutch listeners, /ɛ/ and /æ/ being confusable categories, the first syllable of the auditory target was ambiguous with the first syllable of the competitor (both perceived as [pɛn…]). For native listeners, looks to the competitor were suppressed very early upon hearing the first vowel as the auditory input unfolded. By contrast, Dutch listeners looked longer at the "pencil" during the first syllable, before selecting "panda" upon hearing the second syllable. This finding indicates that for the Dutch, the initial syllable was ambiguous and not as efficient in constraining lexical activation as it was for the native listeners. However, this ambiguity was not visible in Dutch listeners when the target was "pencil" and the competitor "panda". Hence, fixations for targets containing the dominant (e.g. more similar) L2 category /ɛ/ (/pɛnsɪl/) were more selective (earlier rejection[1] of a competitor syllable with the new L2 category /æ/, [pæn]) than fixations for targets containing the new category (/pænda/, which induced later rejection of a competitor syllable with the dominant category, [pɛn]).

In a study using a task similar to Weber and Cutler's, Cutler et al. (2006) examined the categories /l-r/, which are famously difficult for Japanese-English bilinguals. Participants were instructed auditorily to click on the picture of a target word (e.g. a "rocket"), while a phonetically confusable competitor (e.g. "locker") was also displayed on the screen. Just as in Weber and Cutler's findings, results showed that a target with a new, non-dominant category /r/ ("rocket") induced looks to a picture of a "locker" in the bilingual group, but not in the native listeners.

However, when the target contained the dominant category /l/ ("locker"), it did not induce Japanese-English bilinguals to look at the competitor picture of a "rocket".

This effect parallels the findings for Dutch-English bilinguals (for whom /ɛ/ is dominant). When the target was "panda" (non-dominant category /æ/), they looked at the "pencil", but not vice versa.

So in sum, hearing a non-dominant category produces a less selective lexical activation pattern than hearing a dominant category. This finding is important in showing that the two categories in question are not fully merged in lexical representations, and that the contrast is somehow preserved. If the contrasts had been fully merged in lexical representations of their participants, fixations would have been symmetrically (non)selective.

An additional question arises from these reports that L2 learners maintain a distinction at the lexical level between lexical representations containing difficult contrasts. While having separate lexical entries and demonstrating lexical competence is crucial for learners to avoid confusion of minimally different word pairs such as *rock* and *lock*, this does not automatically imply that the coding of this difference in lexical representations is accurate and target-like. To take an example, Darcy et al. (2012) report that L2 French learners did not show repetition priming for minimal pairs differing in vowels that are difficult to discriminate (/ɔ-œ/). The finding has been interpreted as evidence that L2 French learners have achieved separate lexical representations for words containing these categories. Yet, these findings do not tease apart whether L2 learners have established a target-like phonological encoding in the lexical representation for each, or whether the phonological forms are lexically separated but not (yet) target-like. Repetition priming does not allow us to distinguish between these hypotheses. Findings of asymmetries in lexical processing are very important because they suggest that lexical representations might be separated and yet still not target-like. Such a possibility is explicitly mentioned by Cutler et al. (2006) and Hayes-Harb and Masuda (2008). In fact, native speakers of English, for whom representations are expected to be target-like, did not show the asymmetry observed in the L2 learners in Cutler et al. or in Weber and Cutler (2004).

Cutler et al. leave open the question of how the phonological distinction is coded in the lexical representation. While the dominant category is accurately represented at the lexical level, the representation of the non-dominant category is uncertain and compatible with two possible scenarios.

According to the first, the L2 distinction may be accurately represented lexically, that is, in some distinct form for /l/ and /r/ (perhaps due to explicit instruction), but the phonetic input is always misinterpreted as the dominant category (/l/). That this scenario is possible has been shown many times: L2 learners do not always perceive the input faithfully (Sebastián-Gallés, 2005). In this case, even though learners' lexical representations correctly contain the non-dominant category (e.g. /r/), these would not receive positive activation from that stretch of spoken input because the percept would always be [l] (hence the asymmetry, due to temporary ambiguity of the spoken input). Even though listeners misperceive the input and temporarily activate inappropriate lexical representations, this is usually resolved as soon as more input becomes available (e.g. Frauenfelder, Scholten, & Content, 2001) – it would only be a problem in the case of minimal pairs such as *lock* and *rock*, where both pairs might in fact be simultaneously activated (see Gaskell & Marslen-Wilson, 2001, for supporting evidence that this is the case even in native speakers, in case of acoustic/phonetic ambiguity).

According to the second scenario, phonetic perception of the spoken input is accurate, but it is the coding of the phonological distinction in the lexical representation itself that is not target-like and makes reference to the L1 category (for instance /l/ vs. /poor l/). The asymmetry then could arise from this difference in coding: although dominant and non-dominant categories are encoded separately (hence, lexical separation is achieved), the non-dominant category is perhaps represented as a poor match of the dominant category. Accordingly, hearing the non-dominant category in the input would activate both /l/ and /poor l/, whereas hearing a familiar (dominant) category /l/ would only specifically activate /l/-containing representations. Just as we explained above, hearing a non-dominant category like /poor l/ produces a less selective lexical activation pattern (activating both) than hearing the dominant category.

It thus appears that the distinction between these two possibilities hinges on the level of processing at which L2 learners are able to successfully represent the contrast. We developed the following predictions which form the basis of our approach. If the contrast is discriminated correctly during phonetic processing, the asymmetry would arise from a difficulty that is therefore likely located at the lexical coding level (which we term the *lexical coding deficiency* hypothesis). If however phonetic processing indicates that the input containing both categories is interpreted as the dominant category (which we term the *phonetic coding deficiency* hypothesis), then it is possible that lexical representations are accurate, but the ones containing the non-dominant category do not receive (sufficient) activation from auditory input. We develop more specific predictions in the next sections.

Preliminary experimental considerations

The two hypotheses described above (the *phonetic coding deficiency* vs. the *lexical coding deficiency*) allow mapping out the patterns of lexical decision (see Figures 1a and 1b). The basis for auditory lexical decision is to compare the incoming input (stimulus) to stored phonological representations for words. To take a concrete example from German, the only way to correctly reject a non-word which is a potential word (*König* [kønıç] 'king' is a word, whereas **Hönig* [hønıç] is not; it is derived from *Honig* [honıç] 'honey') is to have an accurate phonological representation of existing words at the lexical level. Therefore, lexical decision patterns will reveal the accuracy of lexical representations. We use the example of two German words *Honig* /honıç/ 'honey' and *König* /kønıç/ 'king', and only consider the case where a lexical contrast is present,[2] through explicit instruction or other ways. This is likely to be the case for our learners, who all have been exposed to classroom instruction and orthographic forms (see Escudero et al., 2008).

In parallel to the reaction time advantage for words over non-words commonly observed in native language lexical decision performance (e.g. Forster & Chambers, 1973), it is expected that accuracy will generally be higher for words than for non-words, given that it is easier to accept a form as a word than to reject it as a non-word (all non-words used in this study are well-formed and possible words). Participants will tend to respond "yes" more easily than to respond "no".

According to the phonetic coding deficiency hypothesis (see Figure 1a), we assume that listeners have difficulty correctly perceiving the input. Therefore, in the case of German /o/ and /ø/ or /u/ and /y/, both back and front rounded vowels are perceived as back vowels (/o/, /u/). The lexical representations, by contrast, accurately encode the distinction, even though it is not necessarily the case that the phonological form is target-like. It can simply be different from the dominant category (e.g. "not /o/"), without making reference to it. We represent this in Figure 1a as /X/.

Lexical representation	**/honıç/**		**/kXnıç/**	
	match	match	mismatch ✗	✗ mismatch
Percept	**[honıç]**	***[honıç]**	**[konıç]**	***[konıç]**
Input	**[honıç]**	***[hønıç]**	**[kønıç]**	***[konıç]**
Expected response	yes	no	yes	no
Prediction	easy to accept	difficult to reject	difficult to accept	easy to reject
Ordinal accuracy	1	4	3	2

Note: * indicates a non-word.

Figure 1a. Predictions for lexical decision behavior according to the phonetic coding deficiency hypothesis.

In the case shown in Figure 1a, the word/non-word pairs present in the input will not be perceived as different: both inputs [honıç] and *[hønıç] are perceived as [honıç] (as shown in Figure 1a where the percept sometimes differs from the input). Both members of a pair will thus be compared to existent lexical representations in the same way. Lexical representations containing the dominant ("old") category will be contacted by both words and non-words equally because the percept matches the lexical representation. In the case of lexical representations containing the non-dominant ("new") category (e.g. /kXnıç/), the percepts will in each case be a mismatch, and will not contact the lexical representation that contains the non-dominant category, as suggested by Cutler et al. (2006).

In the context of a lexical decision task, this scenario makes the following predictions. Words containing the old category such as [honıç] in the input will be easy to accept (ordinal accuracy 1), and non-words containing the old category (*[konıç], ordinal accuracy 2) will also be easy to reject, because they mismatch the lexical representation and therefore do not contact it. Conversely, the words containing the new category in the input but perceived as containing the old category ([konıç]) will also mismatch the lexical representation and be difficult to accept (ordinal accuracy 3). Similarly, non-words containing the new category, but perceived as containing the old category (*[honıç]), will be very difficult to reject (ordinal accuracy 4), because the percept matches the lexical representation.

This pattern of decisions would result in higher accuracy for both words and non-words containing old categories ([honıç] and *[konıç]) than for words and non-words containing new categories (*[hønıç] and [kønıç]). This pattern is not

Lexical representation	/honıç/		/ko?nıç/	
	match	mismatch	no mismatch	no mismatch
Percept	[honıç]	*[hønıç]	[kønıç]	*[konıç]
Input	[honıç]	*[hønıç]	[kønıç]	*[konıç]
Expected response	yes	yes	yes	no
Prediction	easy to accept	easy to reject	less easy to accept	difficult to reject
Ordinal accuracy	1	3	2	4

Note: * indicates a non-word.

Figure 1b. Predictions for lexical decision behavior according to the lexical coding deficiency hypothesis.

expected to yield an interaction between lexical status (word vs. non-word) and category type (old vs. new).

According to the lexical coding deficiency hypothesis, shown in Figure 1b, we assume that listeners can correctly perceive the input (so percept and input are the same), and the difficulty is located at the lexical coding level, where lexical representations encode the contrast separately but in a fuzzy way (e.g. /o/ vs. /o?/).

As discussed above, if the L1 does not make use of a certain phonetic category (or acoustic dimension) such as "front rounded vowels" or "long consonants", L2 lexical encoding of this category might be inaccurate or fragmentary compared to native speakers (at first). We therefore predict in this case that lexical representation containing the new (non-dominant) category might be inaccurate. However, this does not necessarily mean that the dominant category is used *in place of* the new category. As suggested by Cutler et al. (2006) and Hayes-Harb and Masuda (2008), it is possible that the new category is encoded as a poor match to the dominant L1 category. What is important for this hypothesis is that the new category makes reference to the dominant L1 category. For the L2 front-rounded /ø/ category for instance, this might be represented as a /poor o/, or /o?/ (henceforth we use /?/ to indicate that a category is represented imprecisely in lexical representations), whereas L2 /o/ itself will be represented clearly as the dominant, similar /o/ category in L1.

This scenario makes the following predictions. First, real words containing the old category will likely be most easily recognized as words (ordinal accuracy 1) since the input exactly matches the lexical representation, e.g. [honıç] matches /honıç/ 'honey'. Second, real words containing the new category (e.g. [kønıç] 'king') might be recognized slightly less accurately if they are encoded as a poor match, perhaps as /ko?nıç/. The input [kønıç] does not exactly match the representation /ko?nıç/, but does not clearly mismatch it either. Rejection patterns for non-words will also be asymmetrical: non-words containing the new category (e.g. *[hønıç]) have to be compared to their real-word counterparts containing the old category (/honıç/) in order to be recognized as fake and rejected. It is easy to reject the non-word with the new category (ordinal accuracy 3) since the lexical representation with the old category is clear. The percept *[hønıç] is clearly a mismatch to /honıç/. Conversely, non-words with an old category (e.g. *[konıç]) have to be compared to fuzzy lexical representations that contain the new category (e.g. /ko?nıç/) before they can be rejected as fake. It becomes clear that in this latter case, the rejection will be more difficult if the real word lexical representation is fuzzy (ordinal accuracy 4). Such an asymmetry in accuracy would indicate that there is lexical separation between the old and the new category, but that this separation is not yet target-like (e.g. /o/ vs. /o?/ instead of /o/ vs. /ø/) and still makes reference to the L1 or dominant category.

This pattern of results would mirror the asymmetry obtained with eye-tracking reported by Cutler et al. (2006) and Weber and Cutler (2004), and should produce an interaction between lexical status (word vs. non-word) and category type (old vs. new). If old and new categories are encoded equally well, no interaction is expected, as in the case of native speakers. Such findings combined with very good categorization at the phonetic level would offer support for the lexical coding deficiency hypothesis according to which learners' encoding of phonological contrasts in lexical representations is not target-like and makes reference to the dominant category.

We turn now to the description of our study, designed to examine both hypotheses.

The current study

The goal of this study is to expand on these early findings of asymmetries in lexical access and to explicitly investigate whether lexical representations are target-like or not, even if they are separate. We examine the degree to which a novel contrast is target-like in learners' lexical representations by looking at asymmetries in lexical decision patterns, combined with phonetic categorization tasks. By establishing categorization performance in the same participants, we will be able to tease apart whether the contrast is misperceived during input categorization or whether the difficulty is located at the lexical coding level.

We also add to the current understanding of L2 lexical encoding by examining developmental patterns in groups of L2 learners who differ in L2 proficiency and experience, in order to see if lexical processing difficulties can be resolved over time.

Two sets of phonemic contrasts, a consonantal and a vocalic contrast in two languages, were used for this study. American English learners of L2 Japanese have difficulties acquiring the durational contrast between long and short consonants (i.e. geminates: *katta* 'bought' vs. singletons: *kata* 'shoulder'). Both are initially mapped onto L1 categories, which in English have only one default duration equivalent to a singleton (Han, 1992; Tajima, Kato, Rothwell, Akahane-Yamada, & Munhall, 2008). Similarly, the German front rounded vowels /y, ø/ (written as <ü, ö>) are confusable with, and thus assimilated to, back rounded vowels /u, o/ for American English listeners (Strange, Weber, Levy, Shafiro, Hisagi et al., 2007). For each language, two experiments were conducted. We tested learners of German and learners of Japanese, and investigated (i) learners' phonetic categorization accuracy by examining their response patterns in an ABX task, and (ii) the degree to which a novel contrast was target-like in learners' lexical representations by observing any potential asymmetries in their lexical decision patterns.

The vowel and consonant categories used for the experiments reported here are divided in two types: "old" (that is, the dominant category according to Cutler et al., 2006) vs. "new" (the non-dominant category). For the German stimuli, the front-rounded vowels (/y/, /ʏ/, /ø/, /œ/) are "new". For the Japanese stimuli, the geminate phonemes (/pː/, /tː/, /kː/) are "new".

Experiments 1 and 2: Japanese

In this section, we report the results of two experiments designed to test participants' ability to categorically discriminate between the Japanese long and short phonemes, and to lexically encode this phonemic difference in their lexical representations for Japanese words.

Experiment 1: Categorical discrimination with ABX

Methods and procedure

Stimuli were pairs of disyllabic non-words in Japanese and English. Test item pairs had the structure CVQV or CVCV, where Q represents a geminate consonant, and C a singleton consonant. An example test pair is [mette] – [mete], where the letter doublet represents a geminate [tː]. Types of consonants used were bilabial, coronal, or velar obstruents, as well as the coronal fricative [s]. Control items only contained singleton consonants (CVCV), and differed in the quality of the last V. An example pair is [moke] – [moki]. There were 12 pairs of test items and 4 pairs of control items. Each pair was then arranged into a triplet (A – B – X) where X is either similar to A or to B. (e.g. A-[mette] B-[mete] X-[mete] (X = B); A-[moke] B-[moki] X-[moke] (X = A)). Four counterbalanced orderings for the triplets were used (ABA, ABB, BAA, BAB), which resulted in a total of 64 test triplets.

These 64 trials were presented in four randomized blocks separated by short breaks through the experimental software DMDX (Forster & Forster, 2003). Participants were instructed to decide whether the third non-word (X) matched the first (A) or the second (B) non-word, and indicate their response as fast as possible. Inter-stimulus interval was set to 500 ms. Participants had 2000 ms to make their response, before the next trial was initiated. Reaction time (RT) was measured from the onset of the third (X) item.

Stimuli were recorded several times by one female Japanese native speaker of the Tokyo dialect. Two renditions were obtained for each non-word, so that the audio stimulus for A, for example in a triplet ABA, would actually be instantiated by two acoustically different tokens. The speaker in this experiment also recorded the lexical decision items (see Experiment 2). The same speaker was used because we were interested in ascertaining that learners were able to perceptually discriminate short from long consonants in the speaker who also produced the lexical decision tokens.

Both experiments were conducted in one single testing session. A demographic and language background questionnaire was given at the beginning of the testing session. Participants were first tested on the discrimination task and then on the lexical decision task.

Participants

Three groups of participants were tested: two groups of English learners of Japanese (advanced learners: n = 14, 7 males and 7 females, mean age = 21; intermediate learners: n = 9, 3 males and 6 females, mean age = 21), and one native speaker group (n = 11, 4 males and 7 females, mean age = 31).

Advanced learners were native speakers of American English, and enrolled either in the second semester of a third-year or fourth-year Japanese class at a large university in the United States, or were teaching Japanese as associate instructors at the same university at the time of recruitment. Average length of time spent living in Japan was 17.8 months. Beginning-Intermediate (henceforth only "intermediate") learners were native speakers of American English and enrolled in the second semester of a first-year Japanese class. None of them had lived in Japan. Native speakers were all enrolled students at the same university in the United States at the time of testing. They all spoke English as a second language with high proficiency, and most of them were also instructors of Japanese at that university. No participant reported any hearing or speech impairment. Participants received a small payment for their participation in the study.

Results

One native speaker (NS) participant and one advanced learner were considered outliers given low accuracy on the control condition (below 2 *SD* from the group mean), and their data excluded from analysis. For each subject, the proportion of accurate answers (%) and mean RT were computed across the four trials for each item, and each condition (test vs. control), resulting in 16 aggregate measures per subject (for 12 test items and four control items). Table 1 presents the mean accuracy and RT in each condition for each group.

Preliminary analysis indicated that the accuracy proportions were not normally distributed, and there was compression towards the upper accuracy range, unsurprisingly given the high and similar scores of all groups. We therefore used

Table 1. Mean accuracy (%), mean RT (ms) and standard error (SE) for each group and each condition.

Condition	Test				Control			
Group	Accuracy	SE	RT	SE	Accuracy	SE	RT	SE
Intermediate	93	1.3	1013	36.9	94	1.7	970	38.5
Advanced	94	1.1	951	29.6	98	1.4	925	30.9
NS	96	1.3	958	35.0	99	1.6	970	36.5

Note: mean RT is computed over correct responses only, NS = native speakers.

an arcsine transform to expand the top of the scale and increase differences in high accuracy ranges.

A linear mixed effects model was conducted in SPSS 20 on the arcsine-transformed accuracy means. It declared the factors *condition* (test, control) and *group* (intermediate, advanced, NS) as fixed effects, and the factors *condition* and *item* as repeated effects within subjects.[3] The significance threshold was set at $p = 0.05$ for this and all following analyses. The visual analysis of residuals confirmed that the model was a satisfactory fit for the data structure. The parameter estimates are presented in Table 2.

When looking at the type III tests of fixed effects, the F-tests showed a main effect of condition ($F(1, 477) = 4.74$, $p < 0.05$), a marginal effect of group ($F(2, 40.9) = 2.73$, $p = 0.08$), and no significant interaction between the two factors ($F < 1$). The control condition yielded more accurate performance than the test condition, and the NS group showed the highest accuracy followed by the advanced learners.

Analysis of RTs was performed similarly; the data were normally distributed. Mean RTs were computed over correct responses and entered into a linear mixed effects model declaring the factors *condition* (test, control) and *group* (intermediate, advanced, NS) as fixed effects, and the factors *condition* and *item* as repeated effects within subjects. The parameter estimates are presented in Table 3.

When looking at the type III tests of fixed effects, the F-tests showed that there was a marginal effect of condition ($F(1, 477) = 3.08$, $p = 0.08$), no effect of group ($F < 1$), and no significant interaction between the two factors ($F(2, 477) = 1.75$, $p > 0.1$). RTs in the control condition were slightly faster overall than in the test condition (955 ms vs. 974 ms).

These data suggest that discrimination of the contrasts between geminate and singleton consonants does not appear to be problematic even in early stages of acquisition. We now turn to Experiment 2, where we examine lexical encoding of this contrast among the same participants, with stimuli produced by the same speaker.

Table 2. Parameter estimate, standard error, t-value, p-value, and 95% confidence interval of the predictors for the ABX accuracy (arcsine transformed).

Fixed effects	Estimate	Std. error	df	t	Sig.	95% Confidence Interval	
						lower	upper
Intercept	1.557706	.035689	180.512	43.647	.000	1.487285	1.628128
[Condition = test]	–.067632	.037787	477.000	–1.790	.074	–.141880	.006617
[Group = Advanced]	–.027187	.047471	180.512	–.573	.568	–.120856	.066482
[Group = Interm.]	–.110538	.051855	180.512	–2.132	.034	–.212857	–.008218
[Condition = test] * [Group = Advanced]	.000503	.050261	477.000	.010	.992	–.098257	.099264
[Condition = test] * [Group = Interm.]	.062783	.054903	477.000	1.144	.253	–.045098	.170665
Covariance parameters	**Estimate**	**Std. error**					
CS diagonal offset (Residual)	.042835	.002774					
CS covariance (Subject)	.002028	.001248					

Note: Interm. = Intermediate.

Table 3. Parameter estimate, standard error, t-value, p-value, and 95% confidence interval of the predictors for the ABX reaction times.

Fixed effects	Estimate	Std. error	df	t	Sig.	95% Confidence Interval	
						lower	upper
Intercept	968.046604	38.168844	39.255	25.362	.000	890.858875	1045.234333
[Condition = test]	−9.584806	19.123175	477.000	−.501	.616	−47.160882	27.991271
[Group = Advanced]	−44.169601	50.769309	39.255	−.870	.390	−146.838878	58.499676
[Group = Interm.]	6.238002	55.458045	39.255	.112	.911	−105.913167	118.389172
[Condition = test] * [Group = Advanced]	36.599469	25.436200	477.000	1.439	.151	−13.381385	86.580323
[Condition = test] * [Group = Interm.]	49.160569	27.785328	477.000	1.769	.077	−5.436204	103.757343
Covariance parameters	**Estimate**	**Std. error**					
CS diagonal offset (Residual)	10970.87	710.39					
CS covariance (Subject)	11825.89	3286.00					

Note: Interm. = Intermediate.

Experiment 2: Lexical decision

Method and procedure

Forty-two common Japanese words were selected from the textbook used by the first-year and second-year students called *Genki* I and II (Banno et al., 1999), to increase familiarity for all learners. More singleton words were available than geminate words (26 vs. 16). Furthermore, 84 additional words were selected as fillers. Forty-two corresponding test non-words were created from the test words by exchanging a singleton consonant for its geminate counterpart (*akeru* 'to open' vs. **akkeru*) or vice-versa (*kippu* 'ticket' vs. **kipu*). Filler non-words were created by exchanging a feature other than length or by changing or inserting a segment (*tenki* 'weather' vs. **tengi*). There were 84 test items (42 singleton and 42 geminate), and 168 fillers, resulting in a total of 252 items, which were randomized.

Stimuli were divided into two blocks, so that participants heard both the word and the non-word of a word/non-word pair, but never in the same block. After a short practice, participants were instructed to decide whether each token they heard was a real word or a fake word of Japanese by pressing buttons labeled "yes" or "no" as fast as possible. Participants had 2200 ms to make their response, before the next trial was initiated. RTs were measured from the onset of the word presentation.

Participants

Three groups participated in this experiment: Japanese native speakers, advanced learners, and intermediate learners of Japanese. Participants in each of these groups were the same as in Experiment 1.

Results

Accuracy on all items was screened to determine if some non-words were accepted as words by a majority of native speakers or vice-versa. Those items for which accuracy was below 2 *SD* of the mean for the native speaker group were excluded, separately for words and non-words. Six words and four non-words were excluded. The resulting mean accuracy of native speakers in this task was 91% (*SD* = 7.7). Two participants (1 native speaker and 1 intermediate) were excluded because their accuracy on the control condition was below 2 *SD* from their group mean. The total number of participants analyzed was 10 native speakers, 14 advanced, and 8 intermediate learners.

The proportion of accurate answers (%) and mean RT for each subject were computed across items for each condition (test vs. control), within the combination of lexical status (word vs. non-word), and consonant (old vs. new). Mean accuracy and RT in each condition for each group are displayed in Table 4.

Table 4. Mean accuracy (%), mean RT (ms) and standard error (SE) in the control vs. test conditions in lexical decision for Japanese words and non-words, for each group.

	Lexical status	Condition	NS		Advanced		Interm.	
			mean	SE	mean	SE	mean	SE
Accuracy	word	control	98	4.4	95	3.7	79	4.9
	non-word	control	91	4.4	81	3.7	72	4.9
	word	test	98	3.5	91	3.0	71	3.9
	non-word	test	93	3.5	53	3.0	51	3.9
RT	word	control	1101	47.3	1214	40.0	1340	52.9
	non-word	control	1232	47.3	1345	40.0	1415	52.9
	word	test	1177	42.5	1301	35.9	1408	47.5
	non-word	test	1288	42.5	1513	35.9	1523	47.5

Note: mean RT is computed over correct responses only, NS = native speakers.

A linear mixed effects model was run in SPSS 20 on the accuracy scores. The factors *group* (native speakers, advanced, intermediates), *lexical status* (word vs. non-word), and *condition* (control vs. test) were declared as fixed effects. The factors *condition, lexical status,* as well as *consonant* (old vs. new) were also entered as repeated effects within subjects. Tables 5 and 6 display the parameter estimates for each model (accuracy and RT).

When looking at the type III tests of fixed effects, the F-tests revealed that there was a main effect of group on accuracy (native speakers, 95%, advanced, 80%, intermediates, 68%, $F(2, 31.2) = 20.4$, $p < 0.01$). Performance for words was more accurate than for non-words (lexical status: $F(1, 157) = 60.8$, $p < 0.01$). Accuracy was also higher in the control condition compared to the test condition (condition: $F(1, 157) = 24.1$, $p < 0.01$). All interactions were significant (all $p < .01$), including the triple interaction between group, lexical status, and condition ($F(2, 151) = 4.4$, $p = 0.013$). Condition had no effect on the native speaker performance only ($p > 0.1$), whereas both learner groups were significantly more accurate in the control over the test condition (both $p < 0.001$). Similarly, lexical status only marginally influenced native speakers' performance ($p = 0.07$), but learners were significantly more accurate for words than non-words (both $p < 0.001$).

Of particular interest is the interaction between lexical status and condition ($F(1, 157) = 9.8$, $p < 0.01$), for which pairwise comparisons indicated that accuracy for words was similar in the test (88%) and the control (92%) condition ($p > 0.1$), but for non-words, accuracy was much higher in the control condition (82%) compared to the test (65%) condition ($p < 0.001$), suggesting that the

Table 5. Parameter estimate, standard error, t-value, p-value, and 95% confidence interval of the predictors for the lexical decision accuracy.

Fixed effects	Estimate	Std. error	df	t	Sig.	95% Confidence Interval	
						lower	upper
Intercept	.977564	.034970	70.253	27.954	.000	.907823	1.047305
[Condition = control]	.002683	.045693	151.000	.059	.953	−.087597	.092963
[Group = Advanced]	−.068681	.045786	70.253	−1.500	.138	−.159993	.022631
[Group = Interm.]	−.267949	.052455	70.253	−5.108	.000	−.372560	−.163338
[Lexical Status = non-word]	−.051522	.037308	151.000	−1.381	.169	−.125236	.022191
[Condition = control] * [Group = Advanced]	.035447	.059826	151.000	.593	.554	−.082757	.153651
[Condition = control] * [Group = Interm.]	.077536	.068539	151.000	1.131	.260	−.057884	.212956
[Lexical Status = non-word] * [Group = Advanced]	−.325366	.048848	151.000	−6.661	.000	−.421880	−.228853
[Lexical Status = non-word] * [Group = Interm.]	−.146374	.055962	151.000	−2.616	.010	−.256944	−.035804
[Condition = control] * [Lexical Status = non-word]	−.015038	.064619	151.000	−.233	.816	−.142713	.112637
[Condition = control] * [Lexical Status = non-word] * [Group = Advanced]	.252057	.084607	151.000	2.979	.003	.084891	.419222
[Condition = control] * [Lexical Status = non-word] * [Group = Interm.]	.146538	.096929	151.000	1.512	.133	−.044975	.338050
Covariance parameters	**Estimate**	**Std. error**					
CS diagonal offset (Residual)	.013919	.001602					
CS covariance (Subject)	.005269	.002011					

Note: Interm. = Intermediate.

Table 6. Parameter estimate, standard error, t-value, p-value, and 95% confidence interval of the predictors for the lexical decision RT.

Fixed effects	Estimate	Std. error	df	t	Sig.	95% Confidence Interval	
						lower	upper
Intercept	1176.561638	42.523051	40.693	27.669	.000	1090.664940	1262.458336
[Condition = control]	−75.246761	35.933487	151.000	−2.094	.038	−146.244105	−4.249417
[Group = Advanced]	124.349338	55.675743	40.693	2.233	.031	11.884161	236.814515
[Group = Interm.]	231.458838	63.784577	40.693	3.629	.001	102.613791	360.303885
[Lexical Status = non-word]	111.704457	29.339569	151.000	3.807	.000	53.735368	169.673546
[Condition = control] * [Group = Advanced]	−11.627803	47.047978	151.000	−.247	.805	−104.585146	81.329541
[Condition = control] * [Group = Interm.]	7.411275	53.900230	151.000	.137	.891	−99.084741	113.907291
[Lexical Status = non-word] * [Group = Advanced]	100.348312	38.414513	151.000	2.612	.010	24.448958	176.247665
[Lexical Status = non-word] * [Group = Interm.]	3.078778	44.009353	151.000	.070	.944	−83.874855	90.032411
[Condition = control] * [Lexical Status = non-word]	19.272912	50.817624	151.000	.379	.705	−81.132495	119.678319
[Condition = control] * [Lexical Status = non-word] * [Group = Advanced]	−100.183328	66.535888	151.000	−1.506	.134	−231.644864	31.278208
[Condition = control] * [Lexical Status = non-word] * [Group = Interm.]	−59.070236	76.226436	151.000	−.775	.440	−209.678346	91.537874
Covariance parameters	**Estimate**	**Std. error**					
CS diagonal offset (Residual)	8608.103	990.681					
CS covariance (Subject)	13778.047	3998.469					

Note: Interm. = Intermediate.

difficulty in rejecting non-words was not generalized to all non-words in the experiment. That this effect is mostly due to the learners is confirmed in the triple interaction: for both learner groups, accuracy for non-words was much higher on the control than on the test condition ($p < 0.001$ for both groups). For words, accuracy was similar in the two conditions ($p > 0.1$ for both groups). For native speakers, neither condition nor lexical status influenced their performance (all $p > 0.1$). The analysis of RTs was conducted similarly.

When looking at the type III tests of fixed effects, the F-tests showed that there was a main effect of group (mean RT, native speakers = 1199 ms; advanced = 1343 ms; intermediate = 1421 ms, $F(2, 29.7) = 7.6$, $p < 0.01$), lexical status (mean RT, words = 1256 ms; non-words = 1386 ms, $F(1, 151) = 78.6$, $p < 0.01$), and of condition (mean RT, control = 1274 ms; test = 1368 ms, $F(1, 151) = 41.2$, $p < 0.01$).

There was a marginal interaction between group and lexical status ($F(2, 151) = 2.6$, $p = 0.08$): For non-words, native speakers were significantly faster than both other groups (both $p < 0.01$), whereas for words, native speakers significantly outperformed only the intermediates ($p < 0.01$), not the advanced ($p > 0.1$). No other interaction reached significance. Globally, participants responded to words faster than to non-words, and this difference was visible across both test and control conditions in all three groups.

We now examine whether asymmetrical patterns are visible in the accuracy rates of each group separately. For the test condition only, the mean accuracy for words vs. non-words for each consonant type (new vs. old) is displayed in Figure 2. Average accuracy was low for both learner groups, a finding that contrasts with their performance in the ABX task.

For each group in turn, a linear mixed effects model declared the mean accuracy as the dependent variable. Fixed factors were *consonant* (old vs. new) and *lexical status* (word vs. non-word). The factors *consonant* and *lexical status* were also entered as repeated effects within subjects. Tables 7, 8, and 9 display the parameter estimates for each group.

For intermediate learners, accuracy was higher for words than for non-words (71% vs. 51%, lexical status: $F(1, 21) = 21.6$, $p < 0.01$), but there was no effect of consonant ($F(1, 21) = 0.3$, $p > 0.1$). The interaction was significant ($F(1, 21) = 4.9$, $p < 0.05$): Intermediate learners were marginally more accurate for words containing the old category (77%) than the new (65%) category ($p = 0.06$). Conversely, there was a (non-significant) trend for non-words containing a new category to be more accurately rejected (55%) than those with an old (48%) category ($p = 0.2$). This pattern conforms to the predicted ordinal accuracy and suggests

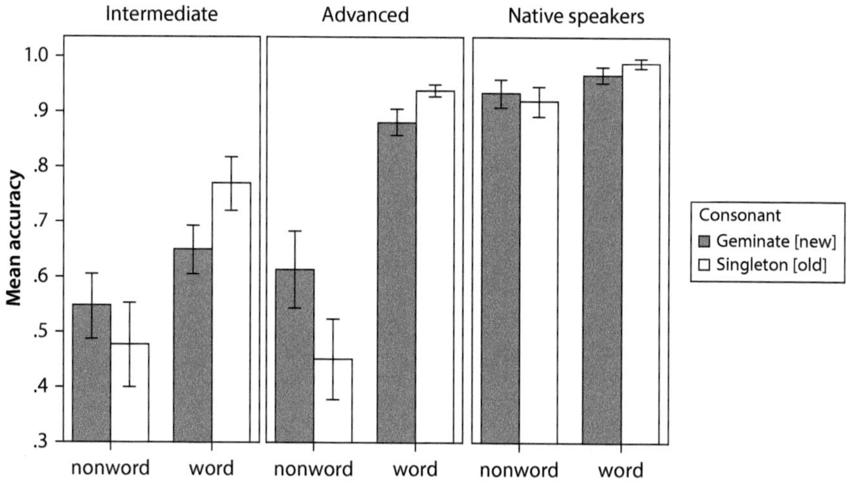

Figure 2. Mean accuracy in lexical decision as a function of consonant type and lexical status for each group. Error bars represent +/− 1 SE.

that there is an asymmetrical pattern in intermediate learners' lexical representations for these old vs. new consonants.

Advanced learners also show a similar pattern of accuracy even though overall accuracy is higher. Type III tests of fixed effects revealed that there was a main effect of lexical status ($F(1, 39) = 75.9$, $p < 0.01$): accuracy was much higher for words (91%) over non-words (53%). Again, the factor consonant had no effect ($F(1, 39) = 1.5$, $p > 0.1$). The interaction was significant ($F(1, 39) = 6.3$, $p < 0.05$). Words containing the old category (94%) were more accurately recognized than those with a new (88%) category, a non-significant trend ($p = 0.3$). Conversely, non-words containing a new category were more accurately rejected (61%) than those with an old (45%) category ($p < 0.01$). This suggests that the advanced learners of Japanese resemble the intermediate learners with respect to non target-like lexical representations.

Native speakers show a clearly different pattern. Type III tests of fixed effects revealed that there was a main effect of lexical status (mean accuracy, words = 98%, non-words = 93%, $F(1, 27) = 7.5$, $p < 0.05$), no effect of consonant ($F < 1$) and importantly, there was no interaction ($F < 1$). This pattern suggests that there is no asymmetry in native speakers' lexical representations for each type of consonants, an expected effect.

Table 7. Parameter estimate, standard error, t-value, p-value, and 95% confidence interval of the predictors for the intermediate group.

Fixed effects	Estimate	Std. error	df	t	Sig.	95% Confidence Interval	
						lower	upper
Intercept	.769231	.058293	16.952	13.196	.000	.646216	.892246
[Lexical Status = non-word]	–.292668	.060237	21	–4.859	.000	–.417938	–.167399
[Consonant = geminate]	–.119231	.060237	21	–1.979	.061	–.244500	.006039
[Lexical Status = non-word] * [Consonant = geminate]	.189543	.085188	21	2.225	.037	.012386	.366701
Covariance parameters	**Estimate**	**Std. error**					
CS diagonal offset (Residual)	.014514	.004479					
CS covariance (Subject)	.012671	.008784					

Table 8. Parameter estimate, standard error, t-value, p-value, and 95% confidence interval of the predictors for the advanced group.

Fixed effects	Estimate	Std. error	df	t	Sig.	95% Confidence Interval	
						lower	upper
Intercept	.936813	.051407	41.373	18.223	.000	.833023	1.040604
[Lexical Status = non-word]	–.485920	.061146	39	–7.947	.000	–.609600	–.362240
[Consonant = geminate]	–.055861	.061146	39	–.914	.367	–.179541	.067819
[Lexical Status = non-word] * [Consonant = geminate]	.218063	.086474	39	2.522	.016	.043153	.392973
Covariance parameters	**Estimate**	**Std. error**					
CS diagonal offset (Residual)	.026172	.005927					
CS covariance (Subject)	.010826	.006972					

Table 9. Parameter estimate, standard error, t-value, p-value, and 95% confidence interval of the predictors for the native speaker group.

Fixed effects	**Estimate**	**Std. error**	**df**	**t**	**Sig.**	**95% Confidence Interval**	
						lower	**upper**
Intercept	.988462	.019842	34.919	49.817	.000	.948177	1.028746
[Lexical Status = non-word]	–.069712	.026598	27.000	–2.621	.014	–.124285	–.015138
[Consonant = geminate]	–.021795	.026598	27.000	–.819	.420	–.076368	.032779
[Lexical Status = non-word] * [Consonant = geminate]	.036378	.037615	27.000	.967	.342	–.040801	.113557
Covariance parameters	**Estimate**	**Std. error**					
CS diagonal offset (Residual)	.003537	.000963					
CS covariance (Subject)	.000400	.000651					

Discussion: Experiments 1 and 2

The results of Experiment 1 clearly show that learners can discriminate the geminate and non-geminate contrast, even at the intermediate level, with high accuracy, closely resembling native speakers' performance.

Experiment 2 looked at how learners lexically encode a new contrast that is not in their L1 (i.e., geminate) in comparison with native speakers' performance. Learners, but not native speakers, exhibited a significant interaction of consonant type with lexical status, triggered by the asymmetrical pattern predicted by the lexical coding deficiency hypothesis. In both learner groups, the lowest accuracy was observed for non-words with singletons, the dominant category. This was not the case for native speakers. The order of accuracy and the interactions between consonant type and lexical status observed in the data mirror the asymmetry reported by Cutler et al. (2006) and Weber and Cutler (2004). In addition, we also showed that this asymmetry persists across learner groups that differ in measurable ways in terms of exposure to Japanese. Despite low accuracy overall on the lexical decision task, even intermediate learners were able to maintain a distinction at the lexical level between lexical representations containing the singleton and the geminate categories.

To answer the question whether the lexical encoding of the contrast is target-like however, it is necessary to consider both experiments together. In the ABX task, learners could discriminate geminate from non-geminate very accurately even in early stages of acquisition. This result corroborates previous findings that learners at low-intermediate and advanced levels can discriminate and identify the contrasts in isolated forms (Hardison & Motohashi-Saigo, 2010). For our purpose, the combined results from Experiments 1 and 2 offered evidence that the L2 learners were able to represent the contrast between geminates and singleton at the phonetic level, and that the difficulty was located at the lexical processing level. Consequently, the observed interaction between category type (old vs. new) and lexical status (word vs. non-word) suggests that the contrast between geminate and singleton was encoded phonologically at the lexical level, but not in a target-like manner. Indeed, it appears that the way this distinction was encoded is dependent on the L1 category, that is, makes reference to the dominant category: the geminate category appears to be encoded as a poor match to the singleton (dominant) category. When lexical representations were target-like, as was the case for native speakers, no interaction was observed.

It is however possible to object that our categorization task was not sensitive enough to truly establish excellent phonetic categorization. It is worth emphasizing that the cognitive load in this task was low given the limited phonetic variability in stimuli induced by the use of only one voice. The results are comparable to those obtained by Polka (1995) for example. While these findings might not be generalizable to all learners, they served our purpose of examining whether these specific participants were able to discern the singleton-geminate contrast as produced by that particular speaker. However, it would be more compelling to use a more demanding task to establish categorization performance. In Experiment 3, therefore, the design has been slightly modified accordingly. There were more contrasts and two different voices.

Experiments 3 and 4: German

In this section, we report the results of two experiments designed to test participants' ability to categorically discriminate between German front-rounded and back-rounded vowel phonemes, and to lexically encode this phonemic difference in their lexical representations for German words.

Experiment 3: Categorical discrimination with ABX

Methods and procedure

Stimuli were CVC monosyllables which were non-words in German as well as in English. The vowels were surrounded by two consonantal contexts: bilabial (e.g. pVm) or coronal (e.g. sVl). Stimuli included the ten contrasts shown in Table 10.

The front-front contrasts are expected to be easier than front-back according to the Perceptual Assimilation Model for Language Learners (PAM-L2, Best & Tyler, 2007), and constitute the control condition. The front-back comparisons are analyzed as the test condition, and the remaining vowel contrasts (/i-a/, /i-o/) are distractors.

There were two pairs of items in each context for each of the 10 contrasts, hence a total of forty pairs of non-words. Each pair was then arranged into a triplet (A – B – X) where X is either similar to A or to B. (e.g. A-[pom] B-[pøm] X-[pøm] (X = B); A-[pem] B-[pøm] X-[pe:m] (X = A)). Four counterbalanced orderings for the triplets were used (ABA, ABB, BAA, BAB), which resulted in a

Table 10. Contrasts used in the German study.

	Front-back (test)	Front-front (control)	High-non high
high	/u y/	/i y/	/i a/, /i o/
	/ʏ ʊ/	/ɪ ʏ/	
mid	/o ø/	/e ø/	
	/ɔ œ/	/ɛ œ/	

total of 160 triplets. These trials were presented in a block with 3 breaks through the experimental software DMDX (Forster & Forster, 2003). Participants were instructed to decide whether the third non-word (X) matched the first (A) or the second (B) non-word, and indicate their response as fast as possible. Each trial started with a fixation cross at the center of the screen for 250 ms. Interstimulus interval was set at 500 ms. Participants had 2000 ms to make their response, before the next trial was initiated. RT was measured from the onset of the third (X) item in a trial.

To increase task difficulty, contrasts were not blocked: all 10 contrasts could occur in the same block. In addition, two different voices were used. Stimuli were recorded several times by two female German native speakers, and normalized for amplitude. One voice was used for the X token, whereas the other was used for the two different A and B tokens.

Both experiments were conducted in one single testing session. A demographic and language background questionnaire was given at the beginning of the testing session. Participants completed the lexical decision task first, followed by the ABX task. At the end, participants rated their familiarity with the words in the lexical decision task.

Participants

Four groups of participants were tested: two groups of late English learners of German (intermediate, n = 103, vs. advanced, n = 21), one group of American English native speakers without experience with German ("monolingual", n = 31), and one group of German native speakers (n = 18).

Based on demographic and background information recorded in the questionnaire, participants were excluded from further analysis if one or several of the following criteria applied: Father's or Mother's L1 non English; Subject's L1 non English; Residential history too complex or including parts in Germany [for intermediate learners and monolingual English native speakers only]; Exposure to German, French or other languages that contain front rounded vowels at home; Exposure to German, French or other languages that contain front rounded vowels in childhood; Speech or hearing disorder; Having had instruction in French/Turkish/Danish/Mandarin or other languages that may contain front rounded vowels under examination; Missing data/subject questionnaire. In total, 39 intermediate participants were excluded, leaving 64 for analysis; six monolingual English native speakers were also excluded, leaving 25 for analysis. No advanced learner or native speaker of German was excluded.

In addition, nine intermediate learners were further excluded because of low familiarity ratings with the words used in Experiment 4 (see below). A total of 55 intermediate participants were retained for the analysis for Experiments 3 and 4.

Intermediate learners (n = 55; 20 females) were enrolled in third-year classes at a large university in the United States, and had taken a maximum of six semesters of German. None of them had spent any time in a German-speaking country. Their mean age was 20.7 years (SD = 1.7, range: 19–30).

Advanced learners (n = 21, 7 females) were graduate students and instructors, who had taken at least 8 semesters of German. Except for three of them, they had spent between 4 and 36 months in a German-speaking country (M = 15.1 months, SD = 11.1, range: 0–36). Their mean age was 27.2 years (SD = 4.73, range: 21–38).

German native speakers (n = 18; 12 females) served as a control group. All were living in the USA at the time of testing, and so had knowledge of English. Their mean age was 26.6 years (SD = 5.0, range: 18–33).

Naïve American English native speakers (n = 25; 24 females) with no knowledge of German and no experience with any language containing the target phonemes were also tested as a second control. Their mean age was 20 years (SD = 0.85, range 18–22).

None of these participants reported any hearing or speech impairment. They received either course credit or a small monetary compensation for participating.

Results

Two participants were considered outliers (one intermediate, and one German native speaker) given very low accuracy on the control and distractor conditions, and were removed from further analysis. Data for one additional intermediate subject were missing, bringing the total number of intermediate learners to 53, and the German native speakers to 17. For each subject, proportions of accurate answers (%) and RT means were computed across items in each condition, within the combination of *height* (mid vs. high), *tenseness* (tense vs. lax), *context* (bilabial, coronal), and *contrast*. Thus, there were 18 aggregate measures per subject,

Table 11. Mean accuracy (%), mean RT (ms) and standard error (SE) for each group and each condition.

Condition	Test (back-front)				Control (front-front)				Distractor			
Group	Acc.	SE	RT	SE	Acc.	SE	RT	SE	Acc.	SE	RT	SE
Intermediate	87	0.9	942	21.4	92	0.9	896	21.4	95	1.3	846	23.2
Advanced	90	1.5	945	34.0	94	1.5	893	34.0	97	2.1	857	36.8
Native Sp.	96	1.6	840	37.8	95	1.6	845	37.8	95	2.3	791	40.9
Monolingual	83	1.4	1021	31.2	87	1.4	981	31.2	93	1.9	939	33.7

Note: mean RT is computed over correct responses only.

Table 12. Parameter estimate, standard error, t-value, p-value, and 95% confidence interval of the predictors for the ABX accuracy (arcsine transformed).

Fixed effects	Estimate	Std. error	df	t	Sig.	95% Confidence Interval	
						lower	upper
Intercept	1.284536	.025105	173.381	51.167	.000	1.234986	1.334087
[Condition = test]	–.065048	.021177	1964.000	–3.072	.002	–.106580	–.023516
[Condition = control]	.072852	.033484	1964.000	2.176	.030	.007184	.138520
[Group = Int.]	.102200	.030456	173.381	3.356	.001	.042089	.162312
[Group = Adv.]	.126425	.037156	173.381	3.403	.001	.053089	.199761
[Group = NS]	.149915	.039460	173.381	3.799	.000	.072031	.227799
[Condition = test] * [Group = Interm.]	–.035064	.025691	1964.000	–1.365	.172	–.085448	.015320
[Condition = test] * [Group = Adv.]	–.014067	.031343	1964.000	–.449	.654	–.075535	.047402
[Condition=test] * [Group = NS]	.091619	.033286	1964.000	2.752	.006	.026339	.156900
[Condition = control] * [Group = Interm.]	–.026750	.040621	1964.000	–.659	.510	–.106414	.052915
[Condition = control] * [Group = Adv.]	–.004478	.049557	1964.000	–.090	.928	–.101668	.092712
[Condition = control] * [Group = NS]	–.084453	.052631	1964.000	–1.605	.109	–.187671	.018764
Covariance parameters	**Estimate**	**Std. error**					
CS diagonal offset (Residual)	.044847	.001431					
CS covariance (Subject)	.010150	.001691					

Note: Interm. = Intermediate; Adv. = Advanced; NS = Native speakers.

aggregated over two items (and four trials per item). Table 11 presents the mean accuracy and RT in each condition for each group.

An arcsine transform was used for these data for the same reason as in Experiment 1. To compare the performance of the groups, a linear mixed effects model was conducted in SPSS 20 on the arcsine-transformed accuracy means of the four groups. The factors *group* (intermediate, advanced, NS, and monolingual), and *condition* (test, control, and distractor) were entered as fixed effects. The variables of *height* (mid vs. high), *tenseness* (tense vs. lax), and *context* (bilabial, coronal) were declared as repeated effects within subjects. Table 12 displays the parameter estimates for this model.

The main effect of condition was significant: accuracy was highest in the distractor condition (95%), followed by the control (92%), and the test (89%) conditions ($F(2, 1964) = 22.5, p < 0.01$). Performance also varied by group ($F(3, 135.1) = 6.8, p < 0.01$). Pairwise comparisons (with Sidak correction) revealed that only the monolingual group performed significantly less accurately than the other three groups (all $p < 0.05$). No other comparison was significant. There was a significant interaction between the two factors ($F(6, 1964) = 4.6, p < 0.01$). Univariate tests indicated that performance of all non-native groups was influenced by condition (simple effect of condition significant for all three groups at $p < 0.01$), whereas for the native speaker group, condition had no effect ($F < 1$). More specifically, pairwise comparisons (with Sidak correction) show that in all non-native groups, this significance is driven by performance in the test condition, significantly less accurate than in both other conditions (all $p < 0.01$). Performance in the distractor and the control condition was equally accurate in all non-native groups (intermediates and advanced: $p > 0.1$; monolinguals: $p = 0.09$).

Analysis of RTs was performed similarly; the data were normally distributed. Parameter estimates are displayed in Table 13. Type III tests of fixed effects revealed that there was a main effect of condition ($F(2, 1964) = 48.3, p < 0.01$), and of group ($F(3, 115.0) = 3.6, p < 0.05$). Pairwise comparisons (with Sidak correction) indicated that RTs were slowest in the test condition (936 ms), faster in the control (903 ms) and fastest in the distractor condition (858 ms, all $p < 0.01$). Latency differences among the groups were less pronounced: pairwise comparisons showed that only the monolinguals were significantly slower than the native speakers ($p = 0.01$). No other comparison reached significance. There was a significant interaction between the two factors ($F(6, 1964) = 2.5, p < 0.05$). Univariate tests showed that the simple effect of group was significant in each condition (test: $F(3, 119.6) = 4.6, p < 0.01$; control: $F(3, 119.6) = 2.9, p < 0.05$; distractor: $F(3, 164.3) = 2.9, p < 0.05$), and was mainly driven by the significantly slower RT of the monolingual compared to the native speaker group (test: $p < 0.01$; both other conditions: $p < 0.05$). No other pairwise comparison reached significance.

Table 13. Parameter estimate, standard error, t-value, p-value, and 95% confidence interval of the predictors for the ABX RT.

Fixed effects	Estimate	Std. error	df	t	Sig.	95% Confidence Interval	
						lower	upper
Intercept	980.796596	31.151506	119.562	31.485	.000	919.116480	1042.476712
[Condition = test]	40.070043	10.601135	1964.000	3.780	.000	19.279388	60.860699
[Condition = control]	−42.061555	16.761866	1964.000	−2.509	.012	−74.934468	−9.188643
[Group = Interm.]	−85.202285	37.791002	119.562	−2.255	.026	−160.028633	−10.375937
[Group = Adv.]	−87.463574	46.105030	119.562	−1.897	.060	−178.751734	3.824585
[Group = NS]	−135.945198	48.964264	119.562	−2.776	.006	−232.894652	−38.995744
[Condition = test] * [Group = Interm.]	6.080688	12.860615	1964.000	.473	.636	−19.141197	31.302573
[Condition = test] * [Group = Adv.]	11.316010	15.689953	1964.000	.721	.471	−19.454695	42.086715
[Condition = test] * [Group = NS]	−45.063466	16.662975	1964.000	−2.704	.007	−77.742436	−12.384496
[Condition = control] * [Group = Interm.]	−7.689640	20.334417	1964.000	−.378	.705	−47.568942	32.189662
[Condition = control] * [Group = Adv.]	6.021856	24.807993	1964.000	.243	.808	−42.630900	54.674613
[Condition = control] * [Group = NS]	−11.643727	26.346477	1964.000	−.442	.659	−63.313716	40.026262
Covariance parameters	**Estimate**	**Std. error**					
CS diagonal offset (Residual)	11238.406	358.632					
CS covariance (Subject)	22855.607	3137.705					

Note: Interm. = Intermediate; Adv. = Advanced; NS = Native speakers.

Within each group however, latencies were also influenced by condition: notably, pairwise comparisons indicated that all non-native groups, but not the native speakers, were slower in the test condition compared to both other conditions (all $p < 0.01$). In addition, for both intermediates and monolinguals, all other comparisons were also significant ($p < 0.01$). For advanced, RT on the control and distractor conditions did not differ ($p > 0.1$). The native speakers were faster on the distractor condition compared to both others (both $p < 0.05$), but did not differ in the test vs. control condition ($p > 0.1$).

After excluding the monolingual group, both analyses (arcsine-transformed accuracy, and RT) showed a marginal main effect of group (accuracy: $F(2, 105.8) = 2.7, p = 0.07$; RT: $F(2, 90.3) = 1.5, p > 0.1$). The main effect of condition (accuracy: $F(2, 1541) = 14.2, p < 0.01$; RT: $F(2, 1541) = 35.0, p < 0.01$) and the interaction remained significant in both models (accuracy: $F(4, 1541) = 7.2, p < 0.01$; RT: $F(4, 1541) = 3.8, p < 0.01$). Pairwise comparisons between the conditions indicated that accuracy on the test condition was significantly lower (91%), and RTs were slower (908 ms), than on both other conditions (control: 93%, 878 ms; distractor: 96%, 831 ms), which did not differ from each other ($p > 0.1$).

The interaction pattern was further explored for both dependent variables. For the arcsine, univariate tests showed that the simple effect of group was significant for the test condition ($F(2, 135.3) = 13.0, p < 0.01$), but not for the two other conditions ($p > 0.1$). In that condition only, native speakers outperformed both other groups (both $p < 0.01$), who did not differ from each other ($p > 0.1$). For the control and distractor conditions, no comparison reached significance. For the RT, the simple main effect of group was marginal for the test condition ($F(2, 93.9) = 3.1, p = 0.052$), and not significant in the two other conditions ($F < 1$). Native speakers were marginally faster than the intermediate group ($p = 0.06$) on the test condition only. No other comparison was significant.

The persistent significant interactions in terms of accuracy suggest that the test condition, despite overall high accuracy levels, triggered more errors in the learner groups compared to the native speakers. We now explore this condition in more detail. Mean accuracy rates for these three groups for the test items are presented in Figure 3.

As above, a linear mixed effects model was conducted on the arcsine-transformed accuracy scores. The factors *group* (intermediate, advanced, NS), *height* (high vs. mid) and *context* (coronal, bilabial) were entered as fixed effects. *Height* and *context* were also entered as repeated effects within subjects. Parameter estimates are shown in Table 14.

Type III tests of fixed effects showed that there was a significant interaction between height and group ($F(2, 264) = 3.8, p < 0.05$). Mid vowels yielded higher accuracy (on average 94% correct) than high vowels (87% correct), a significant

Table 14. Parameter estimate, standard error, t-value, p-value, and 95% confidence interval of the predictors for ABX with the height and context factors.

Fixed effects	Estimate	Std. error	df	t	Sig.	95% Confidence Interval	
						lower	upper
Intercept	1.459285	.043574	269.342	33.490	.000	1.373497	1.545074
[Height = high]	–.116691	.050822	264.000	–2.296	.022	–.216758	–.016624
[Context = bil]	.011620	.050822	264.000	.229	.819	–.088447	.111687
[Group = Interm.]	–.158209	.050077	269.342	–3.159	.002	–.256801	–.059617
[Group = Adv.]	–.057697	.058615	269.342	–.984	.326	–.173099	.057704
[Context = bil] * [Height = high]	.101058	.071873	264.000	1.406	.161	–.040458	.242574
[Height = high] * [Group = Interm.]	–.091473	.058406	264.000	–1.566	.119	–.206474	.023529
[Height = high] * [Group = Adv.]	–.144462	.068364	264.000	–2.113	.036	–.279071	–.009853
[Context = bil] * [Group = Interm.]	.045559	.058406	264.000	.780	.436	–.069442	.160561
[Context = bil] * [Group = Adv.]	–.021971	.068364	264.000	–.321	.748	–.156580	.112638
[Context = bil] * [Height = high] * [Group = Interm.]	.016990	.082599	264.000	.206	.837	–.145647	.179626
[Context = bil] * [Height = high] * [Group = Adv.]	.025437	.096682	264.000	.263	.793	–.164929	.215803
Covariance parameters	**Estimate**	**Std. error**					
CS diagonal offset (Residual)	.021954	.001911					
CS covariance (Subject)	.010324	.002431					

Note: Interm. = Intermediate; Adv = Advanced; NS = Native speakers; bil = bilabial.

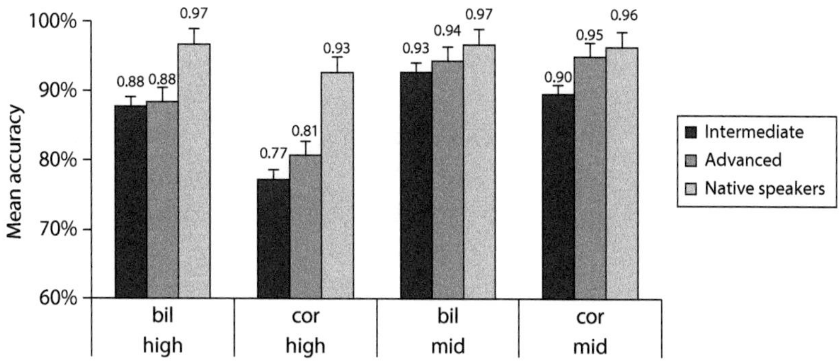

Figure 3. Mean accuracy on the test condition as a function of vowel height and context, for each group. Error bars represent +/– 1 SE.

difference for both learner groups ($p < 0.01$), but only marginal for the native speakers ($p = 0.067$).

There was also a significant interaction between height and context ($F(1, 264) = 10.8, p < 0.01$). Accuracy was higher in the bilabial context than in the coronal context, but for high vowels only (91% vs. 83%, $p < 0.01$), not for mid vowels (95% vs. 94%, $p > 0.1$). There was no interaction between group and context ($F(2, 264) = 1.8, p > 0.1$), nor a significant triple interaction ($F < 1$).

To sum up, this pattern of results indicates that learners displayed lower accuracies in very specific conditions only, such as for high vowels in the coronal context (see Figure 3). In addition, the lack of triple interaction indicated that overall, learners' behavior was not fundamentally different from native speakers' across conditions. Binomial tests confirmed that the scores of the learners in every subcondition (high vs. mid vowels in bilabial vs. coronal contexts) were significantly different from chance (all $p < 0.01$).

Taken together, and despite lower accuracy levels in one specific comparison, the overall high accuracy levels in these data allows us to conclude that learners in our experiment did not have truly serious difficulties in differentiating back from front rounded vowels. We now turn to the examination of lexical encoding of these contrasts among the same learners.

Experiment 4: Lexical decision

Method and procedure

Eighty common German words were selected and matched for frequency and familiarity. They were either mono- or disyllabic words containing one of the vowels under scrutiny. Eighty corresponding non-words were created by exchanging e.g.

a back vowel for its front-rounded counterpart (*Honig* /honɪç/ 'honey' vs. **Hönig* /hønɪç/) or vice-versa (*König* /kønɪç/ 'king' vs. **Konig* /konɪç/). There were 160 test items, and 128 filler items (64 words and 64 similar non-words, e.g. *Kanne* /kanə/ 'teapot', **Blanne* /blanə/, *Pflaume* /pflaʊmə/ 'plum', **Pfeude* /pfɔʏdə/). This resulted in a total number of 288 trials, which were randomized.

Stimuli were divided into two blocks, so that participants heard both the word and the non-word of a word/non-word pair, but never in the same block. Participants listened to stimuli and had to decide whether each token was a real word or a fake word of German by pressing buttons labeled "yes" or "no" as fast as possible. The "yes" button was always the dominant hand of the participant. Participants had 2500 ms to make their response, before the next trial was initiated.

In selecting the target words, we tried as much as possible to match the frequency among words containing the same vowel, and across vowel types (old and new). Therefore, we avoided potential items with extreme frequency values (either very high or very low) that would stand out from the rest of the items. For all the selected word forms (that is, all words including all their homophones), the spoken and written frequency was looked up in the Celex Database (Baayen, Piepenbrock, & Gulikers, 1995), and their average (over spoken and written values) and additive frequency was calculated. In addition to frequency measurements, we also obtained familiarity ratings for these German words from our participants at the end of the experiment in order to verify that the items were known words to them. These averaged measures are included in Table 15 below. A series of two-tailed t-tests revealed that the various measures were very similar for words containing old vs. new vowels.

Stimuli were recorded by a female native speaker of German (who also recorded tokens for the ABX task) in a sound-isolated recording booth. In order to further ensure that L2 learners even at intermediate levels would have established some lexical representations for the words used in the task, we developed a 917-word long "Märchenkrimi" (a detective fairy tale) called "Der schlaue Heinrich" ('the smart Henry'). All the words selected for the experiment were embedded

Table 15. Average frequency and familiarity by contrast for the German words used in lexical decision.

	Frequencies				Familiarity
	spoken	written	mean	sum (S + W)	average
Old	36.1	45.1	40.6	81.2	4.52
New	33.9	35.8	34.9	69.8	3.68
$t(78)$ =	0.15, $p > 0.1$	0.72, $p > 0.1$	0.45, $p > 0.1$	0.45, $p > 0.1$	1.99, $p = 0.05$

in the story. Students in German classes from which recruitment would later be made for this study were presented with the text during their regular classes and worked with it for a few weeks before recruitment began. Students did not know about the upcoming study while they worked with the text. Vocabulary items were explained by teachers, and also used in other exercises. No attention was specifically drawn to the items used as stimuli.

Participants

Three groups participated in this experiment: German native speakers, advanced learners and intermediate learners of German. Participants in each of these groups were the same as in Experiment 3.

Results

Accuracy on all items was screened to determine if some non-words were accepted as words by a majority of native speakers or vice-versa. Those items for which accuracy was below 2 *SD* of the mean for this group were excluded, separately for words and non-words. Four words and three non-words were excluded. These items did not yield high enough convergence in lexical decision responses among the native speakers for various reasons (e.g. indistinct pronunciation or dialectal differences in lexical status). The resulting mean accuracy of native speakers in this task was 95%. For participants, no further outlier was excluded.

The proportion of accurate answers (%) and mean RT for each subject were computed across items for each condition within the combination of lexical status (word vs. non-word), and vowel (old vs. new). They are presented in Table 16.

Table 16. Mean accuracy (%), mean RT (ms) and standard error (SE) in the control vs. test conditions in lexical decision for German words and non-words, for each group.

	Lexical status	Condition	NS		Advanced		Interm.	
			mean	SE	mean	SE	mean	SE
Accuracy	word	control	96	1.4	90	1.7	67	1.4
	non-word	control	95	1.4	87	1.7	72	1.4
	word	test	96	1.4	89	1.7	70	1.4
	non-word	test	91	1.4	72	1.7	45	1.4
RT	word	control	943	36.2	1092	33.6	1096	20.7
	non-word	control	1051	36.2	1267	33.6	1247	20.7
	word	test	918	36.2	1131	33.6	1105	20.7
	non-word	test	1062	36.2	1353	33.6	1283	20.7

Note: mean RT is computed over correct responses only, NS = native speakers.

A linear mixed effects model was conducted in SPSS 20 on the accuracy means. It declared the factor *group* (native speakers, advanced, intermediates), *condition* (control vs. test) and *lexical status* (word vs. non-word) as fixed effects. The factors *condition, lexical status,* as well as *vowel* (old vs. new) were entered as repeated effects within subjects. Parameter estimates are presented in Table 17.

Type III tests of fixed effects indicate that there was a main effect of group on accuracy (native speakers, 95%, advanced, 85%, intermediates, 64%, $F(2, 107.9) = 317$, $p < 0.01$). Performance for words (85%) was more accurate than for non-words (77%, lexical status: $F(1, 461) = 55.2$, $p < 0.01$). Accuracy was also higher in the control condition (85%) compared to the test (77%) condition (condition: $F(1, 461) = 53.0$, $p < 0.01$). All interactions were significant (all $p < 0.01$), including the triple interaction between group, lexical status, and condition ($F(2, 461) = 18.4$, $p < 0.01$). Condition had no effect on the native speaker performance only ($p > 0.1$), whereas both learner groups were significantly more accurate in the control over the test condition (both $p < 0.01$). Similarly, lexical status did not influence native speakers' performance ($p > 0.1$), but learners were more accurate for words than non-words (both $p < 0.01$).

Of particular interest is the interaction between lexical status and condition ($F(1, 461) = 62.0$, $p < 0.01$), for which pairwise comparisons indicated that accuracy for words was similar in the test (85%) and the control (84%) condition ($p > 0.1$), but for non-words, accuracy was much higher in the control condition (85%) compared to the test (70%) condition ($p < 0.01$), suggesting that the difficulty in rejecting non-words was not generalized to all non-words in the experiment but rather specific to the test non-words.

That this effect is mostly due to the learners (see Table 16), is confirmed in the triple interaction: for both learner groups, accuracy for non-words was higher on the control than on the test condition ($p < 0.01$ for both groups). For words, accuracy was similar in the two conditions ($p > 0.1$ for the advanced, $p = 0.045$ for the intermediates). For native speakers, neither condition nor lexical status influenced their performance (all $p > 0.1$).

The analysis of RTs was conducted similarly (Table 18). A linear mixed effects model was conducted on mean RT scores as the dependent variable. The factors *group, condition,* and *lexical status* were entered as fixed effects, and *lexical status, condition,* and *vowel* were declared as repeated factors within subjects.

According to the type III tests of fixed effects, there was a main effect of group (mean RT, native speakers = 993 ms; advanced = 1210 ms; intermediate = 1183 ms, $F(2, 92.0) = 13.7$, $p < 0.01$), of lexical status (mean RT, words = 1047 ms; non-words = 1210 ms, $F(1, 461) = 478.3$, $p < 0.01$), and of condition (mean RT, control = 1116 ms; test = 1142 ms, $F(1, 461) = 12.5$, $p < 0.01$). All interactions were significant (all $p < 0.05$), except the triple interaction between group, lexical

Table 17. Parameter estimate, standard error, t-value, p-value, and 95% confidence interval of the predictors for the lexical decision accuracy.

Fixed effects	Estimate	Std. error	df	t	Sig.	95% Confidence Interval	
						lower	upper
Intercept	.956771	.017667	384.623	54.154	.000	.922034	.991508
[Condition = control]	.005154	.028797	461.000	.179	.858	–.051435	.061743
[Group = Adv.]	–.066096	.024077	384.623	–2.745	.006	–.113435	–.018758
[Group = Interm.]	–.252225	.020354	384.623	–12.392	.000	–.292245	–.212206
[Lexical Status = non-word]	–.042708	.023512	461.000	–1.816	.070	–.088913	.003496
[Condition = control] * [Group = Adv.]	.004910	.039243	461.000	.125	.900	–.072208	.082028
[Condition = control] * [Group = Interm.]	–.038275	.033176	461.000	–1.154	.249	–.103470	.026919
[Lexical Status = non-word] * [Group = Adv.]	–.123859	.032042	461.000	–3.866	.000	–.186826	–.060893
[Lexical Status = non-word] * [Group = Interm.]	–.208542	.027088	461.000	–7.699	.000	–.261773	–.155310
[Condition = control] * [Lexical Status = non-word]	.034046	.040725	461.000	.836	.404	–.045983	.114075
[Condition = control] * [Lexical Status = non-word] * [Group = Adv.]	.106237	.055498	461.000	1.914	.056	–.002825	.215298
[Condition = control] * [Lexical Status = non-word] * [Group = Interm.]	.265316	.046918	461.000	5.655	.000	.173117	.357515
Covariance parameters	**Estimate**	**Std. error**					
CS diagonal offset (Residual)	.009951	.000655					
CS covariance (Subject)	.000643	.000358					

Note: Interm. = Intermediate; Adv. = Advanced.

Table 18. Parameter estimate, standard error, t-value, p-value, and 95% confidence interval of the predictors for the lexical decision RT.

Fixed effects	Estimate	Std. error	df	t	Sig.	95% Confidence Interval	
						lower	upper
Intercept	918.128	35.536	107.475	25.837	.000	847.686	988.570589
[Condition = control]	25.049	21.392	461.000	1.171	.242	−16.988	67.086171
[Group = Adv.]	212.538	48.427	107.475	4.389	.000	116.541	308.534122
[Group = Interm.]	187.246	40.940	107.475	4.574	.000	106.092	268.400497
[Lexical Status = non-word]	143.867	17.466	461.000	8.237	.000	109.544	178.190643
[Condition = control] * [Group = Adv.]	−64.075	29.152	461.000	−2.198	.028	−121.362	−6.787526
[Condition = control] * [Group = Interm.]	−34.702822	24.645	461.000	−1.408	.160	−83.133	13.727316
[Lexical Status = non-word] * [Group = Adv.]	77.817939	23.802	461.000	3.269	.001	31.043	124.592815
[Lexical Status = non-word] * [Group = Interm.]	34.913220	20.122	461.000	1.735	.083	−4.630	74.456262
[Condition = control] * [Lexical Status = non-word]	−36.147842	30.252	461.000	−1.195	.233	−95.598	23.301988
[Condition = control] * [Lexical Status = non-word] * [Group = Adv.]	−10.630492	41.227	461.000	−.258	.797	−91.647	70.385970
[Condition = control] * [Lexical Status = non-word] * [Group = Interm.]	8.283788	34.853	461.000	.238	.812	−60.207	76.774346
Covariance parameters	**Estimate**	**Std. error**					
CS diagonal offset (Residual)	5491.271	361.691					
CS covariance (Subject)	19984.648	3098.988					

Note: Interm. = Intermediate; Adv. = Advanced.

status, and condition ($F < 1$). Condition had no effect on the native speaker RTs only ($p > 0.1$), whereas both learner groups were significantly faster in the control over the test condition (both $p < 0.01$). Lexical status influenced performance as well: all groups responded faster to words over non-words (all $p < 0.01$). Of particular interest is the interaction between lexical status and condition ($F(1, 461) = 6.1$, $p < 0.05$), for which pairwise comparisons indicated that RTs for words were similar in the test (1051 ms) and the control (1043 ms) condition ($p > 0.1$), but for non-words, RTs were faster in the control condition (1188 ms) compared to the test (1233 ms) condition ($p < 0.01$), suggesting that in parallel to the accuracy data, the difficulty in rejecting non-words was particularly pronounced for the test non-words. The same trends as for the accuracy data are observed again here, even though the triple interaction is not significant: native speakers' RTs are not influenced by condition or lexical status, whereas both factors clearly impact learners' performance. As can be seen in Table 16, the learners have slower RTs mainly on the test non-words.

We turn now to the asymmetries in mean accuracy rates as a function of vowel and lexical status. For the test condition only, the mean accuracy for words vs. non-words as a function of vowel type (new vs. old) is displayed in Figure 4. Average accuracy was low for both learner groups, a finding that contrasts with their performance in the ABX task.

For each group separately, a linear mixed effects model was conducted on the accuracy scores. The factors *vowel* (old vs. new) and *lexical status* (word vs. non-word) were declared as fixed effects. The factors *vowel* and *lexical status* were also entered as repeated effects within subjects. Parameter estimates are displayed in Tables 19, 20, and 21.

For intermediate learners, accuracy was higher for words than for non-words (71% vs. 45%, lexical status: ($F(1, 162) = 240.6$, $p < 0.01$), but there was no effect of vowel ($F < 1$). The interaction was significant ($F(1, 162) = 15.4$, $p < 0.01$): Intermediate learners were more accurate for words containing the old category (74%) than the new (68%) category ($p = 0.004$). Conversely, non-words containing a new category were more accurately rejected (49%) than those with an old (42%) category ($p = 0.009$). This pattern conforms to the predicted ordinal accuracy and suggests that there is an asymmetrical pattern in intermediate learners' lexical representations for these old vs. new vowels.

The pattern shown in Figure 4 for the advanced learners is comparable to that of the intermediate learners, but accuracy is overall higher. There was a main effect of lexical status ($F(1, 60) = 74.7$, $p < 0.01$): accuracy was higher for words (89%) over non-words (72%). There was again no effect of vowel ($F < 1$) but the interaction, this time, was not significant ($F(1, 60) = 1.9$, $p > 0.1$). Words containing the old category (90%) were more accurately recognized than those with a new

Table 19. Parameter estimate, standard error, t-value, p-value, and 95% confidence interval of the predictors for the intermediate group.

Fixed effects	Estimate	Std. error	df	t	Sig.	95% Confidence Interval	
						lower	upper
Intercept	.740191	.015621	206.29	47.380	.000	.709393	.770989
[Lexical Status = non-word]	–.322091	.023435	162.00	–13.740	.000	–.368369	–.275814
[Vowel = new]	–.061555	.023435	162.00	–2.627	.009	–.107833	–.015278
[Lexical Status = non-word] * [Vowel = new]	.130119	.033142	162.00	3.926	.000	.064672	.195565
Covariance parameters	**Estimate**	**Std. error**					
CS diagonal offset (Residual)	.015103	.001678					
CS covariance (Subject)	–.001681	.000582					

Table 20. Parameter estimate, standard error, t-value, p-value, and 95% confidence interval of the predictors for the advanced group.

Fixed effects	Estimate	Std. error	df	t	Sig.	95% Confidence Interval	
						lower	upper
Intercept	.900969	.022555	68.644	39.946	.000	.855969	.945968
[Lexical Status = non-word]	–.197825	.027902	60.000	–7.090	.000	–.253637	–.142012
[Vowel = new]	–.020322	.027902	60.000	–.728	.469	–.076134	.035491
[Lexical Status = non-word] * [Vowel = new]	.054629	.039459	60.000	1.384	.171	–.024301	.133559
Covariance parameters	**Estimate**	**Std. error**					
CS diagonal offset (Residual)	.008174	.001492					
CS covariance (Subject)	.002509	.001487					

Table 21. Parameter estimate, standard error, t-value, p-value, and 95% confidence interval of the predictors for the native speaker group.

Fixed effects	Estimate	Std. error	df	t	Sig.	95% Confidence Interval	
						lower	upper
Intercept	.953058	.017960	39.061	53.066	.000	.916733	.989383
[Lexical Status = non-word]	–.021185	.018015	51.000	–1.176	.245	–.057351	.014981
[Vowel = new]	.008053	.018015	51.000	.447	.657	–.028113	.044219
[Lexical Status = non-word] * [Vowel = new]	–.047283	.025476	51.000	–1.856	.069	–.098430	.003863
Covariance parameters	**Estimate**	**Std. error**					
CS diagonal offset (Residual)	.002921	.000578					
CS covariance (Subject)	.002885	.001248					

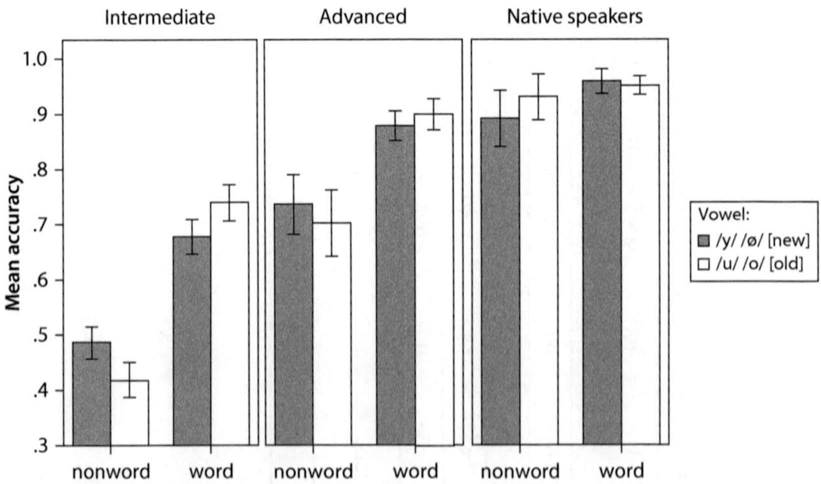

Figure 4. Mean accuracy in lexical decision as a function of vowel type and lexical status for each group. Error bars represent +/– 1 SE.

(88%) category, a non-significant trend ($p > 0.1$). Conversely, non-words containing a new category were more accurately rejected (74%) than those with an old category (70%), again a non-significant trend ($p > 0.1$). This pattern indicates that advanced learners have perhaps resolved a former asymmetry, which is suggested by the accuracy pattern which trends towards the order of accuracy observed in the intermediate learners group.

Native speakers show a different pattern. Again, accuracy was higher for words (96%) than for non-words (91%, $F(1, 51) = 12.4, p < 0.01$), and there was no effect of vowel ($F(1, 51) = 1.5, p > 0.1$). The interaction was marginal ($F(1, 51) = 3.4, p = 0.07$), but not due to the same pattern of accuracy found in the learner groups. Rather, as shown in Figure 4, non-words containing a new category were *less* accurately rejected (89%) than those with an old category (93%, $p = 0.04$), the opposite pattern than the one observed for learners. For words, there was no difference. While the difference found for non-words clearly drives the marginal interaction, the fact that it is against the predicted accuracy pattern does not make the presence of this interaction problematic for our hypothesis. This pattern suggests that there is no such asymmetry in native speakers' lexical representations for each type of vowels as the one found for intermediate learners.

Discussion: Experiments 3 and 4

The results of Experiment 3 demonstrated the overall highly accurate performance of both learner groups in the ABX categorization task, and indicate that the learners in this experiment were able to clearly perceive a difference between back and front rounded German vowels.

In Experiment 4, where the same learners were asked to recognize real German words, we observed a very high error rate on non-words that contain difficult phonemes: just as was the case for the long obstruent consonants [pː, tː, kː] in Japanese, this was observed again for the front rounded vowels (e.g., [y, ø]) in German. This high error rate could be due to a generalized bias to say "yes" in this lexical decision experiment, but this is ruled out by the performance on control items, for which accuracy was much more similar for the word and non-word conditions than for test items. Another possible explanation is based on the fact that the test items contain difficult contrasts whereas the control items do not, perhaps implying that listeners did not actually perceive the non-words containing the difficult contrasts accurately. However, the fact that phonetic perception was rather accurate in most conditions in these same listeners (Experiments 1 and 3) makes the possibility that these non-words were not perceived accurately very remote. Therefore, a more likely explanation for the high error rate in rejecting these non-words is that the lexical representations which are being contacted by the stimuli do not allow their rejection as easily in the case of non-words. The results of Experiment 4 again reproduced the asymmetry of Experiment 2, suggesting that learners are able to maintain a contrast, at the lexical level, between lexical representations containing the German categories under scrutiny.

Combined results from Experiments 3 and 4 reveal a striking picture: given accurate phonetic discrimination between both back and front rounded vowels in German, the asymmetric pattern we found in lexical decision suggests that the lexical encoding of new vowels categories is not target-like. The asymmetry itself shows that, early on, learners are able to establish a contrast at the lexical level, but their specific encoding of the phonological contrast in these lexical representations is not fully target-like and most likely references L1 categories, as suggested by Cutler et al. (2006).

Interestingly, the interaction was not significant for advanced learners, even though there was a trend for accuracy rates to conform to the asymmetrical pattern. This suggests that perhaps advanced learners have recovered from asymmetric lexical access because their representations for each category are now less dependent on L1/dominant categories.

General discussion

The goal of this study was to expand on recent reports of asymmetries in lexical access for L2 learners, and to explicitly investigate whether lexical representations are target-like or not, even if they are separate. We examined the degree to which a novel contrast is target-like in learners' lexical representations by looking at asymmetries in lexical decision patterns, combined with phonetic categorization tasks, in two different languages and different groups of L2 learners. This study is the first to examine both perceptual categorization ability and asymmetries in lexical access within the same listeners. By establishing categorization and lexical decision patterns in the same participants, our experiments allowed us to tease apart the level at which the contrast is not adequately represented: phonetic or lexical. The findings are very clear and consistent in two very different learner populations. Asymmetric lexical decision patterns, coupled with highly accurate categorization performance, suggest that L2 learners' lexical encoding of difficult phonological contrasts remains imprecise for some time, and offers rather clear support for the lexical coding deficiency hypothesis.

We were able to replicate and strengthen previously reported findings of asymmetric mapping from phonetic to lexical representations (Weber & Cutler, 2004; and Cutler et al., 2006) during lexical processing, and we also expand these findings to two different languages, German and Japanese, and with two different sets of contrasts: vowels and consonants. We also used a different method, lexical decision, which strengthens the robustness of the findings.

Our findings indicate that L2 learners' lexical representations are, in fact, quite detailed, even if their lexical encoding of difficult contrasts still makes reference to dominant categories due to L1 influence. This conclusion contrasts with findings of homophonous lexical representations, for instance with those of Pallier et al. (2001), or with some findings reported in Darcy et al. (2012). While it is possible that these studies were unable to uncover asymmetries because of their specific experimental design, it is also possible that such cases where lexical representations fail to clearly separate contrasts exist (see also Ota et al., 2009, for further evidence). The question then arises whether it is more difficult to establish separate lexical representations for certain contrasts than for others, perhaps because of how well they map onto L1 categories. In other words, if a contrast cannot be mapped as a dominant vs. non-dominant category in a given L1 (perhaps because both phones are allophones or equally good exemplars of the L1 category, as is likely the case for the Catalan /e/-/ɛ/ contrast for Spanish listeners; Bosch, Costa, & Sebastián-Gallés, 2000), it is possible that establishing a lexical contrast in any form will be more difficult. Purely phonetic mapping explanations aside, it is also possible that the degree to which explicit instruction, metalinguistic representations, and/or orthographic support are available for a given contrast or linguistic dimension will influence the difficulty with which a lexical contrast can initially be established.

In addition, this study is also the first to provide new evidence that such asymmetries can be resolved with more experience in an L2. In the case of learners of Japanese (Experiments 1 and 2), both intermediate and advanced learners displayed asymmetric mapping, suggesting that the phonological geminate/singleton contrast is not fully accurately encoded lexically, even though contrast is maintained between the two. In the case of learners of German, however (Experiments 3 and 4), advanced learners did not show any significant interaction, which we interpreted as the absence of asymmetry in lexical processing, suggesting that they were in the process of establishing a more efficient, native-like lexical access, and that their lexical representations were gradually encoding all phonological contrasts accurately.

This difference between Japanese and German learners can be due to a number of factors, such as the contrast examined: a consonantal contrast involving duration, and a vocalic contrast involving mainly spectral differences. As mentioned above, it is possible that different contrasts lead to different acquisition speeds. Another possibility is that the learner groups are different. They cannot be directly compared, even though all the learners recruited for these studies were from very similar populations, mainly young college-educated adults. The advanced learners of Japanese might be slightly less advanced than the advanced learners of German. Their overall intensity of exposure to the language might differ, and class-level is obviously not a sufficiently objective basis for comparison. Interestingly, the advanced learners of Japanese and of German in our study had spent overall a similar amount of time abroad (17.8 vs. 15.1 months) on average. It is striking that the advanced learners of German appeared to resolve the asymmetry, while the advanced learners of Japanese in our study (or the advanced learners of English in Weber & Cutler, 2004) did not. Nevertheless, it is possible that the length of time spent abroad is an important factor in acquisition.

Finally, while phonetic accuracy during perception is ultimately important for efficient word recognition in an L2, it is clear from our data and others that even a high accuracy in phonetic categorization will not guarantee accurate lexical encoding of a difficult contrast. The exact mechanisms L2 learners used to resolve initial asymmetries, as well as the factors that facilitate this acquisition, remain mysterious. Our experiments do not allow us to make strong claims about this point yet. A logical possibility is that length or intensity of exposure and perhaps vocabulary size in the L2 eventually promote accuracy, including the ability to lexically encode the new category in a target-like fashion. Similarly, orthography and explicit instruction might provide first indications to learners to bootstrap the contrast separation lexically – but we still need to understand how phonological representations at the lexical level are updated. Indeed, a consequence of such lexical "fuzziness" is to increase lexical competition during spoken word recognition in L2 learners (Broersma, 2012; Broersma & Cutler, 2011). Thus, further studies should investigate what triggers phonological update at the lexical level in the course of second language learning, in order to understand when and how unwelcome lexical competition can be reduced, that is, when and how the input [konɪç] stops being an acceptable rendition of the word *König*.

Acknowledgements

We thank John H. G. Scott for creating the *Märchenkrimi* and for substantial help with data collection and coding, as well as Christiane Kaden, Franziska Krüger and Justin Glover for help with running participants, Laurent Dekydtspotter, Rex Sprouse and Jeffrey Holliday for discussion and feedback, Stephanie Dickinson and Pan Yi from the IU Statistical Consulting Center for their invaluable help with statistical analysis, the Department of Germanic Studies and the Department of Second Language Studies at Indiana University, and the Second Language Psycholinguistics Lab members for comments, help and support. We also thank audiences at the 18th Germanic Linguistics Annual Conference (2012), the 8th International Conference on the Mental Lexicon (2012), the Second Language Research Forum (2012), as well as the Princeton Japanese Pedagogy Forum (2012).

Notes

1. The use of the word "rejection" here only refers to the fact that participants look away from the competitor earlier when the competitor contains the new category – while the ambiguity persists longer when the competitor contains a similar category.

2. The full range of possibilities would be four combinations of perceptual categorization and lexical contrast: *absence* of lexical contrast, with or without accurate perceptual distinction, vs. *presence* of lexical contrast, with or without accurate perceptual distinction. However, we only consider the case when a lexical contrast is present because the two hypotheses do not apply to the case when a lexical contrast is absent. In addition, the stimuli used in the lexical decision experiments reported here do not use lexical minimal pairs with which the absence of lexical contrast could reliably be tested, but only pairs of word/non-word.

3. In SPSS 20, this model uses repeated effects within each subject (with compound symmetry correlation structure within subject) in a way that is equivalent to declaring subjects as random effects.

References

Baayen, R. H., Piepenbrock, R., & Gulikers, L. (1995). *The CELEX lexical database (CD-ROM)*. Philadelphia, PA: Linguistic Data Consortium, University of Pennsylvania.

Banno, E., Ohno, Y., Sakane, Y., & Shinagawa, C. (1999). *Genki: An integrated course in elementary Japanese* [volume 1,2]. Tokyo: Japan Times.

Best, C. T., & Tyler, M. D. (2007). Nonnative and second language speech perception. Commonalities and complementarities. In O.-S. Bohn & M. J. Munro (Eds.), *Language experience in second language speech learning: In honor of James Emil Flege* (pp. 13–34). Amsterdam: John Benjamins. DOI: 10.1075/lllt.17.07bes

Bosch, L., Costa, A., & Sebastián-Gallés, N. (2000). First and second language vowel perception in early bilinguals. *European Journal of Cognitive Psychology*, 12, 189–221. DOI: 10.1080/09541446.2000.10590222

Broersma, M., & Cutler, A. (2008). Phantom word activation in L2. *System*, 36, 22–34. DOI: 10.1016/j.system.2007.11.003

Broersma, M. (2002). Comprehension of non-native speech: Inaccurate phoneme processing and activation of lexical competitors. In *Proceedings of the 7th international conference on spoken language processing* (pp. 261–264).

Broersma, M. (2012). Increased lexical activation and reduced competition in second-language listening. *Language and Cognitive Processes*, 27, 1205–1224. DOI: 10.1080/01690965.2012.660170

Broersma, M., & Cutler, A. (2011). Competition dynamics of second-language listening. *The Quarterly Journal of Experimental Psychology*, 64, 74–95. DOI: 10.1080/17470218.2010.499174

Cutler, A., Weber, A., & Otake, T. (2006). Asymmetric mapping from phonetic to lexical representations in second-language listening. *Journal of Phonetics*, 34, 269–284. DOI: 10.1016/j.wocn.2005.06.002

Darcy, I., Dekydtspotter, L., Sprouse, R. A., Glover, J., Kaden, C., McGuire, M., & Scott, J. H. G. (2012). Direct mapping of acoustics to phonology: On the lexical encoding of front rounded vowels in L1 English-L2 French acquisition. *Second Language Research*, 28, 5–40. DOI: 10.1177/0267658311423455

Dijkstra, A. & Van Heuven, W. J. B. (1998). The BIA model and bilingual word recognition. In J. Grainger & A. M. Jacobs (Eds.), *Localist connectionist approaches to human cognition* (pp. 189–225). Mahwah, NJ: Lawrence Erlbaum Associates.

Dupoux, E., Sebastián-Gallés, N., Navarrete, E., & Peperkamp, S. (2008). Persistent stress 'deafness': The case of French learners of Spanish. *Cognition*, 106, 682–706. DOI: 10.1016/j.cognition.2007.04.001

Escudero, P., Hayes-Harb, R., & Mitterer, H. (2008). Novel second-language words and asymmetric lexical access. *Journal of Phonetics*, 36, 345–360. DOI: 10.1016/j.wocn.2007.11.002

Forster, K. I., & Chambers, S. M. (1973). Lexical access and naming time. *Journal of Verbal Learning and Verbal Behavior*, 12, 627–635. DOI: 10.1016/S0022-5371(73)80042-8

Forster, K. I., & Forster, J. C. (2003). DMDX: A windows display program with millisecond accuracy. *Behavior Research Methods Instruments and Computers*, 35, 116–124. DOI: 10.3758/BF03195503

Frauenfelder, U. H., Scholten, M., & Content, A. (2001). Bottom-up inhibition in lexical selection: Phonological mismatch effects in spoken word recognition. *Language and cognitive processes*, 16, 583–607. DOI: 10.1080/01690960143000146

Gaskell, M. G., & Marslen-Wilson, W. D. (2001). Lexical ambiguity resolution and spoken word recognition: Bridging the gap. *Journal of Memory and Language*, 44, 325–349. DOI: 10.1006/jmla.2000.2741

Han, M. (1992). The timing control of geminate and single stop consonants in Japanese: A challenge for non-native speakers. *Phonetica*, 49, 102–127. DOI: 10.1159/000261906

Hardison, D. M., & Motohashi Saigo, M. (2010). Development of perception of second language Japanese geminates: Role of duration, sonority, and segmentation strategy. *Applied Psycholinguistics*, 31, 81–99. DOI: 10.1017/S0142716409990178

Hayes-Harb, R., & Masuda, K. (2008). Development of the ability to lexically encode novel second language phonemic contrasts. *Second Language Research*, 24, 5–33. DOI: 10.1177/0267658307082980

Jared, D., & Szucs, C. (2002). Phonological activation in bilinguals: Evidence from interlingual omograph naming. *Bilingualism: Language and Cognition*, 5, 225–239. DOI: 10.1017/S1366728902003024

Ju, M., & Luce, P. A. (2004). Falling on sensitive ears: Constraints on bilingual lexical activation. *Psychological Science*, 15, 314–318. DOI: 10.1111/j.0956-7976.2004.00675.x

Ju, M., & Luce, P. A. (2006). Representational specificity of within-category phonetic variation in the long-term mental lexicon. *Journal of Experimental Psychology: Human Perception and Performance*, 32, 120–138. DOI: 10.1037/0096-1523.32.1.120

Marian, V., & Spivey, M. J. (2003). Competing activation in bilingual language processing: Within- and between-language competition. *Bilingualism: Language and Cognition*, 6, 97–115. DOI: 10.1017/S1366728903001068

Marslen-Wilson, W. D. (1987). Functional parallelism in spoken word-recognition. *Cognition*, 25, 71–102. DOI: 10.1016/0010-0277(87)90005-9

McMurray, B., Tanenhaus, M. K., & Aslin, R. N. (2002). Gradient effects of within-category phonetic variation on lexical access. *Cognition*, 86, B33–B42. DOI: 10.1016/S0010-0277(02)00157-9

Ota, M., Hartsuiker, R. J., & Haywood, S. L. (2009). The KEY to the ROCK: Near-homophony in nonnative visual word recognition. *Cognition*, 111, 263–269. DOI: 10.1016/j.cognition.2008.12.007

Pallier, C., Bosch, L., & Sebastián-Gallés, N. (1997). A limit on behavioral plasticity in speech perception. *Cognition*, 64, B9–B17. DOI: 10.1016/S0010-0277(97)00030-9

Pallier, C., Colomé, A., & Sebastián-Gallés, N. (2001). The influence of native-language phonology on lexical access: exemplar-based versus abstract lexical entries. *Psychological Science*,12, 445–449. DOI: 10.1111/1467-9280.00383

Polka, L. (1995). Linguistic influences in adult perception of non-native vowel contrasts. *Journal of the Acoustical Society of America*, 97, 1286–1296. DOI: 10.1121/1.412170

Sebastián-Gallés, N. (2005). Cross-Language Speech Perception. In D. B. Pisoni & R. E. Remez (Eds.), *The Handbook of Speech Perception* (pp. 546–566). Malden, MA: Blackwell Publishing. DOI: 10.1002/9780470757024.ch22

Sebastián-Gallés, N., Echeverría, S., & Bosch, L. (2005). The influence of initial exposure on lexical representation: Comparing early and simultaneous bilinguals. *Journal of Memory and Language*, 52, 240–255. DOI: 10.1016/j.jml.2004.11.001

Sebastián-Gallés, N., Rodríguez-Fornells, A., de Diego-Balaguer, R., & Díaz, B. (2006). First and second-language phonological representations in the mental lexicon. *Journal of Cognitive Neuroscience*, 18, 1277–1291. DOI: 10.1162/jocn.2006.18.8.1277

Spivey, M. J., & Marian, V. (1999). Cross talk between native and second languages: Partial activation of an irrelevant lexicon. *Psychological Science*, 10, 281–284. DOI: 10.1111/14679280.00151

Strange, W., & Shafer, V. (2008). Speech perception in second language learners: The re-education of selective perception. In J. G. Hansen Edwards & M. L. Zampini (Eds.), *Phonology and Second Language Acquisition* (pp. 153–191). Amsterdam: John Benjamins. DOI: 10.1075/sibil.36.09str

Strange, W., Weber, A., Levy, E., Shafiro, V., Hisagi, M., & Nishi, K. (2007). Acoustic variability within and across German, French, and American English vowels: Phonetic context effects. *The Journal of the Acoustical Society of America*, 122, 1111–1129. DOI: 10.1121/1.2749716

Sumner, M., & Samuel, A. G. (2009). The effect of experience on the perception and representation of dialect variants. *Journal of Memory and Language*, 60, 487–501. DOI: 10.1016/j.jml.2009.01.001

Tajima, K., Kato, H., Rothwell, A., Akahane-Yamada, R., & Munhall, K. G. (2008). Training English listeners to perceive phonemic length contrasts in Japanese. *Journal of Acoustical Society of America*, 123, 397–413. DOI: 10.1121/1.2804942

Trofimovich, P., & John, P. (2011). When three equals tree. In P. Trofimovich & K. McDonough (Eds.), *Applying priming methods to L2 learning, teaching and research: Insights from Psycholinguistics* (pp. 105–129). Amsterdam: John Benjamins. DOI: 10.1075/lllt.30

Weber, A., & Cutler, A. (2004). Lexical competition in non-native spoken-word recognition. *Journal of Memory and Language*, 50, 1–25. DOI: 10.1016/S0749-596X(03)00105-0

Testing the viability of webDMDX for masked priming experiments

Jeffrey Witzel,[i] Samantha Cornelius,[i] Naoko Witzel,[i]
Kenneth I. Forster,[ii] and Jonathan C. Forster[ii]
[i] University of Texas at Arlington / [ii] University of Arizona

The DMDX software package (Forster & Forster, 2003) is a Windows-based application that displays stimuli and records responses. Recent developments in this program have made it possible to deploy DMDX experiments over the Internet. This study evaluates the viability of the web-deployable implementation of DMDX, or webDMDX, for masked priming experiments. A lexical decision task (LDT) with masked repetition priming on high- and low-frequency words and an e/a letter detection task were conducted with both lab-based DMDX (labDMDX; Experiment 1) and webDMDX. The webDMDX experiments were run on lab computers (Experiments 2) and on different (unknown) hardware (Experiment 3). The labDMDX and webDMDX experiments yielded comparable results on the LDT. In the e/a-detection task, the only important difference observed among the tests was between the lab-based experiment (Experiment 1) and the first webDMDX experiment (Experiment 2), at the 50 ms display duration. However, after a minor change in keyword coding (Experiment 2 follow-up) and an adjustment to the millisecond-to-retrace conversion process (Experiment 3), the detection rates at all display durations were similar in both labDMDX and webDMDX. Taken together, these results indicate the utility of webDMDX for masked priming experiments as well as for other time-sensitive methodologies.

Keywords: DMDX, webDMDX, masked priming, e/a-detection, word frequency, prime duration

The DMDX software package (Forster & Forster, 2003), a Windows-based application that displays stimuli and records responses, is used widely in experimental psychology and for psycholinguistics research in particular. Recently, a web-deployable version of this program was developed at the University of

DOI 10.1075/bct.80.06wit

Arizona. This version makes it possible to conduct DMDX experiments over the Internet. In the present study, this web-deliverable implementation of DMDX will be referred to as *webDMDX*. These experiments can be deployed by combining the following in a self-extracting .zip file (using, for instance, WinZip™ Self-Extractor): (i) DMDX.exe (version 4.2.0.1 or later[1]), (ii) a rich text file (.rtf) that specifies the parameters, input, and commands for the experiment, (iii) poster.exe, a Windows executable (.exe) file that sends each participant's data to a server at the University of Arizona (accessible at http://psy1.psych.arizona.edu/DMDX/), and (iv) a batch (.bat) file with the commands necessary to run the experiment and the data delivery program. If the experiment requires additional sound files or picture files, these should also be packaged in the self-extracting .zip. A link to this .zip file can then be posted online so that participants can download and run the experiment.[2] (To download the most recent, web-deployable version of DMDX, visit http://www.u.arizona.edu/~kforster/dmdx/dmdx.htm. For more information on how to create and distribute webDMDX experiments, see the DMDX help pages at http://psy1.psych.arizona.edu/~jforster/dmdx/help/dmdxhdmdx.htm and http://psy1.psych.arizona.edu/~jforster/dmdx/help/dmdxhremotetestingoverview.htm. These help pages also provide information on updates to DMDX/webDMDX.) This is an important development because a reliable web-deliverable tool for conducting behavioral experiments allows researchers greater flexibility as well as a convenient way to test otherwise difficult-to-access participant populations. This software thus has the potential to expand the range of research questions that can be practicably addressed by experimental psychologists. For psycholinguists in particular, webDMDX offers a useful way to investigate the processing of languages whose speakers are unrepresented or underrepresented in their communities.

One of the most important features of DMDX is that it is able to display stimuli and measure response times with millisecond accuracy. The purpose of this study was to evaluate the viability of webDMDX for experimental paradigms that require such precise timing. Of particular interest were experiments that use very brief stimulus display durations. In psycholinguistics, experiments that involve these so-called tachistoscopic displays, such as masked priming experiments (Forster & Davis, 1984), have often been used to shed light on automatic language processing. These experiments have been conducted to investigate a wide range of research questions at various levels of processing, including morphological processing (Frost, Forster, & Deutsch, 1997; Grainger, Colé, & Segui, 1991), lexical processing (Carreiras & Perea, 2002; Gollan, Frost, & Forster, 1997; Grainger & Ferrand, 1996; Kim & Davis, 2003) and sentence processing (Novick, Kim, & Trueswell, 2003; Trueswell & Kim, 1998). The present study was designed to determine whether such experiments can be reliably conducted using webDMDX and, by extension, whether this program can be used for other time-sensitive methods in experimental psychology.

Of course, running such experiments online poses a number of potential problems. One potential pitfall relates to communicating information over the web. If input for the experiment and response data are transmitted between the testing computer and the server that houses the experiment throughout the study session, both display and response timing could be influenced by the stability and speed of the participant's Internet connection. This is obviously undesirable. While there are a number of ways to deal with this potential problem, including creating plugins that would allow a web browser to run the experiment code locally, this problem is largely avoided in webDMDX. This is because webDMDX experiments are run purely locally (i.e., from the participant's computer itself), with the output transmitted over the web only at the completion (or termination) of the session.

As mentioned above, a participant in a webDMDX experiment downloads a self-extracting .zip file from a link on the researcher's web page. This file should contain DMDX, the .rtf script that controls the experiment, the .bat file that runs the experiment, and the poster.exe file that sends off its results (as well as any other files – for instance, sound or picture files – that are required for the study). The participant then follows the necessary procedures to run downloaded applications, which will vary depending on the browser and its settings. Typically, the self-extracting .zip appears as an .exe file in a list of recent downloads, and once this file is selected, the experiment begins automatically. At the completion of the experiment, the output is sent over the web to a data repository at the University of Arizona, and the data are deleted from the host computer. It is important to note that during this process, neither DMDX nor any of its support files are installed in the programs folder(s) on the host computer. There is therefore no need for the participant to uninstall anything after completing the experiment. Rather, like other downloaded applications, the self-extracting .zip that runs the experiment is typically stored in the host computer's Downloads folder, which is often cleared as part of normal system maintenance. The researcher can access the participant's data from the University of Arizona data repository (accessible at http://psy1.psych.arizona.edu/DMDX/).[3] At this site, datasets are listed as links that correspond to .rtf file names.[4] When the researcher clicks on the link for a given file name, the data for all of the participants that have completed this experiment are displayed just as they are in standard DMDX .azk or .zil output files. The researcher can then copy the dataset into a text editor, save it as an .azk or .zil file, and proceed with the analyses following his/her preferred procedures.[5]

For accurate display timing in these experiments, DMDX must be synchronized with the host computer's display raster. To achieve this, the program needs to know the refresh rate of the monitor on the testing computer. Without this information, DMDX will not run. In the traditional lab-based implementation of DMDX (which, for ease of exposition, will hereafter be referred to as *labDMDX*), this information is supplied by a companion program, TimeDX, which determines the screen refresh interval and stores it in the registry. For a web-deployable application, however, it is not feasible to run TimeDX in advance of each experiment. This would require the participant to follow a relatively complicated set of instructions and would thus largely negate the benefits of distributing the experiment online. This problem is solved in webDMDX by relying on the operating system of the host computer to report its refresh rate, something that was not possible in older versions of Windows (e.g., Windows 98). In this case, DMDX runs in what is called auto mode.

It is also important to determine the refresh interval of the testing computer in order to code the durations of tachistoscopic displays. Such displays can only be presented for an integer number of refresh intervals. When designing a lab experiment in DMDX, the refresh interval of the testing computer is determined in advance (again, using TimeDX). Display durations can then be expressed as the desired number of refresh intervals. This is done using the keyword `<% N>` in the .rtf input file for the experiment. For instance, on a computer with a 60 Hz monitor, and thus with a refresh interval of 16.67 ms, a 50 ms display duration would be coded as `<% 3>` (i.e., 3 * 16.67 ms). For web-deployed experiments, however, the refresh interval of each host computer is not known at the experimental design stage. In order to allow webDMDX experiments to be run consistently on a range of hardware, display durations can therefore be expressed in keywords that make reference to milliseconds (e.g., `<%ms N>`). For each host computer, DMDX then calculates the number of refresh intervals that gives the closest approximation to the requested duration. For example, in the .rtf file for a webDMDX experiment, a 50 ms display duration might be coded as `<%ms 50>`. If this experiment were run on a computer with a 60 Hz monitor, DMDX would present the stimulus for 3 refresh intervals (3 * 16.67 ms); however, on a computer with a 100 Hz monitor, the stimulus would be presented for 5 refresh intervals (5 * 10 ms).

In light of these differences between the lab-based and web-deployable implementations of DMDX, the purpose of the present study was to investigate the viability of webDMDX for experiments that require brief and tightly controlled display durations. Specifically, three experiments were conducted – one on labDMDX (Experiment 1) and two on webDMDX (Experiment 2, Experiment 3) – using tasks that involve tachistoscopic displays. The first of these tasks was a standard lexical decision task (LDT) with masked repetition priming. The targets were high- and low-frequency words, and there were two prime durations – 33 ms and 67 ms. The second was an e/a-detection task, which is an adjusted

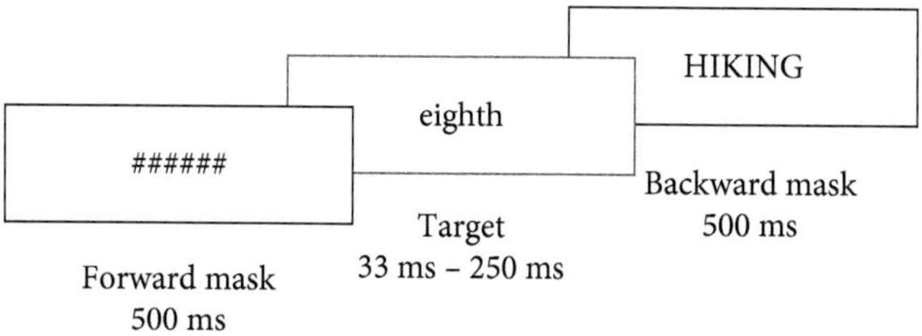

Figure 1. The presentation of test items in an e/a-detection task.

form of e-detection (see e.g., Finkbeiner, Forster, Nicol, & Nakamura, 2004). In e-detection, target words are presented for different display durations between forward and backward masks, and participants indicate whether or not they see the letter 'e' in each target. The e/a-detection task in the present study involved the same display procedures, but participants decided whether they saw the letter 'e' or the letter 'a' in each target (see Figure 1). This adaptation to e/a-detection is important because it eliminates criterion effects inherent to Yes/No detection tasks and thus allows for a measure that is potentially more sensitive to perceptual differences with subtle changes in display duration.

Experiment 1 – LabDMDX

In this experiment, an LDT with masked repetition priming and an e/a-detection task were conducted using labDMDX (version 4.0.4.8). The testing computers had liquid crystal display (LCD) monitors with 60 Hz refresh rates, and display durations were coded using keywords that specified the number of refresh intervals for each stimulus. That is, 33 ms display durations were coded as <% 2>, 50 ms display durations as <% 3>, 67 ms display durations as <% 4>, and so on. In the LDT, standard word frequency and repetition priming effects were predicted at both the 33 ms and 67 ms prime durations (Forster, Mohan, & Hector, 2003). In the e/a-detection task, error rates were predicted to decrease with increasing stimulus display durations. The results of this experiment acted as a baseline for comparison with those of the webDMDX experiments (Experiments 2 and 3).

Method

Participants
Thirty-two (32) students at the University of Texas at Arlington (UTA) participated in the experiment for course credit. All participants were native speakers of English.

Materials and design

Lexical decision task. Forty-eight (48) high-frequency words and 48 low-frequency words were selected as targets. The high-frequency words had a mean CELEX written frequency of 195.90 per million (SD = 52.92, range = 119.10–329.70), while the low-frequency words had a mean of 7.45 per million (SD = 2.69, range = 1.99–15.96) (Baayen, Piepenbrock, & van Rijn, 1995). All target words were 5–7 letters in length (high frequency length: M = 6.00, SD = 0.82; low frequency length: M = 5.98, SD = 0.83). Related primes were the same as the target words, while control primes were completely different, unrelated words (i.e., *result-RESULT* vs. *slowly-RESULT*). At each prime duration (33 ms, 67 ms), there were 12 related and 12 control items for each of the high- and low-frequency word types. Ninety-six (96) length-matched, orthographically legal nonwords (e.g., *POOST*) served as distractors. Just as for the word targets, half of these nonwords were preceded by 33 ms primes, while the other half were preceded by 67 ms primes.

E/a-detection task. Eighty-four (84) *e-words*, or words that contained the letter 'e' but not the letter 'a' (e.g., *behind*), and 84 *a-words*, or words that contained the letter 'a' but not the letter 'e' (e.g., *adjust*), were selected as targets. All of the target words were six letters in length, and the position of the critical letter ('e', 'a') varied across words. There were 7 different target durations, and at each of these display durations, there were 12 e-words and 12 a-words.

Four counterbalanced lists of items were created. For the LDT, high- and low-frequency targets appeared under each combination of the prime duration (33 ms, 67 ms) and prime type (related, control) conditions across lists. For the e/a-detection task, targets in the four shortest display durations (33 ms, 50 ms, 67 ms, and 83 ms) were presented under each of these durations across lists.

Procedure

Stimulus presentation and data collection were conducted using DMDX software (version 4.0.4.8). All stimuli were displayed in the center of the screen on an LCD monitor, in black, bold 12-point Courier New font against a white background.

Lexical decision task. For the LDT, each trial consisted of a forward mask (a row of hash marks #######) for 500 ms, immediately followed by a prime for either 33 ms or 67 ms and a target for 500 ms. Primes were presented in lower case, and targets were presented in upper case. Participants were asked to decide whether each target letter string was a real word or a nonword as quickly and as accurately as possible. They pressed the right Ctrl key if the target string was a word and the left Ctrl key if it was not a word.[6] After each trial, participants were given feedback on the speed and accuracy of their response. Items were presented in a different random order for each participant, in blocks of 32. At the beginning of the task, participants were given 12 practice trials.

E/a-detection task. The LDT was followed after a short break by the e/a-detection task. For this task, each trial consisted of a forward mask (a row of hash marks ######) for 500 ms, immediately followed by a target for one of seven display durations – 33 ms, 50 ms, 67 ms, 83 ms, 100 ms, 150 ms, or 200 ms – and a backward mask for 500 ms. The backward masks were 6-letter words that did not contain an 'a' or an 'e' (e.g., *COURTS*). Targets were presented in lower case, and backward masks were presented in upper case. Participants were asked to decide whether each target word contained the letter 'e' or the letter 'a' as accurately as possible. They pressed the right Ctrl key if the target contained an 'e' and the left Ctrl key if the target included an 'a'. After each trial, participants were given feedback on the accuracy of their response. Items were presented in a different random order for each participant, in blocks of 24. At the beginning of the task, participants were again given 12 practice trials.

Results

No participant in the experiment had an overall error rate of over 20% on the LDT (M = 8.25%, SD = 4.80). The data from all participants were therefore included in the analyses reported below.

Lexical decision task. Reaction times (RTs) for items on which the participant made an error were not included in the RT analyses. Items with RTs shorter than 300 ms and longer than 1500 ms were also discarded, and outlier data points were adjusted to two SD units above and below the mean for each participant. These trimming procedures affected 5.77% of the data. The mean RT and error rate (ER) for each condition are shown in Table 1.

Table 1. Mean reaction times (RTs) and percentage error rates (ERs) for the lexical decision task in Experiment 1 (labDMDX).

	33 ms prime duration				67 ms prime duration			
	HF		LF		HF		LF	
	RT	ER	RT	ER	RT	ER	RT	ER
Related	546	4.4	591	12.0	520	3.9	562	7.6
Unrelated	569	4.9	610	17.4	563	4.9	612	13.5
Priming	23**	0.5	19^	5.4	43***	1.0	50***	5.9*

*** $p < .001$ ** $p < .01$ * $p < .05$ ^ $p = .07$

The primary analyses of the RT data consisted of 2x2x2x4 ANOVAs for both subjects (*F*1) and items (*F*2), with prime duration (33 ms, 67 ms), word frequency (high, low), and prime type (related, unrelated) as predictor variables and list as a grouping factor. These analyses revealed robust main effects of prime duration ($F1(1,28) = 13.69, p < .001, F2(1,88) = 13.24, p < .001$), word frequency ($F1(1,28) = 89.18, p < .001, F2(1,88) = 44.85, p < .001$), and prime type ($F1(1,28) = 87.34, p < .001, F2(1,88) = 77.71, p < .001$) as well as a significant interaction of prime duration and prime type ($F1(1,28) = 9.22, p < .01, F2(1,88) = 8.61, p < .005$; all other interactions: *F*'s < 1). These results thus indicate a standard frequency effect – that is, high-frequency words were responded to more quickly than low-frequency words. They also show repetition priming effects regardless of word frequency at both the 33 ms and 67 ms prime durations, with greater priming at the longer prime duration.

In order to investigate the interaction of prime duration and prime type in more detail, 2x2x4 ANOVAs were conducted by subjects and items at each prime duration, with word frequency (high, low) and prime type (related, unrelated) as predictor variables and list as a grouping factor. At the 33 ms prime duration, there were significant main effects of word frequency ($F1(1,28) = 45.40, p < .001, F2(1,88) = 31.13, p < .001$) and prime type ($F1(1,28) = 11.94, p < .005, F2(1,88) = 18.16, p < .001$), but no interaction between these factors (both *F*'s < 1). At the 67 ms prime duration, the main effects of word frequency ($F1(1,28) = 57.97, p < .001, F2(1,88) = 31.00, p < .001$) and prime type ($F1(1,28) = 90.82, p < .001, F2(1,88) = 67.52, p < .001$) were statistically reliable, and there was again no interaction between these factors (both *F*'s < 1). The findings at each prime duration therefore show standard frequency effects and priming for both high- and low-frequency words.

Finally, at the 33 ms prime duration, tests of the simple effect of prime type revealed statistically reliable repetition priming for high-frequency words ($F1(1,28) = 15.07, p < .001, F2(1,44) = 12.17, p < .005$) and marginal priming for low-frequency words ($F1(1,28) = 3.58, p = .07, F2(1,44) = 7.38, p < .01$). At the 67 ms prime duration, there was robust repetition priming for both high-frequency ($F1(1,28) = 33.31, p < .001$, $\mathrm{F}2(1,44) = 43.69, p < .001$) and low-frequency words ($F1(1,28) = 65.37, p < .001, F2(1,44) = 29.90, p < .001$).

The primary ER analyses followed the ANOVA procedures detailed above. Under these analyses, there were significant main effects of prime duration ($F1(1,28) = 5.58, p < .05, F2(1,88) = 4.31, p < .05$), word frequency ($F1(1,28) = 52.71$, $\mathrm{p} < .001$, $F2(1,88) = 25.09, p < .001$), and prime type ($F1(1,28) = 9.82, p < .005, F2(1,88) = 5.51, p < .05$) as well as a marginally significant interaction of word frequency and prime type ($F1(1,28) = 5.09, p < .05, F2(1,88) = 3.18, p = .08$; word frequency x prime duration: $F1 = 2.81, F2 = 3.35, p = .07$; all other interactions: *F*'s < 1). These results again indicate a standard frequency effect, with high-frequency words responded to more accurately than low-frequency words. They also show repetition priming at both the 33 ms and 67 ms prime durations, with greater priming for low-frequency words at each duration.

To further investigate these effects, 2x2x4 ANOVAs were conducted by subjects and items at each prime duration, with word frequency (high, low) and prime type (related, unrelated) as predictor variables and list as a grouping factor. At the 33 ms prime duration, there was a significant effect of word frequency ($F1(1,28) = 46.79$, $p < .001$, $F2(1,88) = 21.11$, $p < .001$) and a marginal effect of prime type ($F1(1,28) = 5.36$, $p < .05$, $F2(1,88) = 2.87$, $p = .09$). And although the interaction between these factors was not significant ($F1 = 3.04$, $p = .09$, $F2 = 1.96$), tests of the simple effect of prime type at this prime duration revealed a marginal priming effect only for low-frequency words (high frequency: both F's < 1; low frequency: $F1(1,28) = 5.05$, $p < .05$, $F2(1,44) = 2.78$, $p = .10$). Comparably, at the 67 ms prime duration, the main effects of word frequency ($F1(1,28) = 12.30$, $p < .005$, $F2(1,88) = 13.81$, $p < .001$) and prime type ($F1(1,28) = 4.74$, $p < .05$, $F2(1,88) = 4.87$, $p < .05$) were significant, but the interaction between these factors was not ($F1 = 2.88$, $F2 = 2.41$). However, tests of the simple effect of prime type at this prime duration again revealed a priming effect only for low-frequency words (high frequency: both F's < 1; low frequency: $F1(1,28) = 5.55$, $p < .05$, $F2(1,44) = 4.49$, $p < .05$).

E/a-detection task. Figure 2 shows the mean ER at each display duration in the e/a-detection task. The ER at 33 ms ($M = 0.46$, $SD = 0.10$) was just slightly, yet statistically-reliably lower than chance ($t(31) = 2.37$, $p < .05$), with an essentially linear decrease in ERs as display durations increased.

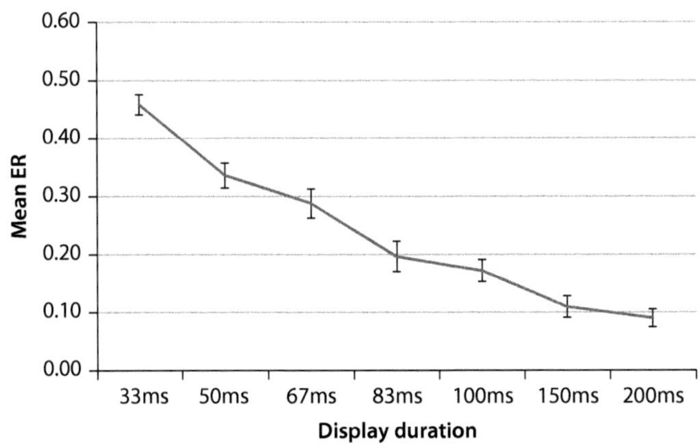

Figure 2. Mean error rate (ER) and standard error bar at each display duration for the e/a-detection task in Experiment 1.

Discussion

The results of this experiment provide essential baseline data for the webDMDX experiments to follow (Experiments 2 and 3). In the LDT, the RT results revealed (i) a robust frequency effect, with high-frequency words responded to more quickly than low-frequency words, (ii) repetition priming effects for high- and low-frequency words at both the 33 ms and 67 ms prime durations, and (iii) greater priming at 67 ms than at 33 ms. The weaker priming effect at the 33 ms prime duration was particularly evident for low-frequency words. Simple comparisons revealed only a marginal priming effect for low-frequency words at this duration. The ER results also showed (i) a clear frequency effect, with high-frequency words responded to more accurately than low-frequency words, and (ii) repetition priming effects for low-frequency targets at both the 33 ms and 67 ms prime durations – an effect that was marginal at the shorter of these prime durations. With respect to the RT results, it is also important to note that the magnitude of the priming effect did not exceed the prime duration in any condition. This is important because if primes were regularly displayed for longer than the time specified in the .rtf input file, priming effects that are much longer than the prime duration might be obtained. Finally, the results of the e/a-detection task revealed clear increases in response accuracy as a function of display duration.

Experiment 2 – WebDMDX with "known" hardware

In Experiment 2, the same LDT and e/a-detection task as in Experiment 1 were conducted, but this time using webDMDX. The experiment was run on the same testing computers as the previous experiment, but was deployed exactly as if it had been downloaded from the Internet. Specifically, the experiment was run from a self-extracting .zip file that contained a web-deployable version of DMDX (version 4.0.4.8), the .rtf input file, the data delivery program, and the .bat command file. The relevant display durations were coded using the following millisecond values: 33 ms as <%ms 33>, 50 ms as <%ms 50>, 67 ms as <%ms 66>, 83 ms as <%ms 83>, 100 ms as <%ms 100>, 150 ms as <%ms 150>, and 200 ms as <%ms 200>. This coding assumed a screen refresh rate of 60 Hz, which is consistent with the specifications of the testing computers and which is fairly standard for both desktop and laptop LCD screens, and was done by rounding down to the nearest integer millisecond value for each display duration. Note that this procedure meant that the 67 ms display duration was coded not as <%ms 67>, but as <%ms 66> (i.e., (1000 ms / 60 Hz) * 4 = 66.67 ms, rounded down to 66 ms). It was predicted that if the display timing in webDMDX matches that of labDMDX, the results of this LDT and e/a-detection task should overlap with those obtained in Experiment 1.

Method

Participants

Thirty-four (34) students at UTA participated in the experiment for course credit. All participants were native speakers of English.

Materials and design

The materials were exactly the same as in Experiment 1.

Procedure

The experiment followed the same procedures as in Experiment 1, except in this case, it was run using webDMDX (see above).

Results

The data from two participants with overall ERs of over 20% on the LDT were excluded from the analysis. For the remaining thirty-two (32) participants, the mean overall ER was 5.59% ($SD = 3.15$).

Lexical decision task. The analysis procedures followed those used for the LDT in Experiment 1. The same trimming procedures as in Experiment 1 were applied, affecting 4.77% of the RT data. The mean RT and ER for each condition are shown in Table 2.

As in Experiment 1, the primary analyses of the RT data consisted of 2x2x2x4 ANOVAs for both subjects ($F1$) and items ($F2$), with prime duration (33 ms, 67 ms), word frequency (high, low), and prime type (related, unrelated) as predictor variables and list as a grouping factor. These analyses revealed robust main effects of word frequency ($F1(1,28) = 157.68, p < .001$, $F2(1,88) = 42.37, p < .001$) and prime type ($F1(1,28) = 118.18, p < .001$, $F2(1,88) = 46.52, p < .001$), but not of prime duration ($F1 = 1.65$, $F2 < 1$). There was also a significant interaction of prime duration and prime type ($F1(1,28) = 6.54, p < .05$, $F2(1,88) = 8.72, p < .005$; word frequency x prime type interaction: $F1 = 4.41, p < .05$, $F2 = 1.56$; all other interactions: F's < 1). That is, as in Experiment 1, high-frequency words were responded to more quickly than low-frequency words, and there was repetition priming for both high- and low-frequency words at the 33 ms and 67 ms prime durations, with greater priming at the longer prime duration.

Table 2. Mean reaction times (RTs) and percentage error rates (ERs) for the lexical decision task in Experiment 2 (webDMDX).

	33 ms prime duration				67 ms prime duration			
	HF		LF		HF		LF	
	RT	ER	RT	ER	RT	ER	RT	ER
Related	564	2.6	601	6.3	546	1.3	577	6.5
Unrelated	582	2.9	628	11.5	589	1.8	636	13.8
Priming	18^	0.3	27*	5.2*	43***	0.5	59***	7.3**

*** $p < .001$ ** $p < .01$ * $p < .05$ ^ $p = .06$

In order to investigate the interaction of prime duration and prime type in more detail, 2x2x4 ANOVAs were conducted by subjects and items at each prime duration, with word frequency (high, low) and prime type (related, unrelated) as predictor variables and list as a grouping factor. At the 33 ms prime duration, there were significant main effects of word frequency ($F1(1,28) = 71.15, p < .001$, $F2(1,88) = 24.53, p < .001$) and prime type ($F1(1,28) = 12.22, p < .005, F2(1,88) = 9.76, p < .005$), but no interaction between these factors (both *F*'s < 1). At the 67 ms prime duration, the main effects of word frequency ($F1(1,28) = 46.45$, $p < .001$, $F2(1,88) = 26.48, p < .001$) and prime type ($F1(1,28) = 54.73, p < .001$, $F2(1,88) = 37.40, p < .001$) were statistically reliable, but there was again no interaction between these factors ($F1 = 3.14, p = .09, F2 = 1.25$). The findings at each prime duration therefore again reveal standard frequency effects and priming for both high- and low-frequency words.

Finally, at the 33 ms prime duration, tests of the simple effect of prime type revealed marginal repetition priming for high-frequency words ($F1(1,28) = 4.54$, $p < .05$, $F2(1,44) = 3.60, p = .06$) and statistically reliable priming for low-frequency words ($F1(1,28) = 7.38, p < .05, F2(1,44) = 6.23, p < .05$). At the 67 ms prime duration, there was robust repetition priming for both high-frequency ($F1(1,28) = 32.14, p < .001, F2(1,44) = 18.67, p < .001$) and low-frequency words ($F1(1,28) = 42.95, p < .001, F2(1,44) = 19.66, p < .001$).

The primary ER analyses followed the ANOVA procedures detailed above. Under these analyses, there were significant main effects of word frequency ($F1(1,28) = 93.99, p < .001, F2(1,88) = 21.07, p < .001$) and prime type ($F1(1,28) = 15.39, p < .001, F2(1,88) = 8.25, p < .01$) as well as a significant interaction of word frequency and prime type ($F1(1,28) = 29.35, p < .001, F2(1,88) = 6.43, p < .05$; word frequency x prime duration: $F1 = 1.40, F2 = 2.99, p = .09$; all other effects: *F*'s < 1). As in Experiment 1, these ER results show a standard frequency effect, with high-frequency words responded to more accurately than low-frequency words, and repetition priming at both the 33 ms and 67 ms prime durations, with greater priming for low-frequency words at each duration.

To further investigate these effects, 2x2x4 ANOVAs were conducted by subjects and items at each prime duration, with word frequency (high, low) and prime type (related, unrelated) as predictor variables and list as a grouping factor. At the 33 ms prime duration, there was a significant main effect of word frequency ($F1(1,28) = 31.75$, $p < .001$, $F2(1,88) = 13.03$, $p < .001$), a marginal effect of prime type ($F1(1,28) = 5.41$, $p < .05$, $F2(1,88) = 3.78$, $p = .06$), and a marginal interaction between these factors ($F1(1,28) = 10.94$, $p < .01$, $F2(1,88) = 3.09$, $p = .08$). Tests of the simple effect of prime type at this prime duration revealed a priming effect only for low-frequency words (high frequency: both *F*'s < 1; low frequency: $F1(1,28) = 11.20$, $p < .01$, $F2(1,44) = 4.07$, $p < .05$). Comparably, at the 67 ms prime duration, there were significant main effects of word frequency ($F1(1,28) = 34.11$, $p < .001$, $F2(1,88) = 22.48$, $p < .001$) and prime type ($F1(1,28) = 12.26$, $p < .005$, $F2(1,88) = 8.84$, $p < .005$) and a significant interaction of these factors ($F1(1,28) = 11.21$, $p < .005$, $F2(1,88) = 6.64$, $p < .05$). Tests of the simple effect of prime type at this prime duration again revealed a priming effect only for low-frequency words (high frequency: both *F*'s < 1; low frequency: $F1(1,28) = 12.88$, $p < .005$, $F2(1,44) = 8.64$, $p < .01$).

E/a-detection task. Figure 3 shows the mean ERs at each display duration for the e/a-detection tasks in Experiments 1 and 2. These data were analyzed using a 2x7x4 ANOVA with experiment type (labDMDX, webDMDX) and display duration as predictor variables and list as a grouping factor. This analysis revealed a significant main effect of display duration ($F(6,336) = 152.66$, $p < .001$), with ER decreasing as a function of increasing display durations, but no statistically reliable effect of experiment type ($F(1,56) = 1.54$, $p = .22$). There was, however, a significant interaction of these factors ($F(6,336) = 2.28$, $p < .05$), indicating that detection rates differed between the two experiments at specific display durations. And indeed planned comparisons at each display duration showed a significant difference between the experiments at 50 ms ($F(1,56) = 9.01$, $p < .01$; 67 ms: $F = 2.17$, $p = .15$; 100 ms: $F = 2.53$, $p = .12$; all other *F*'s < 1.2), with fewer errors made in the webDMDX experiment (Experiment 2: $M = 0.25$, $SD = 0.11$) than in the labDMDX experiment (Experiment 1: $M = 0.34$, $SD = 0.12$).

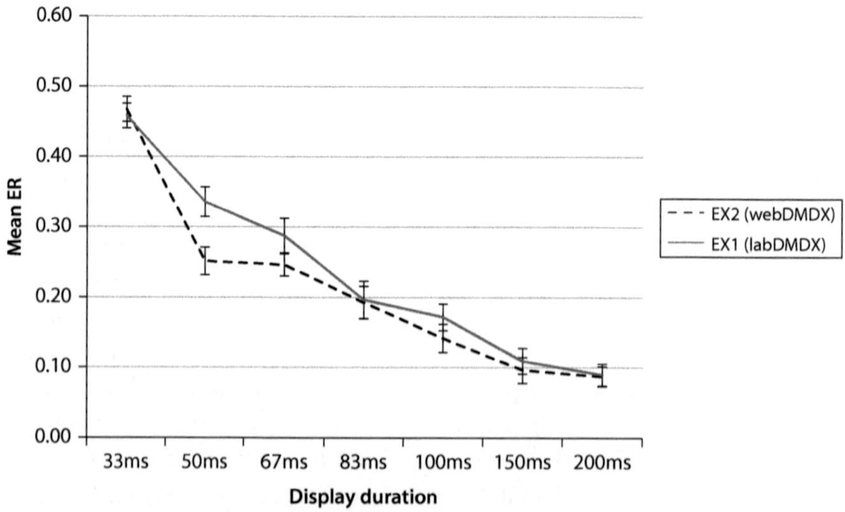

Figure 3. Mean error rates (ERs) and standard error bars at each display duration for the e/a-detection tasks in Experiment 1 (EX1) and Experiment 2 (EX2).

Discussion

The results of this webDMDX experiment match well with those of the labDMDX baseline experiment, Experiment 1. In the LDT, as in the previous experiment, the RT results revealed (i) a robust frequency effect, with high-frequency words responded to faster than low-frequency words, (ii) repetition priming effects for high- and low-frequency words at both prime durations, and (iii) greater priming at 67 ms than at 33 ms. The weaker priming effect at the 33 ms prime duration was particularly evident for high-frequency words. Indeed, simple comparisons revealed only a marginal priming effect for high-frequency words at this duration. This contrasts with Experiment 1, in which marginal priming at this duration was obtained for low-frequency words. Importantly for the purposes of the present study, this minor disparity in the RT results from Experiments 1 and 2 cannot be straightforwardly attributed to display timing differences between the two experiments. Moreover, again as in the previous experiment, the ER results in the LDT yielded (i) a clear frequency effect, with high-frequency words responded to more accurately than low-frequency words, and (ii) repetition priming effects for low-frequency targets at both the 33 ms and 67 ms prime durations. It is important to note that as in Experiment 1, the magnitude of the RT priming effect did not exceed the prime duration under any condition. This can be taken to suggest that the primes in this experiment were not regularly displayed for longer than the duration specified in the .rtf input file.

As an additional check on the degree of overlap between the LDT results of Experiments 1 and 2, 2x2x2x2x4 ANOVAs were conducted by subjects ($F1$) and items ($F2$) on both the RT and ER data, with experiment type (labDMDX, webDMDX), prime duration (33 ms, 67 ms), word frequency (high, low), and prime type (related, unrelated) as predictor variables and list as a grouping factor. In the RT analysis, there were no statistically reliable interactions of experiment type with any of the other predictor variables or combinations thereof (experiment type x prime duration: $F2 = 3.39$, $p = .07$; all other F's < 1.75). In the ER analysis, although there was a statistically reliable experiment type x word frequency x prime duration interaction ($F1(1,56) = 4.14$, $p < .05$, $F2(1,88) = 5.58$, $p < .05$), experiment type did not interact significantly with any of other predictor variables or combinations thereof (experiment type x prime duration: $F1 = 2.85$, $p = .10$, $F2 = 2.85$, $p = .10$; all other F's < 1). While the significant three-way interaction noted above indicates that there was not perfect overlap between the ER results in these experiments, it is crucially the case that experiment type did not interact reliably with prime type (in a two-way interaction) or with prime type and any of the other predictor variables (in a three-way or four-way interaction).

The results of the e/a-detection task were also very similar in Experiments 1 and 2. However, there was a significant ER difference between the experiments at the 50 ms display duration. This difference is particularly troubling in light of the fact that in Experiment 2, the ER at 50 ms ($M = 0.25$, $SD = 0.11$) was essentially the same as the ER at 67 ms ($M = 0.25$, $SD = 0.09$). This would appear to indicate that the 50 ms targets were actually presented for 67 ms, or for one refresh interval (16.67 ms) longer than expected. In fact, this is is exactly what happened. After the experiment was completed, it was discovered that there was a problem in the keyword coding used in the .rtf input file for the webDMDX experiment. Recall that in Experiment 1, the 50 ms display duration was coded as `<% 3>`, which means that these stimuli were presented for three refresh intervals. On the testing computers, all of which had 60 Hz LCD monitors, three refresh intervals adds up to a display duration of exactly 50 ms ((1000 ms / 60 Hz) * 3 = 50.00 ms). In Experiment 2, the coding for this display duration was `<%ms 50>` – a keyword with a millisecond value that equaled the desired display duration. It is important to note, however, that the millisecond values in the keywords for the other tachistoscopic displays – `<%ms 33>`, `<%ms 66>`, and `<%ms 83>` – were just slightly less than the desired display durations. That is, the keywords `<%ms 33>`, `<%ms 66>`, and `<%ms 83>` were not meant to code exactly these values, but rather 33.33 ms, 66.67 ms, and 83.33 ms, respectively. This difference is important because in the version of DMDX used for this experiment (version 4.0.4.8), the number of refresh intervals that gives the closest approximation to the requested millisecond display duration is computed by dividing the requested number of milliseconds plus an additional refresh interval by the refresh interval itself (i.e., the number of refresh intervals in the display = (the requested time + the refresh interval) / the refresh interval)), with the result truncated down to the nearest integer value. The addition of the refresh interval to the requested time is meant to ensure that the millisecond request is "rounded up" to the next closest display duration, or, in other words, that a request for 33 ms will yield a 33.33 ms display, not a 16.67 ms display (on a 60 Hz monitor). And for the <%ms 33>, <%ms 66>, and <%ms 83> millisecond requests, this method of approximating the number of refresh intervals for the display yields the desired values (i.e., (33 ms + (1000 ms / 60 Hz)) / (1000 ms / 60 Hz) = 2.98 refresh intervals (truncated to 2 refresh intervals); (66 ms + (1000 ms / 60 Hz))/ (1000 ms / 60 Hz) = 4.96 refresh intervals (truncated to 4 refresh intervals); (83 ms + (1000 ms / 60 Hz)) / (1000 ms / 60 Hz) = 5.98 refresh intervals (truncated to 5 refresh intervals)). But in the case of the <%ms 50> keyword, where the millisecond request was exactly equal to the desired display duration, this method yields a value that is one refresh interval greater than expected (i.e., (50 ms + (1000 ms / 60 Hz))/ (1000 ms / 60 Hz) = 4.00 refresh intervals (truncated to 4 refresh intervals)).

In order to verify that the disparity in the e/a-detection results was due to this coding problem, an additional experiment ($N = 32$) was run with corrected code. The procedures were the same as in Experiment 2, except that only the e/a-detection task was conducted. The display durations for the target words were coded using the following millisecond values: 33 ms as <%ms 33>, 50 ms as <%ms 48>, 67 ms as <%ms 66>, 83 ms as <%ms 83>, 100 ms as <%ms 100>, 150 ms as <%ms 150>, and 200 ms as <%ms 200>. These values were exactly the same as in Experiment 2, except for the coding of the 50 ms display duration. In order to address the coding problem noted above, this duration was coded with a value that was two milliseconds less than the desired display time. The mean ERs at each display duration for the e/a-detection tasks in Experiments 1 and this follow-up experiment are shown in Figure 4. A 2x7x4 ANOVA with experiment type (labDMDX, webDMDX) and display duration as predictor variables and list as a grouping factor revealed only a significant main effect of display duration ($F(6,336) = 125.97$, $p < .001$), with ERs decreasing with increasing display durations (both other F's < 1). Planned comparisons did not show statistically reliable ER differences between the experiments at any display duration (all F's < 1.4).

In order to investigate the disparity between the e/a-detection results of Experiments 1 and 2 in more detail, the emit option was added to the <%ms N> keywords for Experiment 2 and its follow-up. When this option is used (e.g., <%ms 33 emit>), DMDX (versions 4.0.6.0 and later) reports its computation for the display duration in the output file. Specifically, it outputs the number of refresh intervals (of a specific duration) that it used to approximate the millisec-

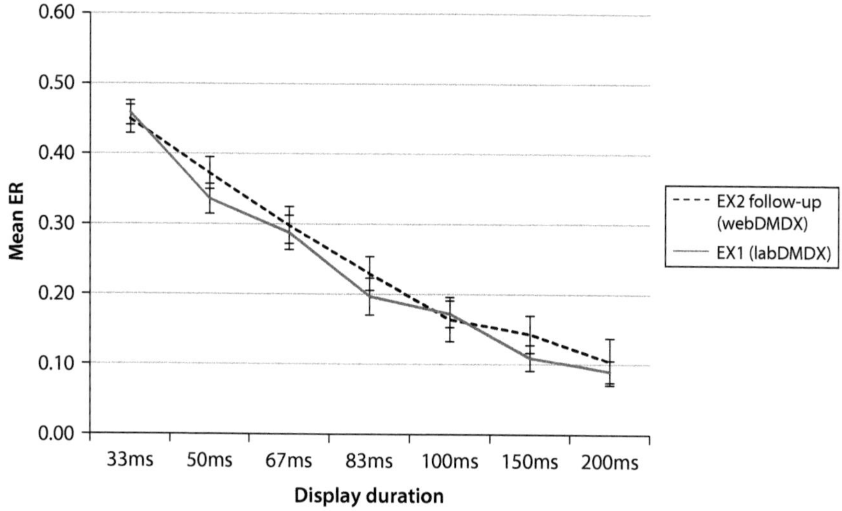

Figure 4. Mean error rates (ERs) and standard error bars at each display duration for the e/a-detection tasks in Experiment 1 (EX1) and the follow-up to Experiment 2 (EX2 follow-up).

ond keyword request. When this keyword was applied to the e/a-detection task in Experiment 2, the number of refresh intervals (again, 16.67 ms) reported for each millisecond request was as follows:

<%ms 33> → 2 refresh intervals
<%ms 50> → 4 refresh intervals
<%ms 66> → 4 refresh intervals
<%ms 83> → 5 refresh intervals
<%ms 100> → 7 refresh intervals
<%ms 150> → 9 refresh intervals
<%ms 200> → 12 refresh intervals.

The follow-up experiment, however, yielded these values:

<%ms 33> → 2 refresh intervals
<%ms 48> → 3 refresh intervals
<%ms 66> → 4 refresh intervals
<%ms 83> → 5 refresh intervals
<%ms 100> → 7 refresh intervals
<%ms 150> → 9 refresh intervals
<%ms 200> → 12 refresh intervals.

As can be seen above, when the 50 ms display duration was coded as <%ms 50>, it resulted in four refresh intervals (or 66.67 ms); however, when it was coded as <%ms 48>, it yielded the desired three refresh intervals (or 50 ms). It is also interesting to note that in both Experiment 2 and its follow-up, seven refresh intervals were used for the 100 ms display duration, not six as in the Experiment 1. This means that for this display duration, the stimuli in the webDMDX experiments were actually presented for 116.67 ms. Despite this disparity, the e/a-detection tasks yielded no detection rate differences at this display duration in the labDMDX and webDMDX versions of the experiment.

Experiment 3 – WebDMDX with "unknown" hardware

In Experiment 3, the same LDT and e/a-detection task as in Experiments 1 and 2 were conducted, but this time by running webDMDX on the computer of the participant's choice. That is, unlike in Experiment 2 (and its follow-up experiment), which used lab testing units, this experiment was conducted on "unknown" hardware. This is an important test because it corresponds more closely to the way that webDMDX will likely be used by researchers. Of interest again was whether the behavioral results on both tasks in this experiment would be comparable to those obtained in the labDMDX experiment, Experiment 1.

It is also important to note that for this experiment, a different version of DMDX was used – version 4.2.0.1. For this version of the program, partly in response to the problem that Experiment 2 revealed with respect to coding display durations in terms of millisecond keywords (<%ms N>), the millisecond-to-retrace code was adjusted. As detailed above, in earlier versions of DMDX and in the version used for Experiment 2 (version 4.0.4.8), the number of refresh intervals for a requested millisecond display duration is calculated as follows (with the result truncated down to the nearest integer value):

# of refresh intervals in the display =
(the requested time + the refresh interval) / the refresh interval

As of version 4.2.0.1, however, this value is computed in the following way (again, with the result truncated down to the nearest integer value):

# of refresh intervals in the display =
(the requested time + the refresh interval/2) / the refresh interval

The key difference between these codes is that in earlier versions of DMDX, a full refresh interval is added to the requested time in order to "round up" to the next nearest display duration. As of DMDX version 4.2.0.1, however, only half of the refresh interval is used for this rounding procedure. The importance of this change can be seen when considering the <%ms 50> keyword that was problematic in Experiment 2. As illustrated above, for this keyword, the millisecond-to-retrace code in earlier versions of DMDX yields a display duration that is one full refresh interval longer than expected. More specifically, assuming a testing computer with a 60 Hz monitor, the number of refresh cycles in the display would be calculated as (50 ms + (1000 ms / 60 Hz)) / (1000 ms / 60 Hz), which equals 4.00 refresh intervals (truncated to 4) and thus a display duration of 67 ms. Under the millisecond-to-retrace code in version 4.2.0.1, however, this value would be computed as (50 ms + (1000 ms / 60 Hz) / 2) / (1000 ms / 60 Hz), which equals 3.5 refresh intervals (truncated to 3) and thus the desired display duration of 50 ms.

This adjustment to the millisecond-to-retrace calculation meant that the relevant display durations could be coded with the same keywords as in Experiment 2 – 33 ms as <%ms 33>, 50 ms as <%ms 50>, 67 ms as <%ms 66>, 83 ms as <%ms 83>, 100 ms as <%ms 100>, 150 ms as <%ms 150>, and 200 ms as <%ms 200> – with no change to the keyword for the 50 ms display duration. This coding again assumed a screen refresh rate of 60 Hz, which is consistent with the specifications of most current desktop and laptop LCD monitors. As an additional check on whether this coding would yield the desired display durations, the emit option was included in each of the millisecond keywords (e.g., <%ms 33 emit>).

Method

Participants
Forty-four (44) participants took part in the experiment.

Materials and design
The materials were exactly the same as in Experiments 1 and 2.

Procedure
The procedures for the experimental tasks were the same as in Experiments 1 and 2. In this case, however, the experimental session was run using webDMDX on a computer of the participant's choice (see above). This was done as follows: A link to the informed consent document for the experiment was placed on the UTA Psycholinguistics Lab website. The participant clicked on a link at the bottom of this document to agree to continue with the experiment. The participant then answered the following language screening question: *Is English your first (or*

native) language? YES NO. Participants who clicked 'YES' in answer to this question were routed to a page with instructions and a link to the experiment; participants who selected 'NO' were routed to a different page, which included the same instructions and a link to the experiment under a different .zip/.rtf file name. This was done in order to ensure that the datasets analyzed for Experiment 3 contained data only from participants who self-identified as English native speakers (as was the case for Experiments 1 and 2). The participant then read a short set of instructions on how to download and run the experiment as well as on how to complete the experimental tasks. (Instructions were also provided before each task during the experiment.) A link to a self-extracting .zip file appeared at the end of these directions, which the participant clicked on to download and run the experiment. Each of the four experimental lists was packaged as its own self-extracting .zip file. The experimenters regularly changed the .zip file referenced by the link so that participants were randomly assigned to lists.

Results

Seven (7) participants indicated that English was not their first (or native) language. As discussed above, datasets for these participants were collected under a different file name from the native-speaker datasets. The data from these non-native-speaker participants were not analyzed. Thirty-seven (37) participants identified themselves as native speakers of English. Four (4) of these participants had overall ERs of over 20% on the LDT and were excluded from the analysis. Another participant's dataset was removed from the analysis because the output indicated display errors on nearly every trial. These errors meant that display frames during the experiment – including those for the primes in the LDT and targets in e/a-detection – were presented for 0.16–10.94 ms longer than anticipated. For the thirty-two (32) participants included in the analyses reported below, the mean overall ER on the LDT was 8.34% (SD = 4.30).

As expected, most of the testing units used by these participants (25 out of 32) had refresh rates of 60 Hz. (DMDX reports this information, along with screen resolution specifications, at the beginning of each output file.) Seven participants (list A: 1, list B: 3, list C: 0, list D: 3), however, used computers with 59 Hz monitors. The standard refresh interval for computers with 59 Hz and 60 Hz screens are 16.95 ms and 16.67 ms, respectively. In the LDT, this difference amounts to a .57 ms disparity at the shorter prime duration (33.90 ms vs. 33.33 ms) and a 1.13 ms disparity at the longer prime duration (67.80 ms vs. 66.67 ms). In the e/a-detection task, this difference amounts to a disparity of less than 1.5 ms at the four shortest display durations. These slight timing differences did not warrant

Table 3. Mean reaction times (RTs) and percentage error rates (ERs) for the lexical decision task in Experiment 3 (webDMDX).

	33 ms prime duration				67 ms prime duration			
	HF		LF		HF		LF	
	RT	ER	RT	ER	RT	ER	RT	ER
Related	537	4.7	577	11.7	513	4.7	545	8.9
Unrelated	559	5.2	614	16.7	553	4.7	614	15.6
Priming	22**	0.5	37**	5.0	40***	0.0	69***	6.7*

*** $p < .001$ ** $p < .01$ * $p < .05$

exclusion of the datasets from the 59 Hz testing units. For all of these units, the refresh intervals reported by DMDX (again, by applying the `emit` option) were exactly as expected for all of the millisecond keyword requests:

`<%ms 33>` → 2 refresh intervals
`<%ms 50>` → 3 refresh intervals
`<%ms 66>` → 4 refresh intervals
`<%ms 83>` → 5 refresh intervals
`<%ms 100>` → 6 refresh intervals
`<%ms 150>` → 9 refresh intervals
`<%ms 200>` → 12 refresh intervals.

Lexical decision task. The analysis procedures followed those used for the LDT in Experiments 1 and 2. The same trimming procedures as in these previous experiments were applied, affecting 4.62% of the RT data. The mean RT and ER for each condition are shown in Table 3.

As in Experiments 1 and 2, the primary analyses of the RT data consisted of 2x2x2x4 ANOVAs for both subjects (*F*1) and items (*F*2), with prime duration (33 ms, 67 ms), word frequency (high, low), and prime type (related, unrelated) as predictor variables and list as a grouping factor. These analyses revealed robust main effects of prime duration ($F1(1,28) = 18.02$, $p < .001$, $F2(1,88) = 17.60$, $p < .001$), word frequency ($F1(1,28) = 67.74$, $p < .001$, $F2(1,88) = 60.00$, $p < .001$), and prime type ($F1(1,28) = 76.72$, $p < .001$, $F2(1,88) = 68.76$, $p < .001$). There were also significant interactions of prime duration and prime type ($F1(1,28) = 15.82$, $p < .001$, $F2(1,88) = 11.29$, $p < .005$) as well as of word frequency and prime type ($F1(1,28) = 12.35$, $p < .005$, $F2(1,88) = 4.21$, $p < .05$; prime duration x word frequency: both *F*'s < 1; prime duration x word frequency x prime type interaction: $F1 = 1.68$, $F2 = 1.18$). That is, as in Experiments 1 and 2, high-frequency words were responded to more quickly than low-frequency words, and there was repetition priming for both high- and low-frequency words at the 33 ms and 67 ms prime durations, with greater priming at the longer prime duration. The interaction of word frequency and prime type further suggests that low-frequency words produced stronger priming effects than high-frequency words.

In order to investigate the significant 2-way interactions in more detail, 2x2x4 ANOVAs were conducted by subjects and items at each prime duration, with word frequency (high, low) and prime type (related, unrelated) as predictor variables and list as a grouping factor. At the 33 ms prime duration, there were significant main effects of word frequency ($F1(1,28) = 43.88, p < .001, F2(1,88) = 47.84, p < .001$) and prime type ($F1(1,28) = 33.71, p < .001, F2(1,88) = 17.19, p < .001$), but no interaction between these factors ($F1 = 2.58, F2 < 1$). At the 67 ms prime duration, there were significant main effects of word frequency ($F1(1,28) = 54.52, p < .001, F2(1,88) = 44.68, p < .001$) and prime type ($F1(1,28) = 73.76, p < .001, F2(1,88) = 75.43, p < .001$) as well as a statistically reliable interaction between these factors ($F1(1,28) = 13.86, p < .001, F2(1,88) = 5.36, p < .05$). The findings at each prime duration therefore again reveal standard frequency effects and priming for both high- and low-frequency words, with greater priming for low-frequency targets only at the 67 ms prime duration.

Finally, at the 33 ms prime duration, tests of the simple effect of prime type revealed repetition priming for both high-frequency ($F1(1,28) = 10.51, p < .005, F2(1,44) = 7.40, p < .01$) and low-frequency words ($F1(1,28) = 29.23, p < .001, F2(1,44) = 9.86, p < .005$). At the 67 ms prime duration, there was also robust repetition priming for both high-frequency ($F1(1,28) = 26.20, p < .001, F2(1,44) = 29.14, p < .001$) and low-frequency words ($F1(1,28) = 92.99, p < .001, F2(1,44) = 46.41, p < .001$).

The primary ER analyses followed the ANOVA procedures detailed above. Under these analyses, there were significant main effects of word frequency ($F1(1,28) = 85.34, p < .001, F2(1,88) = 28.71, p < .001$) and prime type ($F1(1,28) = 10.09, p < .005, F2(1,88) = 5.80, p < .05$) as well as a significant interaction of word frequency and prime type ($F1(1,28) = 12.88, p < .005, F2(1,88) = 4.85, p < .05$; prime duration: $F1 = 1.11, F2 = 1.54$; all other effects: F's < 1). As in Experiments 1 and 2, these ER results show a standard frequency effect, with high-frequency words responded to more accurately than low-frequency words, and repetition priming at both the 33 ms and 67 ms prime durations, with greater priming for low-frequency words at each duration.

To further investigate these effects, 2x2x4 ANOVAs were conducted by subjects and items at each prime duration, with word frequency (high, low) and prime type (related, unrelated) as predictor variables and list as a grouping factor. At the 33 ms prime duration, there was a significant main effect of word frequency ($F1(1,28) = 50.63, p < .001, F2(1,88) = 22.61, p < .001$) and a marginal effect of prime type ($F1(1,28) = 4.67, p < .05, F2(1,88) = 2.42, p = .13$). The interaction of these factors was not statistically reliable ($F1$ = 2.78, $F2$ = 1.58). Tests of the simple effect of prime type at this prime duration revealed a marginal priming effect only for low-frequency words (high frequency: both F's < 1; low frequency: $F1(1,28) = 4.85, p < .05, F2(1,44) = 2.52, p = .12$). Comparably, at the 67 ms prime duration, there was a significant main effect of word frequency ($F1(1,28) = 43.77, p < .001, F2(1,88) = 20.93, p < .001$), a marginal effect of prime type ($F1(1,28) = 4.16, p = .05, F2(1,88) = 5.00, p < .05$), and a significant interaction of these factors ($F1(1,28) = 7.33, p < .05, F2(1,88) = 5.00, p < .05$). Tests of the simple effect of prime type at this prime duration again revealed a priming effect only for low-frequency words (high frequency: both F's < 1; low frequency: $F1(1,28) = 7.28, p < .05, F2(1,44) = 6.42, p < .05$).

E/a-detection task. Figure 5 shows the mean ERs at each display duration for the e/a-detection tasks in Experiments 1 and 3. These data were analyzed using a 2x7x4 ANOVA with experiment type (labDMDX, webDMDX) and display duration as predictor variables and list as a grouping factor. This analysis revealed a significant main effect of display duration ($F(6,336) = 131.92, p < .001$), but no statistically reliable effect of experiment type ($F(1,56) = 2.56, p = .12$) or interaction of experiment type and display duration (F<1). These findings therefore indicate (i) that ERs decreased with increasing display durations and (ii) that these rates did not differ between the two experiments. Planned comparisons at each display duration, however, revealed a significant difference at 50 ms ($F(1,56)$ =

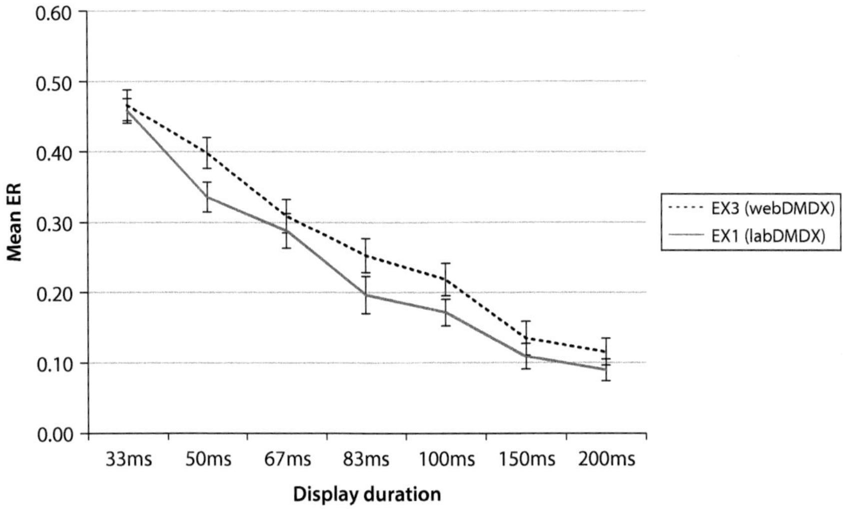

Figure 5. Mean error rates (ERs) and standard error bars at each display duration for the e/a-detection tasks in Experiment 1 (EX1) and Experiment 3 (EX3).

Table 4. Mean error rates as proportions (with standard deviations in parentheses) for the e/a-detection tasks in Experiments 1–3.

	Display duration						
	33ms	50ms	67ms	83ms	100ms	150ms	200ms
EX1 (labDMDX)	.46 (.10)	.34 (.12)	.29 (.14)	.20 (.15)	.17 (.11)	.11 (.10)	.09 (.09)
EX2 (webDMDX)	.47 (.10)	.25 (.11)	.25 (.09)	.19 (.13)	.14 (.11)	.10 (.10)	.09 (.08)
EX2 follow-up (webDMDX)	.45 (.12)	.37 (.13)	.30 (.15)	.23 (.14)	.16 (.18)	.14 (.15)	.10 (.19)
EX3 (webDMDX)	.47 (.12)	.40 (.12)	.31 (.13)	.25 (.14)	.22 (.13)	.14 (.14)	.12 (.11)

4.19, $p < .05$; 83 ms: $F = 2.66$, $p = .11$; 100 ms: $F = 2.53$, $p = .12$; all other F's < 1.1). It is important to note that unlike in Experiment 2, the ER at this display duration was higher than in the labDMDX baseline experiment (Experiment 1). (The mean ERs at each display duration for the e/a-detection tasks in all experiments are presented in Table 4.)

Discussion

The results of this webDMDX experiment, which in this case was run on "unknown" hardware, again match well with those of the labDMDX baseline experiment, Experiment 1. In the LDT, as in Experiment 1, the RT results revealed (i) a robust frequency effect, with high-frequency words responded to faster than low-frequency words, (ii) repetition priming effects for high- and low-frequency words at both prime durations, and (iii) greater priming at 67 ms than at 33 ms. In Experiment 1, the weaker priming at 33 ms was particularly evident for low-frequency words, which showed only marginal priming in the simple comparisons. In the present experiment, however, statistically reliable priming was obtained for both high- and low-frequency words in these tests. This minor disparity in the RT results is not likely attributable to display timing differences between the experiments (for further evidence in support of this argument, see the results of the ANOVA comparing the LDTs in the two experiments below), but rather to measurement error in the context of what will necessarily be a subtle (i.e., ~ 33 ms or less) priming effect. It is also important to note that the magnitude of the priming effect only slightly exceeded the prime duration for low-frequency targets – by ~ 4 ms under the 33 ms prime duration and by ~ 2 ms under the 67 ms prime duration. As discussed above, this can be taken to suggest that primes were not displayed for longer than the duration specified in the input file. Finally, the ER results in this LDT overlapped almost perfectly with those of Experiment 1. As in the labDMDX experiment, the present study showed (i) a clear frequency effect, with high-frequency words responded to more accurately than low-frequency words, and (ii) repetition priming effects for low-frequency targets at both the 33 ms and 67 ms prime durations – an effect that was marginal at the shorter of these durations.

As an additional check on the degree of overlap between the LDT results of Experiments 1 and 3, 2x2x2x2x4 ANOVAs were conducted by subjects (*F*1) and items (*F*2) on both the RT and ER data, with experiment type (labDMDX, web-DMDX), prime duration (33 ms, 67 ms), word frequency (high, low), and prime type (related, unrelated) as predictor variables and list as a grouping factor. In the RT analysis, there was a significant experiment type x word frequency x prime type interaction in the by-subjects analysis ($F1(1,56) = 5.13$, $p < .05$), but this was not statistically reliable by items ($F2 = 1.26$). There were no statistically reliable interactions of experiment type with any of the other predictor variables or combinations thereof (all *F*'s < 1.8). In the ER analysis, experiment type did not interact significantly with any of the predictor variables or combinations thereof (all *F*'s < 1). The lack of any reliable interactions of experiment type and prime type in these RT and ER analyses again suggests comparable display timing in the webDMDX and labDMDX experiments.

The results of the e/a-detection task were also very similar in Experiments 1 and 3. The main ANOVA did not reveal any significant ER differences between the experiments. And planned comparisons indicated an ER difference between them only at the 50 ms display duration. It is important to note that this disparity is quite different from the discrepancy at the 50 ms display duration in Experiments 1 and 2. First, in Experiment 2, the ER at 50 ms was lower than in Experiment 1. The present experiment, however, yielded a higher ER at this display duration. Furthermore, in Experiment 2, the ER at 50 ms ($M = 0.25$, $SD = 0.11$) was almost exactly the same as the ER at 67 ms ($M = 0.25$, $SD = 0.09$). In Experiment 3, however, the ER at 50 ms was reliably different ($M = 0.40$, $SD = 0.12$) from the ER at 67 ms ($M = 0.31$, $SD = 0.13$; $F(1,28) = 10.83$, $p < .005$) and was part of a clearly linear decline in ER across the four shortest display durations (.47 → .40 → .31 → .25). It seems therefore that the disparity at 50 ms in Experiments 1 and 3 is not due to a display timing difference between these experiments (as it was in Experiments 1 and 2). Rather, we would suggest that this difference is indicative of a more general performance disparity between the participants in these two experiments, with the participants in Experiment 1 generally outperforming the participants in Experiment 3 (though not reliably so, as indicated by the lack of a significant experiment type effect in the main ANOVA).

General discussion and conclusion

The present study shows clear overlap in the results from experiments involving tachistoscopic displays in both labDMDX (Experiment 1) and webDMDX (Experiments 2 and 3). These overlapping results were obtained despite several differences in the way that labDMDX and webDMDX are implemented, particularly in terms of how they determine refresh intervals and how they use these intervals to calculate display durations. Furthermore, these comparable findings were revealed when running the webDMDX experiments on "known" hardware (Experiment 2) as well as on "unknown" hardware (Experiment 3). The latter demonstration would seem to be particularly useful for researchers since webDMDX experiments will likely often be deployed over the Internet (following the procedures outlined above) so that participants can run them at their convenience, on Windows-compatible PCs of their choice.

Despite these overlapping findings, it is important to emphasize that webDMDX experiments should not be considered perfectly equivalent replacements for experiments run in the lab. Indeed, the lab offers a number of advantages that cannot be expected of other environments – including stable hardware with optimized audio-visual settings, input devices other than the keyboard, and a relatively quiet and distraction-free place to run experimental sessions. With respect to hardware issues, recall that one of the datasets in Experiment 3 was excluded from the analysis because there were display errors on nearly every item. This could have happened for a number of reasons, but one possibility is that the experiment was taken on an older PC with an outdated video card and/or driver. Since such units would not be used in the lab, this type of data loss would probably not occur in a labDMDX experiment. Some experiments might also require specific hardware settings, which poses a problem for webDMDX. For instance, in a study with auditory stimuli, the experimenter would want to ensure that the volume settings on the testing computer were appropriate for the sound files before the participant began the experimental session. This can be accomplished quite easily in the lab. However, a webDMDX experiment of this type would require carefully constructed directions for setting the volume appropriately and possibly also an "audio check" test in advance of the experiment. It is also important to note that webDMDX experiments are generally limited to using the keyboard as an input device. As discussed in the endnotes, this might not be ideal for experiments that are designed to test for especially subtle processing time differences – experiments for which millisecond response accuracy is absolutely required. For such experiments, it would be necessary to use a button box or game controller as the input device. A quiet, distraction-free environment might also be necessary for experimental tasks that are particularly cognitively demanding or that require focused concentration over a relatively long period of time. Such an environment can be created in the lab, but cannot be expected if participants are able to access the experiment at their convenience. Finally, although virtually any type of experimental stimulus can be presented with webDMDX, these experiments are relatively limited in terms of response options. For instance, experiments involving production tasks – such as naming or sentence-fragment completion – are currently not possible with webDMDX since the recorded responses would not be available to the researcher.

While it is important to recognize these limitations, the present study indicates that webDMDX can be used to examine language processing with a wide range of experimental methods. These include the masked priming methods of interest in this study, but also other time-sensitive experimental techniques, such as self-paced reading, speeded grammaticality judgment, and probe recognition, among many others that are commonly used in psycholinguistics and in experimental psychology generally. As importantly, webDMDX allows for data collection opportunities that might otherwise be unavailable to researchers. For example, this system could make it easier to investigate languages whose speakers are hard to find locally. It might also facilitate collaboration with researchers who have close ties to language communities of interest, but who might not have lab facilities or extensive experience with DMDX. WebDMDX could also be a useful tool for educators and educational researchers, as it could be used to run a number of different tests in classroom settings. In short, webDMDX offers a free and flexible way to conduct a wide variety of experiments over the Internet. And as indicated by the present study, this is possible even with methods that require brief and tightly controlled display durations.

Notes

1. It has been possible to run webDMDX experiments since DMDX version 4.0.4.0. However, for the reasons discussed in this paper, researchers are advised to use version 4.2.0.1 or later, and preferably the most recent distribution of the software.

2. Note that this self-extracting .zip file should be created such that it can be run by any user of the computer (not only by its administrator). This is possible with WinZip™ Self-Extractor and presumably with other compression programs as well. This specification allows participants to access and run the experiment even on computers that they do not own (e.g., units in university computer labs and libraries).

3. It is also possible to set up the .bat file for the experiment such that the data repository server will send an email notification to the researcher whenever it receives a full or partial dataset. For more on this option, see the DMDX remote testing help page: http://psy1.psych.arizona.edu/~jforster/dmdx/help/dmdxhremotetestingoverview.htm.

4. Currently, datasets are automatically removed from the data repository six months after their last update (i.e., six months after the data from the last participant has been collected on the experiment). Researchers can also manually remove their datasets from the repository following the directions provided at http://psy1.psych.arizona.edu/~jforster/dmdx/help/dmdxhremotetestingoverview.htm. It is of course beyond the scope of the current study to comment on whether these data storage and access procedures will be considered acceptable by all institutions and funding agencies. Researchers are advised to consult carefully with their Institutional Review Board (or equivalent) and funding programs to determine whether these procedures are appropriate. Note also that it is possible for researchers to set up their own server to receive webDMDX data. Requests for information about setting up such a system can be sent to J.C. Forster.

5. A useful analysis tool for many of these datasets is azk2csv.exe, which is available in the DMDXUTILS zip file (http://www.u.arizona.edu/~jforster/dmdx/). This application converts .azk output files into .csv files, a file type that can be opened in standard spreadsheet programs and imported into most statistical computing software packages quite easily.

6. It is generally not advisable to use a keyboard as the response device in experiments that test for subtle differences in reaction time (i.e., differences in milliseconds or tens of milliseconds). This is because keyboard keys are not polled with millisecond accuracy. For the purposes of this experiment, however, it was necessary to use the keyboard as the response device to allow for straightforward comparison with the subsequent webDMDX experiments and in particular with Experiment 3. In this final experiment, participants ran webDMDX on unknown hardware and may have only had access to the keyboard as an input device. Also, the Ctrl keys were used rather than the default Shift keys in order to avoid the "Sticky Keys" problem. Pressing either of the Shift keys several times in rapid succession causes the Sticky Keys shortcut activation window to pop up, which can disrupt DMDX.

References

Baayen, R.H., Piepenbrock, R., & van Rijn, H. (1995). *The CELEX lexical data base. Release 2* [CD-ROM]. Philadelphia, PA: Linguistic Data Consortium, University of Pennsylvania.

Carreiras, M., & Perea, M. (2002). Masked priming effects with syllabic neighbors in a lexical decision task. *Journal of Experimental Psychology: Human Perception and Performance*, 28, 1228–1242. DOI: 10.1037/0096-1523.28.5.1228

Finkbeiner, M., Forster, K.I., Nicol, J., & Nakamura, K. (2004). The role of polysemy in masked semantic and translation priming. *Journal of Memory and Language*, 51, 1–22. DOI: 10.1016/j.jml.2004.01.004

Forster, K.I., & Davis, C. (1984). Repetition priming and frequency attenuation in lexical access. *Journal of Experimental Psychology: Learning, Memory, and Cognition*, 10, 680–698. DOI: 10.1037/0278-7393.10.4.680

Forster, K.I., & Forster, J.C. (2003). DMDX: A Windows display program with millisecond accuracy. *Behavioral Research Methods: Instruments and Computers*, 35, 116–124. DOI: 10.3758/BF03195503

Forster, K. I., Mohan, K., & Hector, J. (2003). The mechanics of masked priming. In S. Kinoshita & S. J. Lupker (Eds.), *Masked priming: The state of the art* (pp. 223–238). Hove, England: Psychology Press.

Frost, R., Forster, K. I., & Deutsch, A. (1997). What can we learn from the morphology of Hebrew? A masked-priming investigation of morphological representation. *Journal of Experimental Psychology: Learning, Memory, and Cognition*, 23, 829–856. DOI: 10.1037/0278-7393.23.4.829

Gollan, T. H., Frost, R., & Forster, K. I. (1997). Translation priming with different scripts: Masked priming with cognates and noncognates in Hebrew-English bilinguals. *Journal of Experimental Psychology: Learning, Memory, and Cognition*, 23, 1122–1139. DOI: 10.1037/0278-7393.23.5.1122

Grainger, J., Colé, P., & Segui, J. (1991). Masked morphological priming in visual word recognition. *Journal of Memory and Language*, 30, 370–384. DOI: 10.1016/0749-596X(91)90042-I

Grainger, J., & Ferrand, L. (1996). Masked orthographic and phonological priming in visual word recognition and naming: Cross-task comparisons. *Journal of Memory and Language*,35, 623–647. DOI: 10.1006/jmla.1996.0033

Kim, J., & Davis, C. (2003). Task effects in masked cross-script translation and phonological priming. *Journal of Memory and Language*, 49, 484–499. DOI: 10.1016/S0749-596X(03)00093-7

Novick, J. M., Kim, A. & Trueswell, J. C. (2003). Studying the grammatical aspects of word recognition: Lexical priming, parsing, and syntactic ambiguity resolution. *Journal of Psycholinguistic Research*, 32, 57–75. DOI: 10.1023/A:1021985032200

Trueswell, J. C., & Kim, A. E. (1998). How to prune a garden path by nipping it in the bud: Fast priming of verb argument structure. *Journal of Memory and Language*, 39, 102–123. DOI: 10.1006/jmla.1998.2565

Learning is not decline

The mental lexicon as a window into cognition across the lifespan

Michael Ramscar,[i] Peter Hendrix,[i] Bradley Love[ii] and Harald Baayen[i]
[i] Eberhard Karls Universität Tübingen / [ii] University College London

As otherwise healthy adults age, their performance on cognitive tests tends to decline. This change is traditionally taken as evidence that cognitive processing is subject to significant declines in healthy aging. We examine this claim, showing current theories over-estimate the evidence in support of it, and demonstrating that when properly evaluated, the empirical record often indicates that the opposite is true.

To explain the disparity between the evidence and current theories, we show how the models of learning assumed in aging research are incapable of capturing even the most basic of empirical facts of "associative" learning, and lend themselves to spurious discoveries of "cognitive decline." Once a more accurate model of learning is introduced, we demonstrate that far from declining, the accuracy of older adults lexical processing appears to improve continuously across the lifespan. We further identify other measures on which performance does not decline with age, and show how these different patterns of performance fit within an overall framework of learning.

Finally, we consider the implications of our demonstrations of continuous and consistent learning performance throughout adulthood for our understanding of the changes in underlying brain morphology that occur during the course of cognitive development across the lifespan.

Learning is not decline: The mental lexicon as a window into cognition across the lifespan

As otherwise healthy adults age, their performance on cognitive tests tends to change. These performance changes have traditionally been taken as showing that the functionality of underlying cognitive processes is subject to significant declines

DOI 10.1075/bct.80.08ram

even in healthy aging (Deary et al., 2009; Salthouse, 2009, 2011; Singh-Manoux et al., 2012). However, in a recent article Ramscar et al. (2014) pointed out that it is impossible to determine whether cognitive processes actually decline across the lifespan in the absence of models of processing, and without an understanding of the way that learning changes the processing demands imposed on the cognitive system. In a series of case studies, Ramscar et al. showed that, over a range of cognitive tasks, once a proper measure of processing load is taken into account, the pattern of performance change typically seen across the lifespan can be accounted for without having to invoke "declines" in otherwise undefined "processes." Once learning processes were formally defined, the performance of older and younger adults on cognitive tests could be more straightforwardly modeled in terms of a set of relatively consistent capacities faced with processing loads of increasing size and complexity.

The central thesis put forward by Ramscar et al. is that the evidence for cognitive decline in healthy minds is weak and that the methods used to argue that our cognitive abilities decline critically fail to account for the growing information processing loads that experience brings. Since this article was published, many researchers have questioned these claims (see e.g., Rabbitt, 2014; Carey, 2014; Brink, 2014). The message coming from these specialists on cognitive aging is that there is good evidence that the minds and brains of healthy adults do decline, and that these declines occur in ways that belie Ramscar et al.'s information processing concerns.

In what follows, we examine these objections, and show that researchers massively over-estimate the extent to which the available empirical evidence actually supports claims to the effect that cognitive processes decline in the course of healthy aging. Indeed, we present evidence that, when properly evaluated, in many case the empirical record indicates that the opposite is true:

First, we show how the models of learning that are tacitly accepted across the aging literature are not only simplistic, but that they ignore all of the progress that has been made in understanding learning over the past half century. We show that the models of learning assumed in aging research are incapable of capturing the most basic of established empirical facts relating to simple "associative" learning processes.

Second, we show how this faulty model lends itself naturally to spurious discoveries of "cognitive decline." We demonstrate how, given the naïve assumptions about learning made by psychometricians, analyses of a large, normative Paired Associate Learning (PAL) data set appears to reveal that PAL performance in otherwise healthy adults is subject to significant declines between 39 and 49 years of age. We show how this conclusion is unwarranted, revealing that once a more accurate model of learning is combined with a more faithful representation of lexical information, it would seem that far from declining, the accuracy of older adults' representation of the lexicon improves continuously across the lifespan.

Third, we consider the confirmation bias that prevails throughout the aging literature: we suggest that researchers find "declines" because they expect to find them, and because their research programs are designed to confirm the "cognitive decline" hypothesis. We identify several measures on which performance does not decline with age, and show how more accurate modeling can make sense of these different patterns of performance within an overall framework of learning.

Finally, we consider the implications of our findings, and of our demonstrations of continuous and consistent learning performance across the lifespan for our understanding of the changes in underlying brain morphology that occur during the course of cognitive development across the lifespan.

The nature of lexical learning across the lifespan

A central part of the argument put forward in Ramscar et al. (2014) is that lexical learning continues throughout the lifespan. This raises a question, where is the evidence of this continued learning? As Rabbitt (2014) puts it:

> Ramscar et al. insist that vocabulary tests cannot be appropriate measures because they are biased towards [sic] low frequency words and so do not accurately assess older people who know more rare words that are not tested. It is questionable whether most older people actually do know more rare words than most young adults, but scores on vocabulary tests are not the only, or the best comparison. … Perhaps Ramscar et al. elide this point because of their need to counter a quite different objection that old people generally have only equal or even lower scores on vocabulary tests than the young.

Ramscar et al. (2004) show how some straightforward facts about sampling and the statistical nature of lexical distributions (Baayen, 2001) guarantee that vocabulary tests will become increasingly less accurate as people get older. If we disregard vocabulary tests as a useful tool for assessing cognitive decline, we are left with Rabbitt's suggestion that older people may not actually know more rare words than young people. Does this actually make sense?

Consider life as a continuous process of sampling the world. In infancy, the part of the world sampled is highly restricted to the cot, the high-chair, and the family (Pereira, Smith, & Yu, 2014). During the school years, pupils are trained to absorb selected samples of the world at a rate far beyond that which individual experience would allow. In their twenties and thirties, speakers marry, and may have children of their own. They move to other places, travel more widely, and

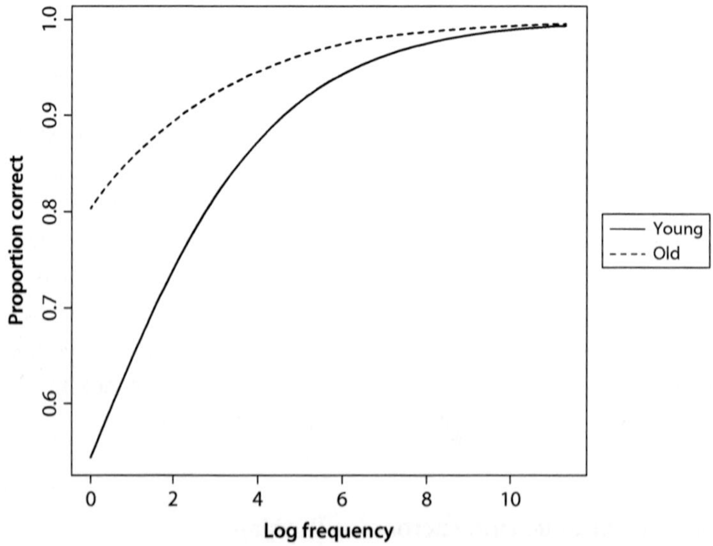

Figure 1. Proportion correct responses in visual lexical decision for the young and old subjects in Balota et al. (1999), plotted as a function of log word frequency in a logistic linear mixed model. The old subjects notably outperform the young subjects on low frequency words.

experience an ever-increasing array of technological innovations. In their sixties, speakers may become grandparents, start a new hobby and become expert bridge players, or captains of industry. It seems likely that as their experiences of the world accumulate, speakers will need a more diverse and more specialized vocabulary to communicate their experiences to other speakers. In other words, given how experience is sampled over the lifetime, it is extremely unlikely that the limited vocabulary acquired by the end of puberty would remain unchanged and sufficient for the remainder of life.

We can supplement this intuitive line of reasoning by an empirical fact. Figure 1 presents the accuracy of young (mean age 21.1 years) and old (mean age 73.6 years) adults in a lexical decision task with 2284 words (Balota et al., 1999) as a function of these words' (log-transformed) frequencies of occurrence in the CELEX lexical database (Baayen et al., 1995; see Table A1 in the Appendix for details of the corresponding statistical model). For the highest-frequency words, both groups perform with comparable accuracy. As frequency decreases, accuracy plummets for the young subjects to approximately chance performance. And while the old participants also make more errors on low frequency than high frequency words, they still outperform the young participants by a wide margin. For the lowest-frequency words, where the young subjects are at chance, the older subjects still get 80% of their responses correct. The markedly different accuracy levels of older adults as compared to the younger adults for the lowest-frequency words are completely incompatible with Rabbitt's suggestion that the former would not know more rare words than the latter.

Given that vocabulary tests clearly misrepresent what older speakers really know, this raises a question: to what extent are current interpretations of scores on other psychometric tests equally guilty of distorting the true extent of lexical knowledge in older adults? As we will now show, because learning in the lexicon involves more than simply adding new items to a list, current interpretations of scores for other psychometric tests are also guilty of underestimating older adults' cognitive abilities.

To demonstrate this point, we take as an example "Paired Associate Learning" (PAL), a common cognitive performance measure in which people are required to memorize associations between two words (e.g., *dig-guilty*, or *lead-pencil*). The test is popular as a clinical measure, and often used as a means for evaluate learning and memory processes in experimental settings. Further, in comparison with other memory measures, researchers consider that, "performance on PAL may be of greater prognostic relevance for day to day functioning where the same associative abilities are required" (desRosiers & Ivison, 1988). In a typical test, participants hear a list of cue (w_1) and response (w_2) words (e.g., *dig-guilty, lead-pencil…*) and are then required to produce w_2 when given w_1 as a cue. Figure 2 plots the performance of 200 30–39 year olds and 200 40–49 year olds, who provided normative data for forms 1 and 2 of the PAL subtest of Wechsler's Memory Scale (WMS; desRosiers & Ivison, 1988).

If we were simply to focus on the changes between the items in the performance of the thirty and forty year-olds shown in Figure 2, then these data would appear to provide evidence that PAL learning capacities decline significantly between ages 39 ($\underline{M}$ PAL Accuracy = 70%), and 49 ($\underline{M}$ Accuracy = 66%; $t(39) = 4.793$, $p < 0.0001$). This finding, though perhaps surprising, would seem to support other claims to the effect that age-related cognitive declines are clearly visible after adults reach their mid-forties (Singh-Manoux et al., 2012).

However, in addition to declining performance, these data also clearly show that PAL performance changes between the two groups in a systematic fashion: "hard" PAL items appear to become proportionally harder to learn over time. This suggests that the initial interpretation we suggested, that these data provide evidence of declining learning abilities in early middle-age, may be premature: All other things being equal, we might expect that, given the association rate in each test is consistent (participants hear each w_1–w_2 pair once, repeated across three list trials), then if we assume that PAL tests are a straightforward measure

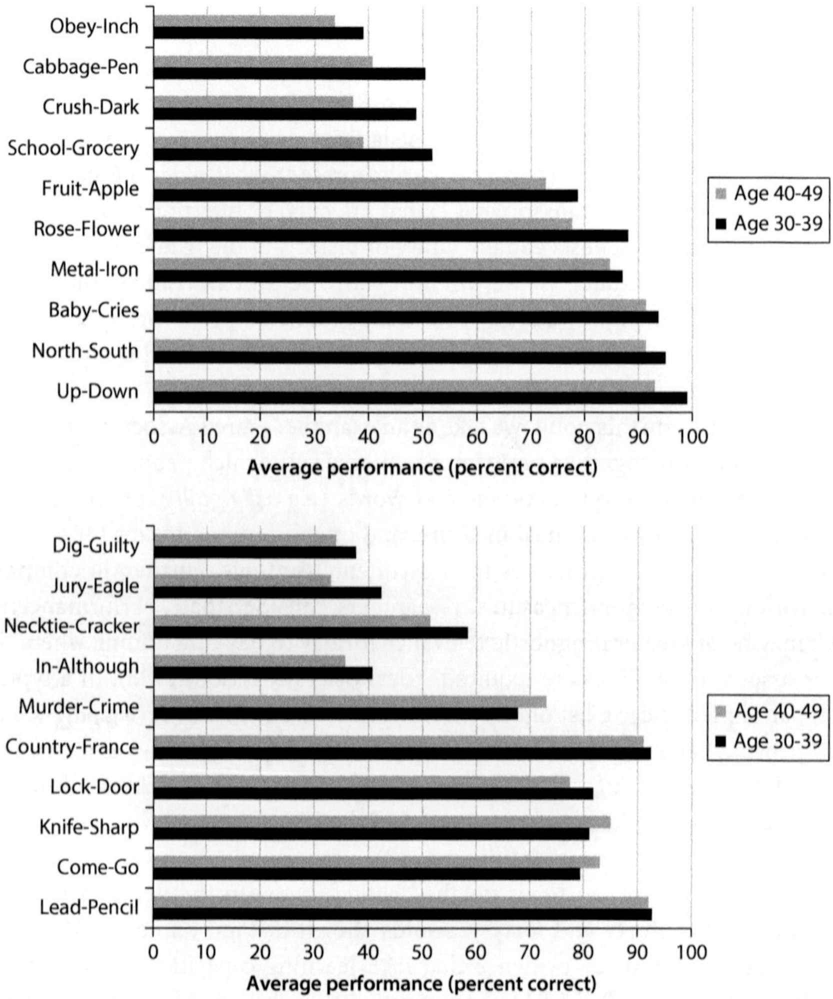

Figure 2. Average by-item performance for adults aged 30-39 and aged 40–49 (50% females in each group), tested on forms 1 (Top Panel, N = 200) and 2 (Bottom Panel, N = 200) of the WMS-PAL subtest (desRosiers & Ivison, 1988). Performance changes systematically: on average, performance differences are greater for harder items than the easier items.

of participants' ability to learn associations, "declines" in this ability ought to be consistent across items.

However, empirically, it has been shown that *association rates* (the frequencies at which items are encountered together) are insufficient to explain the systematic patterns of behavior associated with associative learning. In particular, two additional frequency factors have been shown to exert a significant influence on learning in associative tasks: cue *background rates* (Rescorla, 1968; Ramscar et al., 2013a; in the case of PAL, the frequency with which a cue word appears absent a response word), and *blocking* (the predictability of a response in the learning context based on prior learning, Kamin, 1969; Arnon & Ramscar, 2013, which in the case of PAL, is the predictability of the response word given the cue).

Further, the skewed distribution of language means that the relative influence of the factors that either inhibit (*blocking* and *background rates*) or promote learning (*association rates*) are likely to change as learners sample more and more words over time. This is important, because the *co-occurrence-rates* participants are exposed to in training in a PAL learning study remain constant: a pair is heard, and participants have to learn to associate it. This means that unless the effects that sampling and prior learning can be expected to have on PAL learning are controlled for, it is impossible to know whether changes in PAL performance shown in Figure 2 result from increased experience or cognitive declines.

To illustrate this point, Figure 3 shows what happens when all these factors come into play during associative learning in a very simple model of a lexicon. It depicts a small sample lexicon containing the stock phrases *American – Eagle* and *Obey – Rules*, and the "novel" pairings *Legal – Eagle* and *Obey – Eagle*. The plot shows the outcome of learning simulated using Danks (2003) equations for the Rescorla-Wagner model (a simple model that still embodies sufficient system complexity to account for the basic facts of associative learning; Rescorla & Wagner, 1972). As can be seen, as the frequencies of the stock phrases increase, the association weight between *Obey* and *Eagle* declines. This is despite the fact that the structure of the lexicon remains constant, as does the association rate of *Obey – Eagle* (at a frequency of 1; see the Appendix for full details, and the R code for this simulation).

Figure 3 illustrates the consequences of a basic fact about associative learning that has been known for around half a century: That the outcome of any single learning trial cannot be predicted by considering the association rate that a learner is exposed to on a single trial in isolation (Rescorla & Wagner, 1972; Ramscar et al., 2010). This also explains why it is wrong to think that by-item declines in performance in PAL reveal declines in associative learning capacities: This faulty inference depends on the assumption that PAL performance is determined by association rates alone. This erroneous assumption, which characterized classical behaviorism – and which, disturbingly, still lies at the heart of many contemporary researchers' understanding of learning – has been rejected by all modern learning theories (see Rescorla, 1988, for discussion of both of these points).

To try to get a better estimate of the systematic role that the factors that have actually been shown to determine the outcome of associative learning are playing in this instance, we estimated values for three critical parameters (*background*,

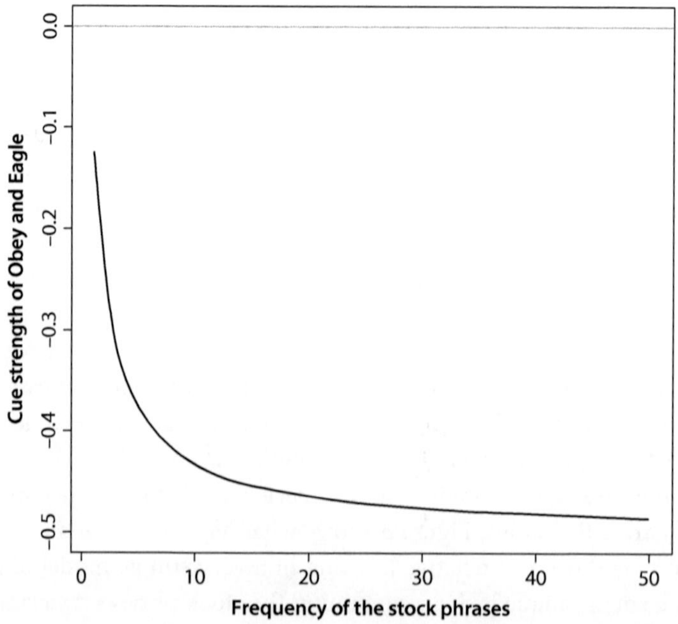

Figure 3. Cue strength for *Obey* to *Eagle* as a function of the frequency of two 'stock phrases' *American – Eagle* and *Obey – Rules*, in a small lexicon with the two stock phrases and two 'novel' pairings *Legal – Eagle* and *Obey – Eagle*. The frequency of the novel pairings is always 1. The plot shows how when learning is simulated using Danks (2003) equations for the Rescorla-Wagner (1972) model, the association weight between *Obey* and *Eagle* declines as the stock phrases' frequencies increase, even though both the structure of the lexicon and the association rate of *Obey – Eagle* remain constant (at 1).

blocking and *association rates*; Kruschke, 2003; Nelson, Dyrdal, & Goodmon, 2005) that can be expected to influence the learning of PAL w_1–w_s word pairs (these parameters were: log transformed, w_1 word frequencies, differences in word frequencies expressed as frequency(w_2)/frequence(w_1), taken for the period 1980–1990 from the Corpus of Historical American English, COHA, Davies, 2012 and w_1–w_2 co-occurrence rates, taken from Google). When these were entered into a linear regression in order to predict the relative performance of 30–39 and 40–49 year olds tested in 1988 (plotted in Figure 2) for each word pair in the normative PAL data, they accounted for over 65% of the observed variance in performance ($r = .82$, $F(4) = 19.385$, $p < 0.01$). Also, as predicted, our estimated *background* and *blocking* rates were associated with lower scores, whereas *association* rates were associated with higher scores (all, $p < .01$).

Once the parameters we estimated from the corpus data are entered into the picture, it would appear that most, if not all of the difference in PAL performance

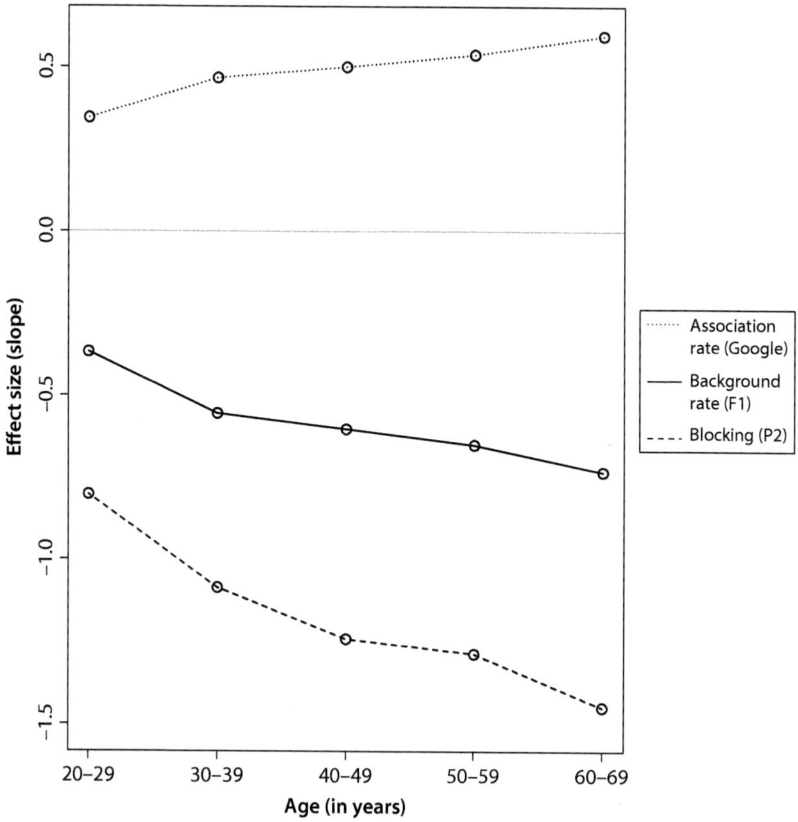

Figure 4. Mixed-effects slope estimates for the three parameters that estimate learnability constraints on the by-item PAL performance of the full set of 60–69, 50–59, 30–39 and 20–29 year-old adults in the normative data set (desRosiers & Ivison, 1988). Larger slope values indicate a greater degree of alignment with the structure of the language. All predictor effects and interactions in the model are significant, and all slopes (except the slope for blocking (P2) for the youngest age group) are significantly different from 0 (see Table 2 in the Appendix). There is no significant main effect of age in the model. This analysis shows how lifelong PAL performance patterns reveal an ever-growing understanding of the systematic structure of the English lexicon as adult age increases, rather than any decline in learning capacity.

seen between adults in their thirties and forties is due to learning. In particular, it appears that over time, learning hard PAL w_1–w_2 word pairs gets harder as language experience increases. As Figure 3 helps illustrate, this is because as learners master the informative details of the lexicon, the learning of a nonsensical link between two unconnected words must increasingly compete with prior learning to the effect that this link *is* nonsensical. It is worth noting here that one reason for this is that the learning of these kinds of *dissociations* is an important part of *discrimination learning*. Virtually all of the models of associative learning that have been developed in the past half-century actually implement discriminative learning principles, because it is these principles that actually appear to govern the processes that we still colloquially refer to as, "associative learning" (see Rescorla, 1988; Ramscar et al., 2010).

Our finding that many of the changes in PAL learning performance observed in early-middle-age are better attributed to learning than cognitive decline raises a further question: To what extent are the changes seen in PAL learning across the rest of the adult lifespan the product of the same, systematic learning factors?

To begin to address this question, we analyzed the full set of normative PAL data collected by desRosiers & Ivison (1988). The data was collected from 1000 adults, 50% of whom were men and 50% women. These were equally divided into the age groups 20–29, 30–39, 40–49, 50–59 and 60–69, and each participant completed either form 1 or form 2 of WMS PAL, such that each of data point represents the average score of 100 tests. The participants in desRosiers & Ivison's study were patients who had been hospitalized for non-neuropsychiatric conditions, and thus were tested in the same, relatively age-neutral context.

Along with our three corpus based learning parameters, these data were entered into a linear mixed effects model with word pair as random-effect factor. The details of this model are reported in the appendix (Table A2). As can be seen from the plot of mixed-effects slope estimates in Figure 4, the impact of the factors that basic learning theory predicts will inhibit the learning of an association – blocking and background rates – grow systematically across the lifespan, as does the influence of the factor that basic learning theory predicts will promote the learning of an association (the *association rate*). *In other words, our analysis of Paired Associate Learning indicates that the changing performance patterns that have been observed across the lifetime in PAL tasks are evidence of an ever-growing understanding of the systematic structure of the English lexicon that develops as age and experience grow.* Not only do these patterns not support the idea that older adults' learning capacities are in decline, they are also clear evidence that, in fact, learning capacities are both retained and fully engaged across adulthood.

Why decline appears to be in the eye of the beholder. And why a cognitive account of lifelong cognitive development matters

Ramscar et al. (2014; see also Ramscar, 2014) point to another serious shortcoming in current approaches to the study of cognitive development in adulthood: whether older participants' performance on even the simplest of cognitive tests improves or declines appears to be a function of the context in which participants are tested. Consider, for example, the FAS task, in which people are asked to generate as many words beginning with F as they can in 60 seconds, followed by as many words beginning with A in 60 seconds, followed by as many words that begin with S. (A couple of rules govern the words that are allowed as responses in the test: Proper names like *Steve* or *France* are not allowed, nor are different versions of the "same" word, e.g., *friends, friendly.*)

In a meta-analysis of 134 studies, Ramscar et al. found that while older participants outperformed younger adults at FAS recall in smaller studies, in very large surveys of the elderly population, older participants' performance declined as the total number of people tested in a study increased. Moreover, this effect was not due to regression to the mean (the analysis presented in Ramscar et al., 2014, controlled for this). Instead, it appears that in the data reported in the literature, there is a clear relationship between the FAS test scores of older adults and the number of older adults tested.

Test performance is both influenced by context, and can vary widely across cohorts (see e.g., Lynn, 1982; Flynn, 1987; Teasdale & Owen, 2005). However, although there is a large historical literature devoted to these very real problems (Schaie, 1959; 1973; 1975; 1977; 1988), and despite the fact that the researchers who employ the current generation of psychometric methods are careful to acknowledge that they cannot conclude anything about causality from the results of any given test, it appears that in practice whenever changes are observed on the correlated results of these tests, the temptation for researchers to interpret them causally – as evidence of decline – invariably proves too strong to resist. Although the cognitive aging literature contains a huge body of work that purports to chart the supposed declines in "cognitive abilities" that are assumed to undermine the minds of adults as they age, the fact is that this literature contains little more than a correlational record showing that scores change on tests that are incapable in themselves of supporting causal inferences about the reasons for change (Naveh-Benjamin & Old, 2008; Deary et al., 2009; Salthouse, 2009; Salthouse, 2011; Singh-Manoux et al., 2012).

Our analysis of PAL learning highlights the worrying shortcomings of these current methodologies. The introduction of even the most elementary discriminative learning model into an analysis of Paired Associate Learning reverses the standard, purely correlational interpretation of PAL test scores. Systematically lower scores do not reveal decline, but rather, they simply show a pattern of changes that any cognitively plausible model of lexical learning would predict. Indeed, the same patterns of change among lexical associations with experience revealed by our analysis can be observed in two-year olds (Ramscar et al., 2013a).

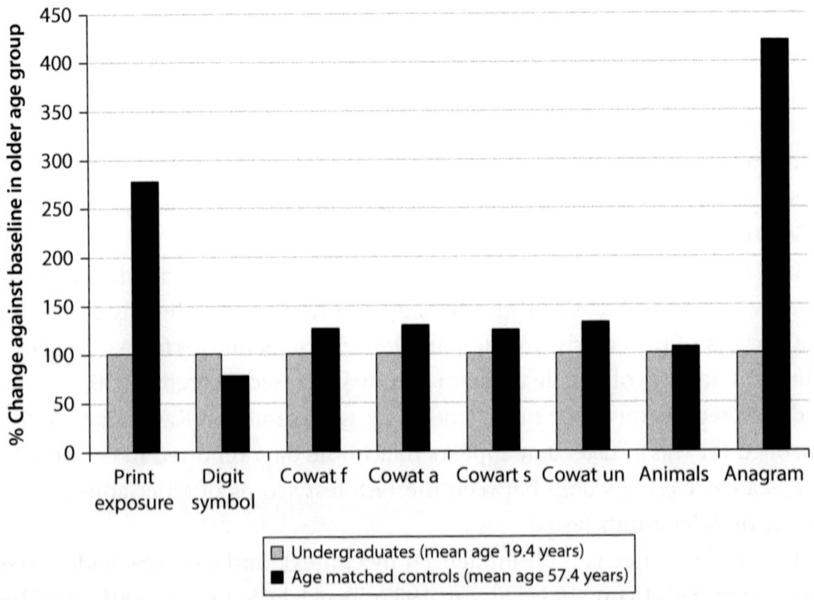

Figure 5. Performance of two control groups (group 1 N = 23; M age 19.4 years; group 2 N = 23; M age 57.4 years) in Hargreaves et al. (2012). Young adult performance is plotted as a reference, and the performance of the older adults reflects the change in their performance against this baseline. The leftmost two bars represent estimates of the relative amount of print exposure each group has experienced, and the remaining bars plot performance in tests of Digit Symbol recall (recalling strings of alphanumeric characters), generating words beginning with F, A, S and UN, animal naming, and anagram solving.

These points matter a great deal. Figure 5 plots the performance of a group of 23 nineteen year olds and a group of 23 fifty-seven year olds on a range of measures of "cognitive performance" (from Hargreaves, Pexman, Zdrazilova, & Sargious, 2012). There are several things to note about this data:

First, it was an experimental study in which participants were carefully matched on a range of control variables, including the number of participants tested in each group.

Second, it was a study of expertise rather than a study of "aging". There are many good reasons to believe that this matters, most notably that making elderly participants aware of their age and of the stereotypes associated with aging, can inhibit their performance on tests (Steele, 1997; Hess et al., 2003; Hess & Hinson, 2006; Hess, Hinson, & Hodges, 2009).

Third, while, perhaps unsurprisingly, older adults' print exposure is greater than that of the younger adults, it is notable that of the 7 cognitive measures tested, the older group outperform the younger group on 6 of them. And even if we collapse all of the FAS related tasks into one, the fact is that the older adults outperform the young on 3 out of 4 of these measures. Further, while the younger adults performance on digit symbol is slightly better than that of the older adults, the younger adults performance on the anagram task is *vastly* inferior to that of the older adults.

Further evidence for the inferior sensitivity of younger adults to the distributional properties of the language can be gleaned from the lexical decision data discussed above, which indicated that adults perform the task more accurately (Figure 1). Figure 6 presents some central partial effects in a generalized additive mixed model fitted to the response latencies, with younger subjects in the left panels and older subjects in the right panels. The top panels present the effect of frequency. As expected, reaction times are longer for lower-frequency words. Older subjects slow down slightly more than younger subjects for the lower-frequency words.

Before we attribute this to cognitive decline, we should first consider the lower panels, which present contour plots for the interaction of two latent variables, PC1 and PC2. PC1 contrasted forward enemies with phonological neighbors (and accounted for 43.5% of the variance in the 10 consistency measures), while PC2 contrasted friends with backward enemies (accounting for 22.2% of the variance; for further details, see Baayen, Feldman & Schreuder, 2006). The non-linear interaction of these two (orthogonal) latent variables was modeled with a tensor product smooth (Wood, 2006, see the appendix Table A3 for the full model). Importantly, the interaction for the younger adults fails to reach significance, in contrast to the interaction for the older adults. Note that the contour lines for the younger adults are 0.005 log RT units apart, whereas those for the older adults are 0.01 log RT units apart. In other words, the younger adults are beginning to show, albeit very weakly, the pattern that characterizes the performance of the older adults. It is the older adults which evidence clear fine-grained sensitivity to the consonances and dissonances between spelling and sound in English.

A difference between older and younger subjects not shown in Figure 6 is that older subjects have longer RTs compared to younger subjects. Older participants' judgments are thus slower and more accurate, a phenomenon that might also be described as a "speed accuracy trade-off". This is consistent with applications of the drift-diffusion model to speed and accuracy data, which also indicates that the quality of information processing is not impaired in healthy aging, and suggests instead that slow downs in aging are largely attributable to other factors (Ratcliff, Thapar, & McKoon, 2011; 2010), such as non-decision time (e.g., motor movement) and boundary separation (i.e., the degree of cautiousness in responding).

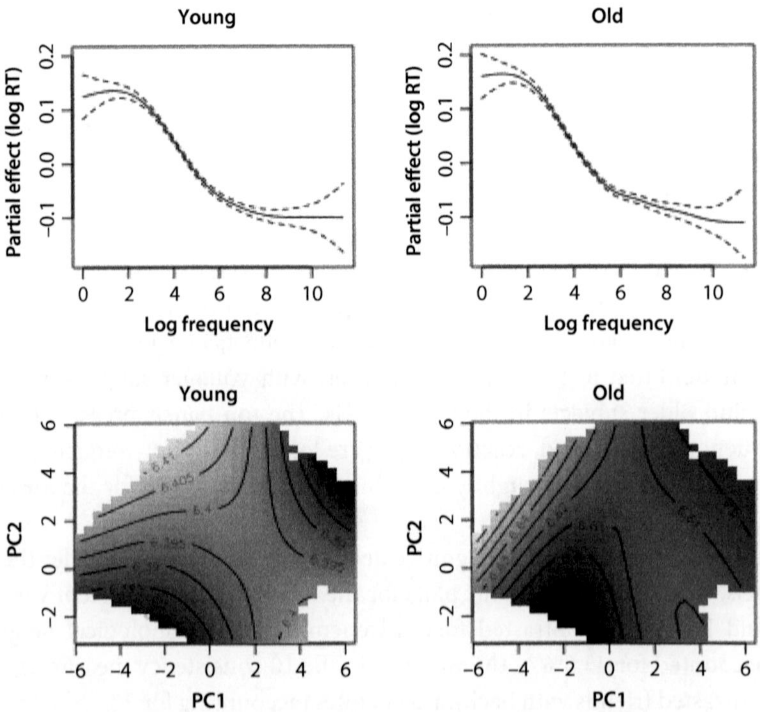

Figure 6. Upper panels: the partial effect of log frequency on log response latency. Younger adults (left) have shorter latencies for the lower-frequency words compared to older adults (right). Lower panels: the nonlinear interaction of two latent variables for orthographic consistency. The interaction does not reach significance for the younger adults, but is highly significant for the older adults, which reveal enhanced sensitivity to the distributional properties of sound-meaning mappings in English.

What is worth noting here is that while the characterization of a lexicality response as accurate or inaccurate in cross-generational lexical decision is made against the background of the lexicon of the total speech community, a young participant classifying a low-frequency word that she doesn't know as a non-word is still making what is to her an accurate and correct response. This has subtle consequences for this speed-accuracy trade-off, because this means that young adults are confronted with materials that contain – for them – a higher proportion of non-words than words, and this will make real words more noticeable and easier to respond to.

While this suggests yet another reason to doubt that the slower responses of older adults present compelling evidence for degraded performance, importantly it also indicates that older and younger adults may be processing *different*

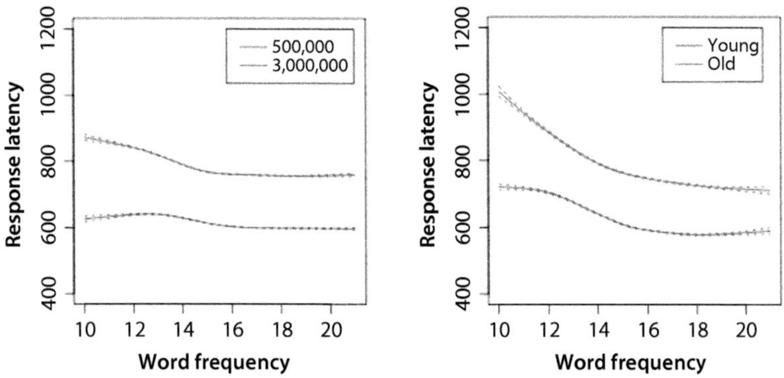

Figure 7. Left panel: fit of a generalized additive model to the simulated response latencies for the 2284 words tested by Balota et al. (1999) taken from the old and young models presented in Ramscar et al. (2014). Right panel: fit of a generalized additive model to the empirical response latencies for the same word taken from young (mean age: 21.1) and old (73.6) adults (Balota et al., 1999). It is well established that lexical decision responses are slower for lower- frequency words (e.g., "whelp") than higher-frequency words ("where"). This overall effect of frequency is present for both young and old adults and in the models. However, while frequency effects asymptote at higher frequencies in both models, they also level off again at the lowest frequencies in the younger model, a pattern also observed in the empirical data (see Figure 6 for more detail).

information in completing this task. Ramscar et al. (2014) presented a large-scale simulation study using the Rescorla-Wagner equations, which correctly predicted the pattern of slower responses to lower frequency words observed in older adults. Figure 7 plots the simulated and empirical reaction times reported in Ramscar et al. (2014) in a way that allows the models' predictions – as well as the empirical effects just described – to be easily apprehended.

These models allow us to develop causal hypotheses about the nature of information in this task, and to explain *why* these particular patterns of response latencies emerge. (Note, simply saying, "because frequency," hardly counts as a causal hypothesis: saying that lower frequency words are read slower because they are lower in frequency – and we know more frequent words get read faster – is a re-description of the data, not an explanation.) First, note that the variance in model's predicted simulated RTs for younger and older adults in the lower frequency-range (Figure 7, left panel) is entirely a function of the weights the models learned from the training sets for the two age groups, which are set without free parameters (save for the selection of the size of the training samples themselves). These weights connect letter conjunctions (*n-gram* cues) in the words the model reads with the lexemes that humans and the models have to discriminate in

Table 1. The 20 lowest frequency items in the set used to train the models and test older and young adults; BLASH has the lowest frequency of these items, and SKULK the highest. As can be seen, many of the letter bigrams in this set of words are fairly rare in English (see also, Nusbaum, 1985).

BLASH	SOUSE	CROME	VELDT
SCHNOOK	WHIG	GIBE	SLOE
LETCH	FILCH	LISLE	CONK
ZOUNDS	RHEUM	FLAYS	FRAPPE
JAPE	PARCH	SPLOTCH	SKULK

reading (i.e. they represent the learned connection between the letters *d o* and *g* and the lexeme *dog*).

In the models, the *n-gram* cues are initially undifferentiated, and their learned values are set competitively, as the models seek to predict words from the letters they 'read.' The logic underlying this process can be intuitively grasped by considering the different cue values of letters in scrabble: if you have Q and A but no U, QA is an excellent cue for the legal scrabble words *qaid, qanat* and *qat*; however, D and I appear in many words, so DI only weakly supports individual words like *oxidize, dim* and *odium*.

As Table 1 shows, when it comes to the test (and hence the training) set that produced the data plotted in Figure 6, the lower frequency words contain significantly more uncommon (low frequency) *n-grams* than the higher frequency words (Ramscar et al., 2014). This means that, while in a smaller vocabulary, these low frequency *n-grams* tend to be very good cues to a given lexeme, as a vocabulary grows, the probability that new words will also contain these *n-grams* increases (suppose someone who knows *qaid*, learns *qanat* playing scrabble, or hears that *qantas* is the name of an airline), then cue competition will increase (this is the same process that produces the changes in the weights of the w_1 cue *obey* to the w_2 response *eagle* in Figure 3).

Thus, in the model, the slower reaction times for lower frequency words for older speakers are the result of learning, and reflect the increasing demands imposed by having to discriminate between more and more lexemes composed of the same set of alphanumeric cues, which is in turn reflected in the increased accuracy of older participants in the lexical decision task. Or, to put it another way, *while we may learn more and more words across our lifetimes, we do not learn any more letters*. And although we can arrange letters in ways that yield more cues, even this process is not infinite. This means that over time, learning more vocabulary items must inevitably increase the information processing demands associated with letter cues. (This point also raises developmental issues, which we return to below.)

We should acknowledge that the models are hypotheses, and that compared to the complexities of actual human experience, their training is absurdly sparse. However, against this we should note that the learning algorithm in the model at least approximates our best understanding of how brains learn (Schultz et al., 1997; Schultz, 2006; Daw, Courville & Dayan, 2008; Daw et al., 2011), and that in practice, even noting their limitations, these models do seem capable of providing insights into human learning that are useful, if not exactly "right" (Box & Draper, 1987; see Ramscar & Yarlett, 2007; Gureckis & Love, 2010; Ramscar et al., 2010; Ramscar et al., 2011; Ramscar et al., 2013a; Ramscar et al., 2013b; Ramscar et al., 2013c; Arnon & Ramscar, 2013; Baayen et al., 2011; Baayen, Hendrix, & Ramscar, 2013).

Moreover, some systematic insights into the complexities of learning and aging can only be gotten from a useful hypothetical model. To return to the empirical data plotted in Figure 5, it clearly suggests that there may be an age-related interaction between digit symbol performance and anagram solving: a model provides a framework in which to examine whether a causal relationship between these facts actually exists. For example, the model we just described suggests that the slowing in older adult's lexical decision responses is the product of loading more and more lexical outcomes on a relatively finite set of combinations of letter cues (see also Anderson, 1974).

We might expect that this will lead to (at least) two outcomes: First, just as virtually any PAL w_1–w_2 pair will become more dissociated as lexical learning increases (Figure 3), we can expect that the association between virtually any two letter unigrams will decrease in exactly the same way for very similar reasons. This means that increased lexical learning will inevitably make the digit symbol task harder in the same way that it makes learning specific PAL pairings harder. However, given that the dissociations in letter *n-grams* are driven at least to some extent by their being learned as cues to more and more words, it follows that increased lexical learning will mean that any given *n-gram* is likely to cue more and more lexemes. Given the role of prefrontal cortex (PFC) in filtering response behavior (Shimamura, 2000; Chrysikou, Weber, & Thompson-Schill, in press), and the way that learning alters the dynamics of the responses that PFC serves to filter (Ramscar & Gitcho, 2007; Thompson-Schill, Ramscar, & Chrysikou, 2009) and helps modulate perseverative behavior (Ramscar et al., 2013b), it is hardly surprising that learning to associate more lexical outcomes with *n-grams* serves to improve people's ability to solve anagrams, or that older scrabble experts should be particularly adept at this (Hargreaves et al., 2012).

Thus, just as a model can help us understand why there is an interaction between speed and accuracy in lexical decision with age, and why slower lexical decisions speed do not necessarily betoken "decline," so it can also help us understand why there is an interaction between digit symbol accuracy and anagram solving with age, and why performance on the two measures in the latter is as inextricably linked as speed and accuracy "performance" in the former.

Why better functional models of behavior across the lifespan are necessary to understanding the aging brain

An improved functional understanding of the behavioral changes we see in healthy adults as they age is necessary to determining which (if any) of these changes can be considered "decline." Model-based analyses (Davis, Love, & Preston, 2012a, 2012b; Turner et al., 2013) of brain imaging data and model selection methods (Kriegeskorte & Kievit, 2013; Mack, Preston, & Love, 2013) have proven invaluable in interpreting brain activity for younger adults. If we are to understand the aging brain, better functional models will also need to be developed, applied, and evaluated. Thus, for example, studies employing a range of imaging techniques and a variety of tasks have revealed a posterior to anterior shift in patterns of task-related activation as adults age, and a concomitant decrease in the degree to which tasks trigger activation patterns that are lateralized to one (in particular the left) hemisphere (Reuter-Lorenz et al. 2000; Cabeza et al. 1997; Grady et al., 2006; Cabeza, 2002; Cabeza et al., 2002; Cabeza et al., 2004; see Park & Reuter-Lorenz, 2009 for a review). In the cognitive neuroscience literature this shifting pattern of activations is thought to reflect the results of a "scaffolding" process, in which contra-lateral and frontal areas step in to pick up the slack in the processing capacity of left-lateral and posterior areas that occurs in "direct response to the magnitude of neural insults that occur with age" (Park & Reuter-Lorenz, 2009).

Although this idea is widely accepted, the literature offers no details (nor even detailed speculations) as to quite how it is that frontal areas come to be aware of the plight of their insulted brethren in posterior regions (it seems reasonable to assume that dead cells don't talk), nor are accounts forthcoming of how it is that ensembles of neurons in functionally distinct areas of cortex are able to acquire the tunings that enable them to replicate the functions of circuits in other regions that have succumbed to the ravages of time. Finally, nor does the literature offer a suggestion, let alone a convincing explanation, of why it is that, for example, posterior regions are systematically more susceptible to insults than anterior regions across the entire human population as it ages.

By contrast, consider the model of the relationship between digit span performance and anagram solving we just described. It outlines a (clearly over-) simple feed-forward network in which the perception of letter cues in turn activate lexemes, and, in the case of anagram solving, any activated lexemes are then filtered along with other task relevant information in prefrontal cortex in order to generate a response. Over the lifetime, the model thus predicts a systematic pattern of changes will occur as a learner's lexical experience grows: First, in posterior regions associated with reading letter forms, such as left posterior occipitotemporal sulcus (pOTS; Mano et al., 2013) the model predicts that more experience will lead to less neural activation, because learning and cue-competition will increasingly serve to tune *n-gram* representations (this is consistent with findings from imaging studies, which show stronger activation of the left pOTS to pseudowords and low frequency words as compared to high frequency words; Kronbichler et al., 2004, 2007; Bruno et al., 2008; Schurz et al., 2010; Mano et al., 2013); Second, since these increasingly tuned *n-gram* representations will become associated with more and more lexemes, which will activate when they are activated, the model predicts that greater experience will result in more activation of the anterior regions associated with lexical processing itself, such as the superior temporal gyrus (STS), inferior frontal gyrus (IFG) and PFC (see e.g., Friederici, 2011), because activating increasingly specialized *n-gram* representations will result in the activation of increasingly larger sets of lexemes.

That is, a simple functional model of reading that incorporates learning can predict and explain the interaction between digit span performance and anagram solving and provide an account of the posterior to anterior shift in activation during lexical processing without having to make the many dubious assumptions involved in theories of "neural scaffolding." Further, the model we have outlined does so in ways that are highly compatible with our best understanding of the functions of the brain regions involved. Moreover, given that this model does not automatically assume that changing patterns of activation are evidence of "neural insults," it is more consistent with biological models of brain aging, which have revealed that the brains of healthy adults do not experience significant cell loss as they age, nor do they undergo dramatic changes in neuronal morphology (in a recent review, Burke & Barnes, 2006, describe the widely held beliefs to the contrary as "the myth of brain aging".)

The patterns of change in neuronal morphology over the lifespan are both more complex and more puzzling than the notion of "brain atrophy" embraced by the scaffolding hypothesis supposes. Most of the typical changes in brain morphology that are observed in healthy aging involve declines in the density and organization of neuronal dendrites and spines (gray matter) and axons (white matter). Although the typical pattern of change that is usually observed in many areas of the dorsal, frontal, and parietal lobes in adulthood involve reductions in grey matter density, in some brain areas, such as the cingulate gyrus, the density of grey matter appears to remain consistent across the lifespan in healthy adults

(Sowell et al., 2003). Moreover, in some brain areas, such as the parahippocampal gyrus, there is evidence of significant dendritic growth in normal human aging (but not in senile dementia, Buell et al., 1979, 1981).

While it goes without saying that the complex and systematic pattern of changes that are actually seen in neural morphology are not going to be explained without the development of functional models of what brain systems actually do, the need for good functional models of cognitive processes is particularly acute because given the changes that typify aging in healthy brains, it is extremely difficult to disentangle "declines" in brain function from the effects of learning. This is because learning is itself reflected in neuronal morphology as changes in the density and composition of grey and white matter (see e.g., Merrill et al., 2001; Zuo et al., 2005; Rapp et al., 1996; Flood et al., 1991, 1993; Burke & Barnes, 2006; Zatorre, Fields, & Johansen-Berg, 2012).

It follows from this that in order to be sure that all of the changes in neural morphology that ones sees in a healthy brain are insults, rather than signs of learning, one first needs a functional model of "normal" learning and processing. For example, studies of 11–17 year-olds have revealed patterns of changes in gray and white matter densities that are remarkably similar to those associated with aging (Alemán-Gómez et al., 2013). Should these findings be interpreted as a marker for the (extremely) early onset of age-related declines in neural plasticity, or as ordinary, business-as-usual learning?

Similarly, consider that more extensive age-related reductions in grey matter density are typically observed in the posterior temporal cortex in the left (as compared to right) hemisphere (Sowell et al., 2003). Are these differences, which are particularly evident in posterior language areas, really just the result of simple (and presumably random) insults, and atrophy caused by "brain aging?" While it is, of course, possible that they are, it seems highly likely that, given that language is one of the most extensive functional systems any brain ever learns, at least some of the systematic changes in neuronal morphology seen in posterior temporal cortex reflect the effect of learning this system. If so, then this means that, again, the process of distinguishing learning from decline – if indeed there is decline in healthy brain aging – is likely to be far more subtle and complex than the literature currently acknowledges.

Understanding lexical processing and understanding lexical learning

Rabbitt (2014) points out that our assumption that greater information processing loads result in slower processing appears to be confounded by empirical results that, in comparing across people of the same age, as opposed to between people of different ages, reveal that people who have larger vocabularies often perform better than people with smaller vocabularies.

> people of any age whose brains are so stuffed with words that they can produce more names of animals within a fixed time also produce words in other categories correspondingly faster and more accurately. This does not support the Ramscar hypothesis that words are retrieved more slowly from a large vocabulary.
> (Rabbitt, 2014)

The reason these findings do not contradict our central hypothesis, is, of course, that the mind and brain are not fixed systems:

> plasticity is not an occasional state of the nervous system; instead, it is the normal ongoing state of the nervous system throughout the lifespan. A full, coherent account of any sensory or cognitive theory has to build into its framework the fact that the nervous system, and particularly the brain, undergoes continuous changes in response to modifications in its input afferents and output targets.
> (Pascual-Leone et al., 2005)

It goes without saying that learning changes the brain. Just 7 days training in something as inconsequential as juggling is sufficient to produce visible changes in gray matter density and to the organization of white matter pathways in the occipito-temporal areas associated with the processing of complex visual motion (Draganski et al., 2004; Driemeyer et al., 2008); notably, these patterns of change are even visible in elderly participants (Boyke et al., 2008; albeit that the elderly learn less well on average over the same time frame).

Because learning changes the brain, prior learning always impacts subsequent learning. As our case study of PAL learning demonstrated, there is no such thing as "learning" in a vacuum. This in turn means that a full, coherent account of lexicial processing across the lifetime can't simply consider the effects of having a large vocabulary in a vacuum: In order to understand the interaction between experience, vocabulary size and processing, one has to consider how people end up with different sized vocabularies, and how this might affect learning and processing at different stages of linguistic development.

Studies of children clearly show that, consistent with Rabbitt's observation, larger vocabulary scores actually predict faster lexical processing in childhood. Children with larger vocabularies process words faster than children with smaller vocabularies (Fernald & Marchman, 2012; Bion, Borovsky, & Fernald, 2013). Perhaps unsurprisingly, these studies have also shown that vocabulary scores and processing speeds are highly correlated with the amount of language a child is exposed to (Fernald & Marchman, 2012; Bion, Borovsky, & Fernald, 2013; Weisleder & Fernald, 2013; Fernald, Marchman, & Weisleder, 2013). Moreover, as Hart &

Risely (1995) revealed in their landmark studies, depending on the social environment a child grows up in, the amount of language she hears can differ dramatically.

These points are of particular importance when we are dealing with human brains, because in children, not only will learning be having an impact on the local morphology of areas processing the various factors that contribute to behavior, but also because the maturation and development of the overall structure of the human brain is occurring throughout childhood (Ramscar & Gitcho, 2007; Thompson-Schill, Ramscar, & Chrysikou, 2009). Given what we know about the way brains learn and develop, it seems at least reasonable to suppose that children who are exposed to large amounts of language develop much richer neural networks in the areas involved in lexical processing than children whose linguistic experience is impoverished. In developing the model we used to predict lexical processing speeds above, we considered the relation between network density and processing speed, and, in theory at least (in practice, we should acknowledge that this is a free parameter), the model predicts that dedicating more processing hardware to a task in the brain will lead to faster processing speeds.

Ultimately, what we want to be able to do is integrate the many strands that influence the development of neural networks in the maturing mind, and the way processing in these networks responds to information gains in mature minds. We don't pretend for a second that our models are even close to doing all this. Yet consider the complexity involved in the task we just described, and in the interactions between experience, weights and learning in the analyses and simulations we described above. However simple and flawed the various models presented above are, they at least offer insight.

This observation highlights an important point in this debate: Researchers in the brain and cognitive sciences are engaged in a tortuous process of trying to reverse engineer a complex physical information processing device. Yet the simple fact is that very few researchers in the field have any training in information processing systems, and of the few that do, most have training at the software rather than the hardware end. Most researchers have only the dimmest idea how increases in data and task complexity impact information processing in the physical systems that actually do the processing. While it is clear that the brain is not a computer in a straightforward sense, the fact is that machine information processing still represents our best model of neural information processing (indeed, formally, it is the only model we have) and it seems highly unlikely that a "no model" approach will lead to meaningful progress in our search to understand the mind, and the effects of age on it.

Conclusion: Learning is not decline

Do the ravages of time inevitably result in declines in cognitive processing in otherwise healthy brains? We remain open to the possibility that the answer to this question is, "yes." What we have sought to show above is that, when it comes to aspects of lexical learning where we now can quantify the environment in which learning takes place (in large part thanks to the development of large corpora), once one controls for the effects of learning on performance, there is precious little variance left to be described in terms of "decline." Not only are the changing patterns of performance observed in paired-associate learning better accounted for by learning models than by vague notions of "cognitive decline," but detailed comparison of the specifics of those performance patterns suggests that instead of declining with age, older adults' lexical knowledge in fact becomes more and more attuned to the information structure of the lexicon.

Similarly, we have shown that if one simply attends to speed in lexical decision tasks, one will inevitably find evidence of decline. Whereas if one integrates a measure of accuracy into one's analysis, a different picture emerges: a picture in which an improvement in one dimension – accuracy – is shown to come at a cost in another, speed.

In one sense, the findings we report are hardly surprising: they simply suggest that one rarely gets something from nothing, and that actions have reactions, and these are hardly new ideas. However, we would suggest what our findings reveal about our folk theories of the mind, and of the effect of aging on the mind ought to surprise us: It would appear that many of the implicit assumptions that serve to underpin received ideas about cognitive declines involve the idea that some things – especially learning – ought to come for free, and that some actions – especially the acquisition of knowledge – ought not to have a reaction. Our findings not only undermine these implicit assumptions, they also undermine the muddled thinking that is embodied in received ideas about cognitive decline, both in the literature, and in society more generally.

We have sought to show how many of the tacit, over-simplified assumptions about the nature of learning in the literature are leading researchers to seriously overestimate of the degree to which cognitive function declines with age. We would not wish to argue that this means that functionality does not change. For instance it may be that a side-effect of some kinds of prior-learning is that subsequent learning is inhibited in ways that, essentially, amount to functional losses, in much the same way that children learning of a native sound system functionally impedes the later learning of non-native phonetic contrasts (Werker & Tees, 1984). Rather, we would suggest that a better understanding of learning can do much to assist our understanding of cognitive functions themselves (see e.g., Baayen et al., 2011), and the way these functions develop across the lifetime.

Finally, in relation to this last point, we should reiterate why all this is important. In numerous studies, Carol Dweck and her colleagues have shown how people who believe that their abilities can be improved through hard work learn far better than those who think that their abilities are fixed (Dweck, 2006, 1999; Dweck & Leggett, 1988; Yeager & Dweck, 2012; see also Mangels et al., 2012; Rattan, Good, & Dweck, 2012; Dweck et al., 1978). Since it is clear from the findings we present here that people's ability to learn stays with them at all ages, and from the work of Dweck and colleagues that thinking of ability as a fixed factor has an adverse influence on children and younger adults' ability to learn, we can only shudder to think what the pervasive mythology of "cognitive decline" is doing to older adults' ability to adopt a positive mindset, or to believe that their efforts can lead to improvement.

Authors' note

This work was supported by an Alexander von Humboldt research award to R. Harald Baayen.

References

Alemán-Gómez, Y., Janssen, J., Schnack, H., Balaban, E., Pina-Camacho, L., Alfaro-Almagro, F., & Desco, M. (2013). The Human cerebral cortex flattens during adolescence. *The Journal of Neuroscience*, 33(38), 15004–15010. DOI: 10.1523/JNEUROSCI.1459-13.2013

Anderson, J. R. (1974). Retrieval of propositional information from long-term memory. *Cognitive Psychology*, 6(4), 451–474. DOI: 10.1016/0010-0285(74)90021-8

Arnon, I., & Ramscar, M. (2012). Granularity and the acquisition of grammatical gender: How order of acquisition affects what gets learned. *Cognition*, 122(3), 292–305. DOI: 10.1016/j.cognition.2011.10.009

Baayen, R. H., Davidson, D. J., & Bates, D. M. (2008). Mixed-effects modeling with crossed random effects for subjects and items. *Journal of Memory and Language*, 59(4), 390–412. DOI: 10.1016/j.jml.2007.12.005

Baayen, R. H. (2001). *Word frequency distributions*. Amsterdam: Kluwer. DOI: 10.1007/978-94-010-0844-0

Baayen, R. H., Milin, P., Đurđević, D. F., Hendrix, P., & Marelli, M. (2011). An amorphous model for morphological processing in visual comprehension based on naive discriminative learning. *Psychological Review*, 118(3), 438–482. DOI: 10.1037/a0023851

Baayen, R. H., Hendrix, P., & Ramscar, M. (2013). Sidestepping the combinatorial explosion: Towards a processing model based on discriminative learning. *Language and Speech*, 56, 329–347. DOI: 10.1177/0023830913484896

Baayen, R.H., Feldman, L.B., & Schreuder, R. (2006). Morphological influences on the rec-og-nition of monosyllabic monomorphemic words. *Journal of Memory and Language*, 55(2), 290–313. DOI: 10.1016/j.jml.2006.03.008

Bion, R.A., Borovsky, A., & Fernald, A. (2013). Fast mapping, slow learning: Disambiguation of novel word–object mappings in relation to vocabulary learning at 18, 24, and 30months. *Cognition*, 126(1), 39–53. DOI: 10.1016/j.cognition.2012.08.008

Box, G.E., & Draper, N.R. (1987). *Empirical model-building and response surfaces*. John Wiley & Sons.

Borovsky, A., Elman, J.L., & Fernald, A. (2012). Knowing a lot for one's age: Vocabulary skill and not age is associated with anticipatory incremental sentence interpretation in children and adults. *Journal of Experimental Child Psychology*, 112(4), 417–436. DOI: 10.1016/j.jecp.2012.01.005

Boyke, J., Driemeyer, J., Gaser, C., Buchel, C., & May, A. (2008). Training-induced brain structure changes in the elderly. *Journal of Neuroscience*, 28, 7031–7035. DOI: 10.1523/JNEUROSCI.0742-08.2008

Bruno, J.L., Zumberge, A., Manis, F.R., Lu, Z.-L., & Goldman, J.G. (2008). Sensitivity to orthographic familiarity in the occipito-temporal region. *Neuroimage*, 39, 1988–2001. DOI: 10.1016/j.neuroimage.2007.10.044

Brink, S. (2014). An aging brain is still pretty smart [Web log article]. Retrieved from *National Geographic*, http://news.nationalgeographic.com/news/2014/01/140128-aging-brain-memory-cognitive-decline-neurology/

Buell, S.J., & Coleman, P.D. (1981). Quantitative evidence for selective dendritic growth in normal human aging but not in senile dementia. *Brain Research*, 214, 23–41. DOI: 10.1016/0006-8993(81)90436-4

Buell, S.J., & Coleman, P.D. (1979). Dendritic growth in the aged human brain and failure of growth in senile dementia. *Science*, 206, 854–856. DOI: 10.1126/science.493989

Burke, S., & Barnes, C. (2006). Neural plasticity in the aging brain. *Nature Reviews Neuro science*, 7(1), 30–40. DOI: 10.1038/nrn1809

Carey, B. (2014). The older mind may just be a fuller mind [Web log article]. Retrieved from *The New York Times*, http://newoldage.blogs.nytimes.com/2014/01/27/the-older-mind-may-just-be-a-fuller-mind

Chrysikou, E.G., Weber, M.J., & Thompson-Schill, S.L. (2013). A matched filter hypothesis for cognitive control. *Neuropsychologia*, S0028–3932(13), 00379–5.

Danks, D. (2003). Equilibria of the rescorla-wagner model. *Journal of Mathematical Psychology*, 47(2), 109–121. DOI: 10.1016/S0022-2496(02)00016-0

Daw, N.D., Courville, A.C., & Dayan, P. (2008). Semi-rational models of conditioning: The case of trial order. In N. Chater & M. Oaksford (Eds.), *The probabilistic mind*. Oxford: Oxford University Press.

Daw, N.D., Gershman, S.J., Seymour, B., Dayan, P., & Dolan, R.J. (2011). Model-based influences on humans' choices and striatal prediction errors. *Neuron*, 69(6), 1204–1215. DOI: 10.1016/j.neuron.2011.02.027

Davies, M. (2012) Expanding horizons in historical linguistics with the 400 million word Corpus of historical American English. *Corpora*, 7, 121–157. DOI: 10.3366/cor.2012.0024

Davies, M. (2009). The 385+ million word corpus of contemporary American English (1990–present). *International Journal of Corpus Linguistics*, 14, 159–190. DOI: 10.1075/ijcl.14.2.02dav

Davis, T., Love, B. C., & Preston, A. R. (2012a). Learning the Exception to the Rule: Model-based fMRI reveals specialized representations for surprising category members. *Cerebral Cortex*, 22, 260–273. DOI: 10.1093/cercor/bhr036

Davis, T., Love, B. C., & Preston, A. R. (2012b). Striatal and hippocampal entropy and recog-ni-tion signals in category learning: Simultaneous processes revealed by model-based fMRI. *Journal of Experimental Psychology: Learning, Memory, and Cognition*, 38, 821–839. DOI: 10.1037/a0027865

Deary, I. J. et al. (2009). Age-associated cognitive decline. *British Medical Bulletin*, 92, 135–152. DOI: 10.1093/bmb/ldp033

des Rosiers, G., & Ivison, D. (1986). Paired-associate learning: Normative data for differences between high and low associate word pairs. *Journal of Clinical Experimental Neuropsychology*, 8, 637–642. DOI: 10.1080/01688638608405184

Draganski, B., Gaser, C., Busch, V., Schuierer, G., Bogdahn, U., & May, A. (2004). Neuroplasticity: Changes in grey matter induced by training. *Nature*, 427(6972), 311–312. DOI: 10.1038/427311a

Driemeyer, J., Boyke, J., Gaser, C., Büchel, C., & May, A. (2008). Changes in gray matter induced by learning – revisited. *PLoS One*, 3(7), e2669. DOI: 10.1371/journal.pone.0002669

Dweck, C. S., Davidson, W., Nelson, S., & Enna, B. (1978). Sex differences in learned helplessness: II. The contingencies of evaluative feedback in the classroom and III. *An experimental analysis. Developmental psychology*, 14(3), 268. DOI: 10.1037/0012-1649.14.3.268

Dweck, C. S. (1999). *Self-theories: Their role in motivation, personality and development.* Philadelphia: Psychology Press.

Dweck, C. S., & Leggett, E. L. (1988). A social-cognitive approach to motivation and personality. *Psychological Review*, 95(2), 256. DOI: 10.1037/0033-295X.95.2.256

Dweck, C. S. (2006). *Mindset: The new psychology of success.* New York: Random House.

Fernald, A., Marchman, V. A., & Weisleder, A. (2012). SES differences in language processing skill and vocabulary are evident at 18 months. *Developmental Science*, 16(2), 234–248. DOI: 10.1111/desc.12019

Fernald, A., & Marchman, V. A. (2012). Individual differences in lexical processing at 18 months predict vocabulary growth in typically developing and late-talking toddlers. *Child Development*, 83(1), 203–222. DOI: 10.1111/j.1467-8624.2011.01692.x

Flynn, J. R. (1987). Massive IQ gains in 14 nations: What IQ tests really measure. *Psychological Bulletin*, 101, 171–191. DOI: 10.1037/0033-2909.101.2.171

Friederici, A. D. (2011). The brain basis of language processing: From structure to function. *Physiological Reviews*, 91(4), 1357–1392. DOI: 10.1152/physrev.00006.2011

Flood, D. G. (1991). Region-specific stability of dendritic extent in normal human aging and regression in Alzheimer's disease. *II. Subiculum. Brain Research*, 540, 83–95. DOI: 10.1016/ 0006-8993(91)90494-G

Flood, D. G. (1993). Critical issues in the analysis of dendritic extent in aging humans, primates, and rodents. *Neurobiology of Aging*, 14, 649–654. DOI: 10.1016/0197-4580(93)90058-J

Gureckis, T. M., & Love, B. C. (2010). Direct associations or transformations of an internal state? Exploring the mechanism underlying sequential learning behavior. *Cognitive Science*, 34, 10–50. DOI: 10.1111/j.1551-6709.2009.01076.x

Hart, B. & Risley, T. T. (1995). *Meaningful differences in the everyday experience of young American children.* Brookes Publishing.

Hess, T.M., Auman, C., Colcombe, S.J., & Rahhal, T.A. (2003). The impact of stereotype threat on age differences in memory performance. *The Journals of Gerontology Series B: Psychological Sciences and Social Sciences*, 58(1), P3–P11. DOI: 10.1093/geronb/58.1.P3

Hess, T.M., & Hinson, J.T. (2006). Age-related variation in the influences of aging stereotypes on memory in adulthood. *Psychology and Aging*, 21(3), 621. DOI: 10.1037/0882-7974.21.3.621

Hess, T.M., Hinson, J.T., & Hodges, E.A. (2009). Moderators of and mechanisms underlying stereotype threat effects on older adults' memory performance. *Experimental Aging Research*, 35(2), 153–177. DOI: 10.1080/03610730802716413

Kriegeskorte, N., & Kievit, R.A. (2013). Representational geometry: Integrating cognition, computation, and the brain. *Trends in Cognitive Science*, 17(8), 401–412. DOI: 10.1016/j.tics.2013.06.007

Kronbichler, M., Bergmann, J., Hutzler, F., Staffen, W., Mair, A., & Ladurner, G. (2007). Taxi vs. Taksi: Orthographic word recognition in the left ventral occipitotemporal cortex. *Journal of Cognitive Neuroscience*, 19, 1584–1594. DOI: 10.1162/jocn.2007.19.10.1584

Kronbichler, M., Hutzler, F., Wimmer, H., Mair, A., Staffen, W., & Ladurner, G. (2004). The visual word form area and the frequency with which words are encountered: evidence from a parametric fMRI study. *Neuroimage*, 21, 946–953. DOI: 10.1016/j.neuroimage.2003.10.021

Kruschke, J.K. (2003). Attention in learning. *Current Directions in Psychological Science*, 12,171–175. DOI: 10.1111/1467-8721.01254

Lynn, R. (1982). IQ in Japan and the United States shows a growing disparity. *Nature*, 297(5863), 222–223. DOI: 10.1038/297222a0

Mack, M.L., Preston, A.R., & Love, B.C. (2013). Decoding the Brain's algorithm for categorization from its neural implementation. *Current Biology*, 23, 2023–2027. DOI: 10.1016/j.cub.2013.08.035

Mangels, J.A., Good, C., Whiteman, R.C., Maniscalco, B., & Dweck, C.S. (2012). Emotion blocks the path to learning under stereotype threat. *Social Cognitive and Affective Neuroscience*, 7(2), 230–241. DOI: 10.1093/scan/nsq100

Mano, Q.R., Humphries, C., Desai, R.H., Seidenberg, M.S., Osmon, D.C., Stengel, B.C., & Binder, J.R. (2013). The role of left occipitotemporal cortex in reading: Reconciling stimulus, task, and lexicality effects. *Cerebral Cortex*, 23(4), 988–1001. DOI: 10.1093/cercor/bhs093

Merrill, D.A., Chiba, A.A., & Tuszynski, M.H. (2001). Conservation of neuronal number and size in the entorhinal cortex of behaviorally characterized aged rats. *The Journal of Comparative Neurology*, 438, 445–456. DOI: 10.1002/cne.1327

Morris, R.G, Moser, E.I., Riedel, G., Martin, S.J., Sandin, J., Day, M., & O'Carroll, C. (2003). Elements of a neurobiological theory of the hippocampus: The role of activity-dependent synaptic plasticity in memory. *Philosophical Transactions of the Royal Society B: Biological Sciences*, 358, 773–786. DOI: 10.1098/rstb.2002.1264

Nelson, D.L., Dyrdal, G.M., & Goodmon, L.B. (2005). What is preexisting strength? Predicting free association probabilities, similarity ratings, and cued recall probabilities. *Psychonomic Bulletin & Review*, 12(4), 711–719. DOI: 10.3758/BF03196762

Nusbaum, H.C. (1985). *A Stochastic account of the relationship between Lexical Density and Word Frequency*. Indiana University, Research on Speech Perception, Progress Report #11.

O'Donnell, C., Nolan, M.F., & van Rossum, M.C. (2011). Dendritic spine dynamics regulate the long-term stability of synaptic plasticity. *The Journal of Neuroscience*, 31(45), 16142–16156. DOI: 10.1523/JNEUROSCI.2520-11.2011

Park, D. C., & Reuter-Lorenz, P. (2009). The adaptive brain: aging and neurocognitive scaffolding. *Annual Review of Psychology*, 60, 173. DOI: 10.1146/annurev.psych.59.103006.093656

Pascual-Leone, A., Amedi, A., Fregni, F., & Merabet, L. B. (2005). The plastic human brain cortex. *Annual Review of Neuroscience*, 28, 377–401. DOI: 10.1146/annurev.neuro.27.070203.144216

Pereira, A. F., Smith, L. B., & Yu, C. (2014). A bottom-up view of toddler word learning. *Psychonomic Bulletin & Review*, 21(1), 178–185. DOI: 10.3758/s13423-013-0466-4

Rabbitt, P. (2014). Age and the overstuffed mind [Web log article]. Retrieved from Outlook from the Hutch: A blog on aging and the mind, http://pmar76.wordpress.com/2014/02/06/age-and-the-overstuffed-mind/

Ramscar, A. (2014). What happens to our minds and memories in healthy aging? [Web log article]. Retrieved from The importance of being wrong, http://ramscar.wordpress.com/2014/01/19/what-happens-to-our-minds-and-memories-in-healthy-aging/

Ramscar, M., Hendrix, P., Shaoul, C., Milin, P., & Baayen, H. (2014). The myth of cognitive decline: Non-linear dynamics of lifelong learning. *Topics in Cognitive Science*, 6, 5–42. DOI: 10.1111/tops.12078

Ramscar, M., & Gitcho, N. (2007). Developmental change and the nature of learning in childhood. *Trends in Cognitive Science*, 11(7), 274–279. DOI: 10.1016/j.tics.2007.05.007

Ramscar, M., & Yarlett, D. (2007). Linguistic self-correction in the absence of feedback: A new approach to the logical problem of language acquisition. *Cognitive Science*, 31, 927–960. DOI: 10.1080/03640210701703576

Ramscar, M. J. A., Yarlett, D. G., Dye, M. W., Denny, K., & Thorpe, K. (2010). The effects of Feature-Label-Order and their implications for symbolic learning. *Cognitive Science*, 34(6), 909–957. DOI: 10.1111/j.1551-6709.2009.01092.x

Ramscar, M., Dye, M., Popick, H. M., & O'Donnell-McCarthy, F. (2011). The enigma of number: Why children find the meanings of even small number words hard to learn and how we can help them do better. *PLoS ONE*, 6(7): e22501. DOI: 10.1371/journal.pone.0022501

Ramscar, M., Dye, M., & Klein, J. (2013a). Children value informativity over logic in word learning. *Psychological Science*, 24(6), 1017–1023. DOI: 10.1177/0956797612460691

Ramscar, M., Dye, M., Gustafson, J. W., & Klein, J. (2013b). Dual routes to cognitive flexibility: Learning and response conflict resolution in the dimensional change card sort task. *Child Development*, 84(4), 1308–1323. DOI: 10.1111/cdev.12044

Ramscar, M., Dye, M., & McCauley, S. (2013c). Error and expectation in language learning: The curious absence of 'mouses' in adult speech. *Language*, 89(4), 760–793. DOI: 10.1353/lan.2013.0068

Rapp, P. R., & Gallagher, M. (1996). Preserved neuron number in the hippocampus of aged rats with spatial learning deficits. *Proceedings of the National Academy of Sciences USA*, 93, 9926–9930. DOI: 10.1073/pnas.93.18.9926

Ratcliff, R., Thapar, A., & McKoon, G. (2011). Effects of aging and IQ on item and associative memory. *Journal of Experimental Psychology: General*, 140(3), 464–487. DOI: 10.1037/a0023810

Ratcliff, R., Thapar, A., & McKoon, G. (2010). Individual differences, aging, and IQ in two-choice tasks. *Cognitive Psychology*, 60, 127–157. DOI: 10.1016/j.cogpsych.2009.09.001

Rattan, A., Good, C., & Dweck, C. S. (2012). "It' s ok – not everyone can be good at math": Instructors with an entity theory comfort (and demotivate) students. *Journal of Experimental Social Psychology*, 48(3), 731–737. DOI: 10.1016/j.jesp.2011.12.012

Rescorla, R. A. (1968). Probability of shock in the presence and absence of CS in fear conditioning. *Journal of Comparative Physiology*, 66, 1–5.
Rescorla, R. A., & Wagner, A. R. (1972). A theory of Pavlovian conditioning: Variations in the effectiveness of reinforcement and nonreinforcement. In A. H. Black & W. F. Prokasy (Eds.), *Classical conditioning II: Current research and theory* (pp. 64–99). New York: Crofts.
Rescorla, R. A. (1988). Pavlovian conditioning: It's not what you think it is. *American Psychologist*, 43, 151–160. DOI: 10.1037/0003-066X.43.3.151
Rizzuto, D. S., & Kahana, M. J. (2001). An autoassociative neural network model of paired-associate learning. *Neural Computation*, 13(9), 2075–2092. DOI: 10.1162/089976601750399317
Salthouse, T. A. (2009). When does age-related cognitive decline begin? *Neurobiology of Aging*, 30, 507–514. DOI: 10.1016/j.neurobiolaging.2008.09.023
Salthouse. T. A. (2011). Consequences of age-related cognitive declines. *Annual Review of Psychology*, 63, 5.1–5.26.
Schaie, K. W. (1977). Quasi-experimental research designs in the psychology of aging. *Handbook of the Psychology of Aging*, 1, 39–69.
Schaie, K. W. (1974). Translations in gerontology-from lab to life. *Intellectual functioning. The American Psychologist*, 29(11), 802. DOI: 10.1037/h0037434
Schaie, K. W. (1973). Methodological problems in descriptive developmental research on adulthood and aging. In J. R. Nesselroade & H. W. Reese (Eds.), *Life-span developmental psychology: Methodological issues* (pp. 253–280). New York: Academic Press. DOI: 10.1016/B978-0-12-515650-9.50018-6
Schaie, K. W. (1959). Cross-sectional methods in the study of psychological aspects of aging. *Journal of Gerontology*, 14(2), 208–215. DOI: 10.1093/geronj/14.2.208
Schaie, K. W. (1988). Internal validity threats in studies of adult cognitive development. In M. L. Howe & C. J. Brainerd (Eds.), *Cognitive development in adulthood: Progress in cognitive development research* (pp. 241–272). New York: Springer-Verlag. DOI: 10.1007/978-1-4612-3852-2_8
Scholz, J., Klein, M. C., Behrens, T. E., & Johansen-Berg, H. (2009). Training induces changes in white-matter architecture. *Nature Neuroscience*, 12, 1370–1371. DOI: 10.1038/nn.2412
Schultz, W. (2006). Behavioral theories and the neurophysiology of reward. *Annual Review of Psychology*, 57, 87–115. DOI: 10.1146/annurev.psych.56.091103.070229
Schultz, W., Dayan, P., & Montague, P. R. (1997). A neural substrate of prediction and reward. *Science*, 275(5306), 1593–1599. DOI: 10.1126/science.275.5306.1593
Schurz, M., Sturm, D., Richlan, F., Kronbichler, M., Ladurner, G., & Wimmer H. (2010). A dual-route perspective on brain activation in response to visual words: Evidence for a length by lexicality interaction in the visual word form area (VWFA). *Neuroimage*, 49, 2649–2661. DOI: 10.1016/j.neuroimage.2009.10.082
Shimamura, A. P. (2000). The role of the prefrontal cortex in dynamic filtering. *Psychobiology*, 28, 207–218.
Singh-Manoux, A. et al. (2012). Timing of onset of cognitive decline: Results from Whitehall II prospective cohort study. *British Medical Journal*, 344, d7622. DOI: 10.1136/bmj.d7622
Sowell, E. R., Peterson, B. S., Thompson, P. M., Welcome, S. E., Henkenius, A. L., & Toga, A. W. (2003). Mapping cortical change across the human lifespan. *Nature Neuroscience*, 6(3),309–415. DOI: 10.1038/nn1008
Steele, C. M. (1997). A threat in the air: How stereotypes shape intellectual identity and performance. *American Psychologist*, 52(6), 613–629. DOI: 10.1037/0003-066X.52.6.613

Teasdale, T.W., & Owen, D.R. (2005). A long-term rise and recent decline in intelligence test performance: The Flynn Effect in reverse. *Personality and Individual Differences*, 39(4), 837–843. DOI: 10.1016/j.paid.2005.01.029

Turner, B.M., Forstmann, B.U., Wagenmakers, E.J., Brown, S.D., Sederberg, P.B., & Steyvers, M. (2013). A Bayesian framework for simultaneously modeling neural and behavioral data. *Neuroimage*, 72, 193–206. DOI: 10.1016/j.neuroimage.2013.01.048

Weisleder, A., & Fernald, A. (2013). Talking to children matters: Early language experience strengthens processing and builds vocabulary. *Psychological Science*, 24(11), 2143–2152. DOI: 10.1177/0956797613488145

Werker, J., & Tees, R. (1984). Cross-language speech perception: Evidence for perceptual re-or-ganization during the first year of life. *Infant Behavior and Development*, 7, 49–63. DOI: 10.1016/S0163-6383(84)80022-3

Yeager, D.S., & Dweck, C.S. (2012). Mindsets that promote resilience: When students believe that personal characteristics can be developed. *Educational Psychologist*, 47(4), 302–314. DOI: 10.1080/00461520.2012.722805

Zatorre, R.J., Fields, R.D., & Johansen-Berg, H. (2012). Plasticity in gray and white: Neuro-imaging changes in brain structure during learning. *Nature Neuroscience*, 15(4), 528–536. DOI: 10.1038/nn.3045

Zucker, R.S. (1999). Calcium-andactivity-dependentsynapticplasticity. *Current Opinion in Neurobiology*, 9, 305–313. DOI: 10.1016/S0959-4388(99)80045-2

Zuo, Y., Lin, A., Chang, P., & Gan, W.B. (2005). Development of long-term dendritic spine stability in diverse regions of cerebral cortex. *Neuron*, 46, 181–189. DOI: 10.1016/j.neuron.2005.04.001

Appendix

Table A1. Fixed-effects estimates in a mixed-effects logistic regression model with word as random-effect factor fitted to the visual lexical decision latencies of old and young participants. Data available in the languageR package (Baayen, 2008), dataset "english". Model fitted with the glmer function from the lme4 package (Bates et al., 2013).

Fixed effects:

	Estimate	Std. Error	z value	Pr(>|z|)
Intercept	1.40760	0.07432	18.940	< 2e-16
WrittenFrequency	0.36847	0.01515	24.320	< 2e-16
AgeSubject=young	-1.23280	0.05348	-23.053	< 2e-16
WrittenFrequency:AgeSubject=young	0.06914	0 .01220	5.666	1.46e-08

R code for the simulation of the PAL task:

```
lex = read.table(“obeyRulesLex.txt”, T)

lex
```

```
   Cues              Outcomes   Frequency
1  Context_American  Eagle      1
2  Context_Obey      Rules      1
3  Context_Obey      Eagle      1
4  Context_Legal     Eagle      1
```

```
ibrary(ndl)
wmlist = list()
for (i in 1:50) {
  cuesOutcomes = lex
  cuesOutcomes$Frequency[1:2] = rep(i, 2)
  wmlist[[i]] = estimateWeights(cuesOutcomes)
  }

frequencies = 1:50
strength = sapply(wmlist, FUN=function(m)return(m[4,1]))
plot(frequencies, strength, ylim=c(-0.5, 0),type="l",
  xlab="frequency of the stock phrases",
  ylab="cue strength of Obey and Eagle")
  abline(h=0, col="darkgray")
```

Table A2. Coefficients in a linear mixed effects model (with Item as random-effect factor) for the results plotted in Figure 4. Slope coefficients estimate the slopes for each age group separately. The t-tests evaluate whether a slope is zero. A separate analysis using treatment contrasts (not shown) indicated that all interactions were highly significant. F1: frequency of the first word (background rate); P2: ratio of the frequency of the first and second word (blocking); Google: google frequency of the first and second word pair (association rate).

	Estimate	Std. Error	t value
Intercept	2.55064	0.68220	3.739
Sex=Male	-0.10740	0.02211	-4.858
F1:AgeGroup20	-0.36897	0.14189	-2.600
F1:AgeGroup30	-0.55493	0.14189	-3.911
F1:AgeGroup40	-0.60279	0.14189	-4.248
F1:AgeGroup50	-0.65100	0.14189	-4.588
F1:AgeGroup60	-0.73176	0.14189	-5.157
P2:AgeGroup20	-0.80059	0.41103	-1.948
P2:AgeGroup30	-1.08672	0.41103	-2.644
P2:AgeGroup40	-1.23984	0.41103	-3.016
P2:AgeGroup50	-1.28778	0.41103	-3.133
P2:AgeGroup60	-1.44944	0.41103	-3.526
Google:AgeGroup20	0.34482	0.06214	5.549
Google:AgeGroup30	0.46774	0.06214	7.528
Google:AgeGroup40	0.50119	0.06214	8.066
Google:AgeGroup50	0.53815	0.06214	8.661
Google:AgeGroup60	0.59641	0.06214	9.599

Table A3. Specification of the generalized additive mixed model predicting log response latency in visual lexical decision from age, log frequency, and two latent variables for orthographic consistency.

Parametric coefficients:

	Estimate	Std. Error	t value	Pr(>|t|)
(Intercept)	6.661213	0.001773	3757.7	<2e-16
age=young	-0.221721	0.001862	-119.1	<2e-16

Approximate significance of smooth terms:

	edf	Ref.df	F	p-value
smooth frequency for age = old	6.555	7.290	218.335	< 2e-16
smooth frequency for age = young	6.245	6.975	229.127	< 2e-16
tensor product PC1 x PC2 for age = old	7.081	8.147	6.804	5.62e-09
tensor product PC1 x PC2 for age = young	3.829	4.147	2.122	0.073
random intercepts word	341.173	2192	1.601	< 2e-16

Index